Approaches to Teaching Chaucer's
Troilus and Criseyde
and the Shorter Poems

Approaches to Teaching
World Literature
Joseph Gibaldi, series editor

For a complete listing of titles,
see the last pages of this book.

Approaches to Teaching Chaucer's *Troilus and Criseyde* and the Shorter Poems

Edited by

Tison Pugh

and

Angela Jane Weisl

The Modern Language Association of America
New York   2007

For information about obtaining permission to reprint material
from MLA book publications, send your request by mail (see address below),
e-mail (permissions@mla.org), or fax (646-458-0030).

Library of Congress Cataloging-in-Publication Data

Approaches to teaching Chaucer's Troilus and Criseyde and the shorter poems /
edited by Tison Pugh and Angela Jane Weisl.
p.   cm.—(Approaches to teaching world literature)
Includes bibliographical references and index.
ISBN-13: 978-0-87352-996-9 (alk. paper)
ISBN-10: 0-87352-996-0 (alk. paper)
ISBN-13: 978-0-87352-997-6 (pbk. : alk. paper)
ISBN-10: 0-87352-997-9 (pbk. : alk. paper)
1. Chaucer, Geoffrey, d. 1400. Troilus and Criseyde.   2. Chaucer, Geoffrey,
d. 1400—Study and teaching.   I. Pugh, Tison.   II. Weisl, Angela Jane, 1963-
PR1896.P84 2007
821'.1—dc22   2006030556
ISSN 1059-1133

Cover illustration of the paperback edition: Woodcut for *Troilus and Criseyde*.
From *The Boke of Caunterbury Tales* with *The Book of Fame* and
The Boke of Troylus and Creseyde, by Geoffrey Chaucer. London: printed by
Richard Pynson, 1526. Glasgow University Library, Hunterian Bv.2.6.

Published by The Modern Language Association of America
26 Broadway, New York, New York 10004-1789
www.mla.org

CONTENTS

Teaching the Poems

Course Contexts

Appendix

PREFACE TO THE SERIES

In *The Art of Teaching* Gilbert Highet wrote, "Bad teaching wastes a great deal of effort, and spoils many lives which might have been full of energy and happiness." All too many teachers have failed in their work, Highet argued, simply "because they have not thought about it." We hope that the Approaches to Teaching World Literature series, sponsored by the Modern Language Association's Publications Committee, will not only improve the craft—as well as the art—of teaching but also encourage serious and continuing discussion of the aims and methods of teaching literature.

The principal objective of the series is to collect within each volume different points of view on teaching a specific literary work, a literary tradition, or a writer widely taught at the undergraduate level. The preparation of each volume begins with a wide-ranging survey of instructors, thus enabling us to include in the volume the philosophies and approaches, thoughts and methods of scores of experienced teachers. The result is a sourcebook of material, information, and ideas on teaching the subject of the volume to undergraduates.

The series is intended to serve nonspecialists as well as specialists, inexperienced as well as experienced teachers, graduate students who wish to learn effective ways of teaching as well as senior professors who wish to compare their own approaches with the approaches of colleagues in other schools. Of course, no volume in the series can ever substitute for erudition, intelligence, creativity, and sensitivity in teaching. We hope merely that each book will point readers in useful directions; at most each will offer only a first step in the long journey to successful teaching.

Joseph Gibaldi
Series Editor

PREFACE TO THE VOLUME

In editing *Approaches to Teaching Chaucer's* Troilus and Criseyde *and the Shorter Poems*, we aim to provide students a unified vision of Chaucer, one that highlights the great variety, breadth, and depth of his body of work. We also hope to offer professors the necessary tools for achieving this goal. No Chaucerian needs convincing that *Troilus and Criseyde* and the shorter poems are as entertaining and as complex as any of the narratives found in *The Canterbury Tales*, but our research on medieval literature syllabi suggests that professors do not as readily turn to these texts when composing their courses. Through this volume, we establish the grounds both for a wider perspective on Chaucer's position as the foundational author of English literature and for a reassessment of his place in the university and the English-department curriculum. Unfortunately, today many English majors graduate having read only selections from *The Canterbury Tales*, since its comic brilliance distracts much attention from Chaucer's other works. Although many excellent courses concentrate solely on Chaucer and his Canterbury pilgrims, our goal is to supply professors of medieval literature with practical suggestions for incorporating Chaucer's lesser-taught works into their courses. When English majors remember their college days, we would like them to look back on *Troilus and Criseyde* and the shorter poems with as much affection as they hold for such Canterbury gems as The Miller's Tale.

Troilus and Criseyde and the shorter poems present unique pedagogical difficulties for both instructors and students. Simply because of its length, *Troilus and Criseyde* requires a major investment in class time and preparation, more than any individual tale of the Canterbury pilgrimage. Teaching an eight-thousand-line poem in Middle English, no matter the level or the preparedness of the students, represents a major undertaking. If professors make a misstep early in the lesson, they suffer the repercussions of a classroom disenfranchised from the pleasures of a long and challenging text. *Troilus and Criseyde* offers innumerable rewards for those who successfully engage it, but it is essential to prepare the necessary groundwork to ensure the student-reader's readiness for such textual pleasures.

Although the shorter poems do not present an educational challenge in terms of their length, they likewise necessitate a sophisticated plan if one is to teach them effectively. Undergraduates are disarmingly candid in their first reaction to the shorter poems and often allege that they are "weird." To counter this charge, a teacher must have patience and a plan, because, from a modern perspective, our students are right: there is a vast disparity between medieval conventions and today's readerly expectations. *The Book of the Duchess*, *The House of Fame*, *The Parliament of Fowls*, *The Legend of Good Women*, and the miscellaneous verses—these poems are unlike anything our lower- or upper-level undergraduate students have typically seen before they enter a medieval literature classroom. The shorter poems require ample contextualization and explication for students bewildered by the unfamiliar tropes of the dream vision and Chaucer's role in his poetry as both character and creator. When students return from the shorter poems perplexed by their ostensible strangeness, professors need to devise stimulating methods of moving beyond such initial disenfranchised responses.

Professors who bring *Troilus and Criseyde* and the shorter poems into the classroom must reconceptualize their courses for these works. Showing how the Trojan romance of *Troilus and Criseyde*, the great varieties of subject matter in the shorter poems, and the manifold narratives of *The Canterbury Tales* are interrelated represents a Herculean task; few literature professors must negotiate such an obstacle course of genres, influences, traditions, and language barriers in their courses. With *Approaches to Teaching Chaucer's* Troilus and Criseyde *and the Shorter Poems*, we hope to give suggestions to professors seeking to introduce their students to the full range of the Chaucerian canon; to that end, this volume interrogates the specific demands of teaching Chaucer's lesser-taught works both by themselves and in conjunction with *The Canterbury Tales*.

Following the format of the Approaches to Teaching World Literature series, part 1 of this volume addresses the necessary materials for successfully teaching the texts. Here we analyze and recommend editions of *Troilus and Criseyde* and the shorter poems, highlighting the benefits and limitations of each text from both a pedagogical and a scholarly perspective. (Throughout this volume, we pay particular attention to the nexus of pedagogy and scholarship, two perspectives that should complement each other. Modeling for our students how scholarship and pedagogy interact is itself one of the most effective pedagogical techniques.) Following our coverage of editions, we discuss the range of translations available and comment on their individual merits, although we encourage teachers to engage their students with the rewarding difficulties of Chaucer's own language. Other sections of the "Materials" unit offer suggested readings for undergraduates, Web sites and other audiovisual materials useful in and out of the classroom, and recommendations for the instructor's library.

In part 2 of the volume, twenty-nine essays address specific context and strategies for teaching these works. The volume concludes with biographical notes on our contributors, the list of survey participants, a list of the works cited, and the index. All parenthetical citations refer to bibliographic entries in the works-cited list; all citations of Chaucer refer to *The Riverside Chaucer,* edited by Larry D. Benson.

Our debts of gratitude for personal and scholarly support throughout this project are immense. We thank the contributors whose teaching strategies form the heart of this volume and the numerous respondents to our survey on teaching *Troilus and Criseyde* and the shorter poems. Thanks, also, to

Thomas LoGiudice, Gordon Sullivan, Kristina Dzwonczyk, and Peter Dona-
hue, our research assistants, whose time and energy helped this volume come
to fruition. Finally, without Joseph Gibaldi's patient guidance and encourage-
ment, the volume would have never achieved its final form.

   We hope that *Approaches to Teaching Chaucer's* Troilus and Criseyde *and
the Shorter Poems* will contribute immeasurably to Chaucerian pedagogy and,
hence, to Chaucerian scholarship. Providing professors with this tool for in-
corporating a wider range of Chaucerian texts within their classrooms will give
future students a deeper understanding of the vast and complex world of
Chaucerian literature. As enthusiastic professors of Chaucer ourselves, we can
vouch for the vast enjoyments arising both from a deep appreciation of the
complete range of Chaucer's canon and from sharing that appreciation with
others. Our work on this volume has been dedicated to this goal.

TP and AJW

Part One

MATERIALS

Editions

Middle English Editions

Complete Works

The current standard edition of Chaucer's complete works is, without question, Larry D. Benson's *The Riverside Chaucer*. This edition supersedes the previous standard-bearing volume, the second edition of F. N. Robinson's *The Works of Geoffrey Chaucer*, and is therefore sometimes referred to as Robinson 3. Since *The Riverside Chaucer* contains all of Chaucer's literature, accompanied by extensive footnotes, explanatory notes, textual notes, a glossary, and a bibliography, it is particularly attractive to professors who wish to teach the full range of the Chaucerian canon.

Although *The Riverside Chaucer* is essential for the education of preprofessional graduate students, its cost and its sheer bulk make it somewhat less attractive for many undergraduate classes. For professors wishing to teach *Troilus and Criseyde* and the shorter poems in addition to *The Canterbury Tales* in their courses but who find *The Riverside Chaucer* unpractical for course adoption, affordable student editions of Chaucer's literature, along with handouts, library reserves, or Web-based editions, may be the solution.

Other editions of Chaucer's complete works that are out of print or otherwise not suitable for general classroom use but that may serve as the basis of an assignment on comparing editions or on the editorial history of Chaucer include John H. Fisher's *The Complete Poetry and Prose of Geoffrey Chaucer*; E. Talbot Donaldson's *Chaucer's Poetry: An Anthology for the Modern Reader*; and Albert C. Baugh's *Chaucer's Major Poetry*. (For a discussion of the relative merits of these texts, see Gibaldi 5–8.) On the history of Chaucerian studies, Walter W. Skeat's seven-volume *The Complete Works of Geoffrey Chaucer*, originally published in 1894–97, is of particular interest.

Troilus and Criseyde

Three affordable editions of *Troilus and Criseyde*, representing the editorial efforts of Stephen Barney, Maldwyn Mills, and R. A. Shoaf, are available for students. Barney's *Troilus and Criseyde*, a volume in the Norton Critical Edition series, contains an introductory essay on the text, which addresses Chaucer's biography, language, and versification. Barney's edition also includes Giovanni Boccaccio's *Il Filostrato* and Robert Henryson's *Testament of Cresseid*, which are quite helpful for professors seeking to teach *Troilus and Criseyde* and to give due consideration to its literary forebears and its afterlife. A range of critical essays on the text, from such luminaries as C. S. Lewis, Donaldson, Sheila Delany, Karla Taylor, Lee Patterson, and Jill Mann, close Barney's edition, along with a bibliography and a compendium titled "Frequent Words in

Troilus and Criseyde." Barney's lucid instructions for teaching the pronunci-ation of Chaucer's English are particularly useful.

Mills's *Troylus and Criseyde* includes "Chronology of Chaucer's Life and Times," as well as a wide-ranging and erudite introduction. Mills's text is pub-lished in the Everyman series, replacing John Warrington's *Geoffrey Chaucer: Troilus and Criseyde.* The text is based on Pierpont Morgan Library MS. M. 817 but features modernized punctuation and slight orthographic alterations (which do not meaningfully detract from its presentation as a medieval text). The edition ends with an instructive range of textual notes and suggestions for further reading. Teachers may debate the appropriateness of Mills's "Text Summary"—beneficial guide or cheater's crib?—but, given the complexity of *Troilus and Criseyde,* we feel that the summary can be used more to facilitate learning than to undermine it.

Shoaf's edition is based on the text that Baugh presents in *Chaucer's Major Poetry.* Shoaf's "Introduction to the Poem" is particularly engaging, and it addresses such essential topics as the poem's date, sources, language, char-acters, contexts, and conclusion, as well as Chaucer's work as translator. After the text of *Troilus and Criseyde,* Shoaf includes "A Brief List of Important Words," which provides an extremely helpful pedagogical tool. In sum, these three editions of *Troilus and Criseyde* are ideal for classroom use. The chief difference is that Barney's volume includes contextual literary and critical sources, whereas Mills's and Shoaf's editions focus exclusively on *Troilus and Criseyde.*

R. K. Gordon's *The Story of Troilus* contains texts and translations of the four major medieval tellings of the legend of Troilus: Benoît de Sainte-Maure's *Le roman de Troie,* Boccaccio's *Il Filostrato,* Chaucer's *Troilus and Criseyde,* and Henryson's *The Testament of Cresseid. Le roman de Troie* and *Il Filostrato* are translated; Gordon uses Skeat's texts of Chaucer and Henryson. The var-iant versions of the same tale in one collection offer excellent opportunities to analyze Chaucer's version in comparison with two of his forebears and one of his followers. However, this edition does not include a sufficient apparatus to assist the first-time student-reader of Chaucer's Middle English.

Barry Windeatt's Troilus and Criseyde: *A New Edition of* The Book of Troilus places the text in dialogue with its manuscript tradition. Boccaccio's *Il Filostrato* and Chaucer's *Troilus and Criseyde* are printed side-by-side on one leaf, with the facing leaf containing voluminous textual and manuscript com-mentary. The introduction includes the essays "The *Troilus* as Translation," "The Scribal Medium," "The Text of the *Troilus,*" "Metre," "This Edition," and "List of Manuscripts." Windeatt's scrupulous editing results in the defin-itive edition of *Troilus and Criseyde* for classes concerned with the text in relation to *Il Filostrato* and its manuscript tradition, but, unfortunately, the book is out of print.

A variety of other notable editions of *Troilus and Criseyde* are out of print or otherwise unsuitable for general course adoption but could provide useful comparative contextualization for discussion and analysis of the text. These include Robert Kilburn Root, *The Book of* Troilus and Criseyde *by Geoffrey Chaucer*; Donald Howard and James Dean, *Geoffrey Chaucer:* Troilus and Criseyde *and Selected Short Poems*; and Daniel Cook, Troilus and Criseyde *by Geoffrey Chaucer.* Georges Bonnard's *Geoffrey Chaucer:* Troilus and Criseyde excerpts passages from the poem, presenting the narrative in a condensed form.

The Shorter Poems

The most comprehensive and affordable edition of Chaucer's shorter poems (exclusive of the miscellaneous verse) is Helen Phillips and Nicholas R. Havely's *Chaucer's Dream Poetry*. It contains complete editions of *The Book of the Duchess*, *The Parliament of Fowls*, and *The House of Fame*, as well as both prologues and "The Legend of Dido" from *The Legend of Good Women*. The volume commences with a succinct and lively introduction, "Chaucer and Dream Poetry," which addresses such topics as classical theories of dreaming, the *Roman de la rose*, and the narrators of dream visions. Kathryn Lynch's Norton Critical Edition of the shorter poems, entitled *The Dream Visions and Other Poems*, includes complete texts of *The Book of the Duchess*, *The House of Fame*, *and The Parliament of Fowls*, as well the complete text of the F prologue, selections from the G prologue, and all the legends from *The Legend of Good Women*. A selection of the shorter lyric poems is also included. The volume contains an exciting array of primary sources for students, such as excerpts from Ovid's *Heroides* and *Metamorphoses*, Vergil's *Aeneid*, *The Dream of Scipio* and Macrobius's commentary on it, Boethius's *The Consolation of Philosophy*, Alain de Lille's *Complaint of Nature*, Dante Alighieri's *Divine Comedy*, Boccaccio's *Il Teseida*, and the "Fountain of Love" by Guillaume de Machaut. The volume concludes with critical essays addressing Chaucer's texts from a variety of theoretical approaches.

Other than these editions, individual and collective editions of the shorter poems are rare and mostly out of print. We recommend library reserves, handouts, and Web-based resources to make these texts readily available to undergraduate students at a reasonable cost.

Translations

Given our commitment to teaching Chaucer in his original Middle English, we feel somewhat hesitant to address the availability of translations; nonetheless, students are quite adept at seeking them out to supplement their course materials. Thus professors should be aware of the various translations of *Troilus and Criseyde* and the shorter poems. Additionally, translations are not without their pedagogical benefit, since they can be used as the foundation of classroom exercises and discussions on the advantages and disadvantages of rewriting Chaucer's literature in modern English. As one respondent noted, "I think it is important to use snippets of translations to see how different each person's rendition can be and how readily changed the original becomes."

A Chaucerian omnibus in translation, Theodore Morrison's *The Portable Chaucer* contains many of the tales from *The Canterbury Tales*; *Troilus and Cressida* in its entirety; and short selections from *The Book of the Duchess*, *The House of Fame*, *The Bird's Parliament*, and *The Legend of Good Women*, along with some of the miscellaneous verse. The translations are, for the most part, crisp, pleasant, and easy to read, and they retain Chaucer's rhyme schemes. As Joseph Gibaldi ponders, however, "[o]ne wonders . . . why any teacher who would take the time and effort to teach the minor works would wish to teach them in translation rather than in the original Middle English" (12). It is difficult to imagine the utility of this volume, since it would be of greatest value in a class on Chaucer taught entirely in translation, which seems an anathema to most Chaucerian scholars.

Poetic translations of *Troilus and Criseyde* include Nevil Coghill's *Troilus and Criseyde*, George Philip Krapp's *Troilus and Cressida*, and Margaret Stanley-Wrench's *Troilus and Criseyde*, each of which maintains Chaucer's rime royal verse scheme. Prose translations of *Troilus and Criseyde* include Windeatt's Troilus and Criseyde: *A New Translation*; James J. Donohue's *Chaucer's* Troilus and Cressida: *Five Books in Present-Day English*; and R. M. Lumiansky's *Geoffrey Chaucer's* Troilus and Criseyde: *Rendered into Modern English Prose*.

Published translations of the shorter poems are rare. Brian Stone's *Love Visions* contains poetic translations of *The Book of the Duchess*, *The House of Fame*, *The Parliament of Birds*, and *The Legend of Good Women*. Brief essays introduce each poem, and endnotes guide student readers through potentially confusing passages. A bibliography and an index of proper names offer further guidance for the new reader of Chaucer. Two translations of *The Legend of Good Women*, by Ann McMillan and Florence Hay Anastasas, are also useful.

Anthologies

One of the primary purposes of *Approaches to Teaching Chaucer's* Troilus and Criseyde *and the Shorter Poems* is to encourage professors to teach these texts both in medieval and in survey literature courses. Unfortunately, the outlook for the inclusion of this poetry in survey courses is somewhat bleak, since most anthologies focus almost exclusively on *The Canterbury Tales*. The most frequently assigned anthology in English literature classes, *The Norton Anthology of English Literature* (8th ed.), foregrounds *The Canterbury Tales* but also includes "Troilus's Song," "Truth," "To His Scribe Adam," and "Complaint to His Purse." *The Norton Anthology of World Masterpieces* and *The Norton Anthology of World Literature* include Morrison's translations of selected tales from *The Canterbury Tales. The Longman Anthology of British Literature* likewise focuses almost exclusively on *The Canterbury Tales*; the lone representatives of the rest of the Chaucerian canon are *The Parliament of Fowls*, "To His Scribe Adam," and "Complaint to His Purse." (The compact edition, however, only anthologizes "To His Scribe Adam" in addition to selected tales from *The Canterbury Tales*.) Likewise, *The Oxford Anthology of English Literature* includes a collection of shorter poems ("Gentilesse," "Truth," "Roundel" from *The Parliament of Fowls*; "Cantus Troili" from *Troilus and Criseyde*; "Balade" from the prologue to *The Legend of Good Women*; "To Rosemounde"; "The Complaint of Chaucer to His Purse"; and "To Adam, His Scribe") to complement its selections from *The Canterbury Tales*.

   The outlook is brighter for professors who seek an anthology for medieval literature courses. Anthologies specifically addressing medieval English literature include J. B. Trapp, Douglas Gray, and Julia Boffey's *Medieval English Literature* and Derek Pearsall's *Chaucer to Spenser: An Anthology. Medieval English Literature* contains the "Cantus Troili" and Book 3 of *Troilus and Criseyde*, "The Legend of Thisbe of Babylon" from *The Legend of Good Women*, and two miscellaneous verses ("Gentilesse" and "Chaucer's Words unto Adam, His Own Scribe"). *Chaucer to Spenser* presents *The Parliament of Fowls*, excerpts from *Troilus and Criseyde* (including sections editorially entitled "The Wooing of Criseyde," "The Winning of Criseyde," "The Loss of Criseyde," and "The Epilogue"), and four short poems ("Adam Scriveyn," "Truth," "The Envoy to Scogan," and "The Complaint of Chaucer to His Purse"). A companion volume of criticism, *Chaucer to Spenser: A Critical Reader*, also edited by Pearsall, includes a range of readings on medieval and early modern literature. (Duncan Wu's abridged edition of *Chaucer to Spenser: An Anthology*, entitled *Poetry from Chaucer to Spenser*, includes only excerpts from *The Canterbury Tales*.)

Required and Recommended Reading
for Undergraduates

On first venturing into the realm of medieval literature, students often feel overwhelmed by the plentitude of unfamiliar materials. In an ideal pedagogical world, students would read a range of classical and medieval authors before entering our classrooms; given the discrepancy between the ideal and the real world, however, professors would do well to offer students a bibliography of accessible primary sources so that they can better acquaint themselves with classical and contemporary influences on Chaucer's literature. A solution to this problem is to assign each student to read one primary source from the bibliography and to present this text to the class as a means of briefly exposing students to the literature of many primary sources without diverting too much classroom attention away from Chaucer. Such a bibliography might include Andreas Capellanus, *The Art of Courtly Love*; Augustine, *Confessions* and *On Christian Doctrine*; selected books of the Bible; Boccaccio, *Il Decameron* and *Il Filostrato*; Boethius, *The Consolation of Philosophy*; Dante, *The Divine Comedy*; Jacobus de Voragine, *The Golden Legend*; Guillaume de Lorris and Jean de Meun, the *Roman de la rose*; Macrobius, *Commentary on the Dream of Scipio*; Ovid, *The Art of Love* and *Metamorphoses*; and Vergil, *Aeneid.* Collections of Old French fabliaux, such as Robert Harrison's *Gallic Salt* or John DuVal's *Fabliaux Fair and Foul,* would help students' appreciate medieval humor and Chaucer's bawdy tales.

If one volume is sought to situate students within the intellectual and social environment of medieval England, a teacher might assign Robert P. Miller's *Chaucer: Sources and Backgrounds,* which collects an array of primary readings and introduces students to Chaucer's literary milieu. Nine units ("Creation and Fall," "Medieval Literary Theory," "Selected Narrative Sources," "The Three Estates," "Antifraternal Texts," "Modes of Love," "Marriage and the Good Woman," "The Antifeminist Tradition," and "End of the World and Last Judgment") consist of materials written by the literary and cultural figures most influential on Chaucer's literature. For sources and analogues related to *Troilus and Criseyde* and the shorter poems, see Gordon, *The Story of Troilus*; Havely, *Chaucer's Boccaccio: Sources of* Troilus *and the Knight's and Franklin's Tales*; and Windeatt, *Chaucer's Dream Poetry: Sources and Analogues.*

For secondary sources, a compact, affordable, and accessible collection of readings to familiarize students with scholarly discussions of Chaucer's literature plays an essential role in the Chaucer class. The revised edition of Beryl Rowland's *Companion to Chaucer Studies* provides a wealth of historical and contextual information on Chaucer and his literature, as well as individual chapters on *Troilus and Criseyde* and the shorter poems. In *The Cambridge Companion to Chaucer*, Piero Boitani and Jill Mann assemble essays that are challenging for the undergraduate and informative for the graduate student and that even provide a refreshing review for the professor. Derek S. Brewer's *A New Introduction to Chaucer* offers an excellent overview of Chaucer's life, texts, and culture. At least one chapter (if not two or three) addresses individually *Troilus and Criseyde, The Book of the Duchess, The House of Fame, The Parliament of Fowls,* and *The Legend of Good Women* and provides introductions to the plot and major themes of the poems.

Despite the death of the author in postmodern literary theory, literary biographies help place Chaucer in his cultural and historical world. The most recent Chaucerian biography, Pearsall's *The Life of Geoffrey Chaucer*, moves seamlessly between historical fact and Chaucer's fictions, creating a vibrant vision of the author's position in the changing world of fourteenth-century England. John C. Gardner's *The Life and Times of Chaucer* and Howard's *Chaucer: His Life, His Works, His World* are both readable biographies. Although each is comprehensible to generalists, Howard's is the more academic of the two. Earlier biographies that might be assigned include Marchette Chute's *Geoffrey Chaucer of England*; Coghill's *The Poet Chaucer*; Edward Wagenknecht's *The Personality of Chaucer*; and G. G. Coulton's *Chaucer and His England*. Martin Crow and Clair Olson's compilation, *Chaucer Life-Records*, provides a range of primary historical sources specifically connected to Chaucer's life, including the infamous deeds of release to Chaucer in respect of the *raptus* of Cecily Champain.

Texts that view the Middle Ages from a primarily sociocultural and historical perspective can nicely complement a literature classroom and provide a forum for considering the intersection of Chaucerian fiction against the (reconstructed) reality of historical life in the vast swath of years constructed as the Middle Ages. William R. Cook and Ronald B. Herzman's *The Medieval World View: An Introduction* and Jacques LeGoff's *Medieval Civilization, 400–1500* offer intriguing and approachable introductions to the medieval mind-set. Other such sources include Lewis, *The Discarded Image: An Introduction to Medieval and Renaissance Literature*; Léopold Génicot, *Contours of the Middle Ages*; A. J. Gurevich, *Categories of Medieval Culture*; Harald Kleinschmidt, *Understanding the Middle Ages*; James Harpur, *Inside the Medieval World*; and Frederick Artz, *The Mind of the Middle Ages*.

Instead of attempting to locate Chaucer in the overarching trajectory of the Middle Ages, instructors may wish their students to focus on the historical, social, and cultural conditions specific to fourteenth-century England. To that end, Brewer's *The World of Chaucer* details Chaucer's life and times in a social biography that contextualizes life in fourteenth-century England. The lavish prints, illustrations, and photographs throughout the book give students an illuminating sense of the medieval world. Although a less visually stunning view of Chaucer's England, Lillian Bisson's *Chaucer and the Late Medieval World* nonetheless provides a succinct yet wide-ranging analysis of three crucial aspects of Chaucer's life and fiction: his relations to religion, to class and commerce, and to gender and sexuality. Other such sources include F. R. H. DuBoulay, *The Age of Ambition: English Society in the Late Middle Ages*; May McKisack, *The Fourteenth Century, 1307–1399*; and Alec Myers, *London in the Age of Chaucer*. Jean Froissart's *Chronicles* is an enlightening primary text to illuminate the political concerns of Chaucer's day in the wider context of European affairs.

Aids to Teaching

Web Sites

The state of the World Wide Web in relation to Chaucer studies brings to mind a familiar metaphor of futility: planting a stake in a riverbed to stop the water's flow. As if to prove the futility of the process, one site that we had planned to comment on disappeared before we could fully document its contributions. As professors are increasingly aware, the ease and accessibility of the Web both facilitate and hamper learning, depending in large part on whether students use technology to enhance their education or to avoid their responsibilities. Regardless of a professor's affinity for or dislike of computer technology, our students often use *Google* or other search engines as their first step in researching a topic. Professors must be wary of the quality of many Web sites, especially in regard to their frequent use of public-domain texts containing errors or insufficient documentation.

Superior Web sites for student research include *Luminarium* (www .luminarium.org), which is organized primarily to support undergraduate research for introductory survey courses of British literature. The site is divided into chronological sections on medieval, Renaissance, and seventeenth-century literatures. The pages devoted to Chaucer offer the texts of most of *The Canterbury Tales*, *Troilus and Criseyde*, and the shorter poems, as well as many of the miscellaneous verses. "Additional Sources" offers links to literary biographies, bibliographies, images, electronic mailing lists, and other Chaucerian Web sites. "Essays on Chaucer" offers both professional and student analyses of Chaucer's literature. Since discussion of their peers' essays assists students to develop their own critical-thinking skills—because they often feel more comfortable debating the work of their fellow undergraduates than they do that of professional scholars—*Luminarium* helps professors engage their students in critical dialogue with other student critics.

The Georgetown University Medieval Studies Program sponsors *The Labyrinth: Resources for Medieval Studies* (www.georgetown.edu/labyrinth/ labyrinth-home.html), an ambitious project featuring texts of medieval literatures in French, Iberian, Italian, Latin, Middle English, and Old English. The site discusses and provides links to various topics relevant to medieval studies, ranging from architecture to paleography, from the Arthurian legend to Vikings, as well as pedagogical resources and information about professional publications and organizations. On the Middle English texts page, several links provide access to Chaucer's major texts as well as links to other Chaucerian sites.

Other excellent Chaucer Web sites include the *Chaucer MetaPage* (www.unc .edu/depts/chaucer/index.html); *The Geoffrey Chaucer Page* (www.courses.fas .harvard.edu/~chaucer); and *Geoffreychaucer.org* (www.geoffreychaucer.org). *The Chaucer Pedagogy Page* (hosting.uaa.alaska.edu/afdtk/pedagogy.html) is an excellent resource for teachers. Professors trying to wean their students off *Google* searches might recommend the *Essential Chaucer Bibliography* (http:// colfa.utsa.edu/chaucer) and the searchable *Chaucer Bibliography Online* (http: /uchaucer.utsa.edu). Web sites that provide texts of medieval literature include The Middle English Collection at the *Electronic Text Center* of the University of Virginia (http://etext.lib.virginia.edu/mideng.browse.html); *Digital Scriptorium* (http://sunsite.berkeley.edu/scriptorium); and *TEAMS Medieval Texts* (http://

www.lib.rochester.edu/camelot/teams/tmsmenu.htm). *The Middle English Dictionary* (http://ets.umdl.umich.edu/m/med) offers an important reference tool for all readers of Middle English.

Video and Audio Materials

We know of no instructional video that focuses exclusively on *Troilus and Criseyde* or the shorter poems; rather, Chaucer videos tend to focus on the author, the development of Middle English, and the literary achievements of *The Canterbury Tales*. *Geoffrey Chaucer and Middle English Literature*, for example, summarizes the development of Chaucer's English from its Anglo-Norman roots; discusses briefly the genres of romance, dream vision, and lyric; mentions *Troilus and Criseyde* and the *Gawain* poet as context; and spends the bulk of its attention on *The Canterbury Tales*. The video would be best used on the first day of a Chaucer class to contextualize Chaucer in the linguistic and literary history of the Western Middle Ages. Other videos of similar scope include *Early English Aloud and Alive: The Language of* Beowulf, *Chaucer and Shakespeare* and Velma Richmond's *A Prologue to Chaucer*.

It is essential for instructors to have an array of audio resources to help them teach students to pronounce Middle English correctly. The Chaucer Studio hosts a Web site (http://english.byu.edu/chaucer) from which instructors can purchase cassettes and CDs of Chaucer being read aloud by prominent Chaucerians at affordable prices. The Chaucer Studio suggests that these audio materials serve a twofold purpose:

> [A]s teaching aids they provide [both] performed readings of texts originally composed for oral delivery and models demonstrating the pronunciation of English at various stages of its development from Anglo-Saxon times onwards as well as other medieval languages. [As] a research resource they provide texts for research into literature in performance and into the relative merits for pedagogic purposes of dramatization and narrative monologue.

The Web site *Librarius* (http://www.librarius.com) and the "Criyng and the Soun" page of *The Chaucer MetaPage Audio Files* (http://academics.vmi.edu/english/audio/audio_index.html) both contain audio clips of various scholars reading passages of Chaucer's literature. Alan T. Gaylord offers further insights into the intersection of the aural and the pedagogical in his essay for this volume and in the appendix at the end.

Electronic and Multimedia Resources

ChaucerNet is the preeminent electronic mailing list for Chaucerians and their students. It provides undergraduates with a sense of the scholarly questions currently being investigated in Chaucer studies, as well as the types of discussions people have about Chaucer's literature. Professors should advise students to read Laura Hodges's "Netiquette" article (www.towson.edu/~duncan/laura.html) before they join; it offers helpful recommendations for students using electronic mailing lists, particularly about posting questions to the discussion list. To subscribe, send an e-mail to listserv@listserv.uic.edu. Leave the subject line blank and, as the message, type the following: Subscribe chaucer [your name]. (That is, if one's name is Jane Doe, one would type: Subscribe chaucer jane doe.) If everything works correctly, subscribers receive an e-mail saying that they are members of *ChaucerNet*, and they will start receiving posts shortly thereafter. To post a message, address it to the network, not to the list. Post messages to chaucer@listserv.uic.edu. To unsubscribe, send a message to listserv@listserv.uic.edu. Leave the subject line blank and, as the message, type the following: Signoff chaucer [your name]. Further commands can be found at www.towson.edu/~duncan/listser2.html.

The *Chaucer: Life and Times CD-ROM* presents an exciting array of materials packaged in one disc, including the text of Chaucer's complete works as they appear in *The Riverside Chaucer*; translations of much of the literature; introductory material for the literature; an analysis of Chaucer's life in relation to medieval culture; a selection of critical essays; a time line; images from museums, libraries, and galleries such as the Huntington, Bodleian, and Tate; a map of pilgrimage routes to Canterbury; a brief lesson on reading a medieval manuscript; audio selections of Middle English; and a glossary. It is difficult to imagine a given day of a Chaucer course for which this CD-ROM could not be used to illuminate a particular aspect of Chaucer's life, culture, and literature.

Murray McGillivray's *Geoffrey Chaucer's* Book of the Duchess: *A Hypertext Edition* contains a reading edition with hypertext glossary and explanatory notes and a critical edition with notes, images from manuscripts (Bodley 638, Fairfax 16, Tanner 346, and the edition in William Thynne's 1532 *Works of Geoffrey Chaucer*), and Chaucer's sources along with translations (including Machaut's *Fonteine amoreuse, Jugement du roi de Behaigne, Remede de Fortune*, and lyrics; Froissart's *Paradis d'amour*; *Le Roman de la rose*; Ovid's *Metamorphoses*; and Statius's *Thebaid*). With its electronic apparatus, this CD-ROM could be used for a variety of pedagogical purposes, including developing Middle English reading skills, discussing paleography and manuscript culture, and analyzing sources. As more CD-ROMs become available, these resources promise to revolutionize our classrooms.

The Instructor's Library

Background Studies

Anyone seeking to teach Chaucer's literature can find discussions of virtually every aspect of the texts from every imaginable approach. The following overview provides a selection of the scholarship, which answers a range of questions and concerns about the poem. Understandably, the sheer bulk of Chaucerian criticism precludes an expansive account of the field here.

Studies of Chaucer's relation to the biblical and classical past include Lawrence Besserman's *Chaucer's Biblical Poetics*, as well as his *Chaucer and the Bible: A Critical Review of Research, Indexes, and Bibliography*. The essays collected in David Lyle Jeffrey's *Chaucer and Scriptural Tradition* provide insight into an eclectic range of biblical topics in Chaucer's literature. Classical studies include John Fyler's *Chaucer and Ovid*; Anne Payne's *Chaucer and Menippean Satire*; and Michael Calabrese's *Chaucer's Ovidian Arts of Love*. Edgar Shannon's *Chaucer and the Roman Poets* looks at Chaucer primarily through the literature of Ovid and Vergil; to complete the volume, Shannon considers the influences of such writers as Statius, Lucan, Horace, and Juvenal. Christopher Baswell's *Virgil in Medieval England: Figuring the* Aeneid *from the Twelfth Century to Chaucer* traces Vergil's influence on Chaucer's literature.

Regarding Chaucer's relation to the Italian tradition, Nicholas R. Havely's *Chaucer's Boccaccio* offers a translation of *Il Filostrato*, selections from Benôit de Sainte-Maure's *Roman de Troie* and Guido delle Colonne's *Historia Destructionis Troiae*, as well as commentary on "The Fortunes of Troilus" in earlier classical and medieval texts. David Wallace, in *Chaucer and the Early Writings of Boccaccio*, takes a critical approach to the same material, offering investigations of all Chaucer's poems with Italian sources. A new entry into the discussion of Chaucer's Boccaccian heritage is Robert R. Edwards's *Chaucer and Boccaccio*, which considers the dialectic between antiquity and modernity in relation to the two authors. Piero Boitani's *Chaucer and Boccaccio* focuses on Boccaccio's *Teseida* and Chaucer's reliance on it. Warren Ginsberg's *Chaucer's Italian Tradition* investigates Chaucer's relationships to Dante, Boccaccio, and Petrarch. Karla Taylor explores Chaucer's exposure to Dante in *Chaucer Reads* The Divine Comedy; additional Dantean studies include Howard H. Schless's *Chaucer and Dante: A Revaluation* and Richard Neuse's *Chaucer's Dante*.

For an exploration of Chaucer's relationship to French writers, Charles Muscatine's *Chaucer and the French Tradition* provides essential information on the dream visions. Beginning with a discussion of the courtly and bourgeois traditions and then addressing their intersections with particular attention to the *Roman de la rose*, Muscatine subsequently includes a useful chapter on Chaucer's early poems that pays individual attention to *The Book of the Duchess*, *The House of Fame*, and *The Parliament of Fowls*. The rest of the volume addresses French influences on *Troilus and Criseyde* and *The Canterbury Tales*. James I. Wimsatt's *Chaucer and His French Contemporaries* explores Chaucer's literary relationships to Machaut, Froissart, Granson, and Deschamps. Dean Fansler's *Chaucer and the* Roman de la rose analyzes the critical question of Chaucer's relationship to this enormously influential French work. Barbara Nolan's *Chaucer and the Tradition of the Roman Antique* reads *Troilus and Criseyde* and The Knight's Tale in the light of romance's French and Italian constructions and their generic forebears.

Books that view Chaucer within the social, political, and artistic milieu of fourteenth-century England include Wallace's *Chaucerian Polity: Absolutist Lineages and Associational Forms in England and Italy*, which examines Chaucer's literature alongside the cultural shifts occurring in England and Italy. Seth Lerer places Chaucer within the context of fourteenth-century English literature in *Chaucer and His Readers: Imagining the Author in Late-Medieval England*, which slyly examines "the self-conscious invention of an author by those apparently least qualified to do so" (3). Peggy Knapp, in *Chaucer and the Social Contest*, considers Chaucer in the context of social estates, Wycliffite controversies, and constructions of gender. Studies of Chaucer's afterlife in the Renaissance include Alice Miskimin's *The Renaissance Chaucer* and Theresa Krier's collection of essays, *Refiguring Chaucer in the Renaissance*.

Chaucer's language often proves difficult for undergraduates meeting his poetry for the first time, and teaching linguistic skills is a challenge for many medievalists trained more in literary analysis than linguistic form. Norman Davis's *Chaucer Glossary* is a useful supplement to any Chaucer edition, including *The Riverside Chaucer*. More extended commentary can be found in David Burnley's *A Guide to Chaucer's Language*, which focuses more on grammar than on vocabulary building and provides an excellent short course in late Middle English. *The Language and Metre of Chaucer*, originally published in 1901, and listed as being "Set forth by Bernhard Ten Brink, revised by Friedrich Kluge, translated by M. Bentinck Smith," takes an even more detailed philological approach, examining phonology, accidence, and structure and style. This may be too much for anyone reading the poem outside a historical linguistics course, although it can provide a useful reference book for any query that arises about Chaucer's language. Christopher Cannon's *The Making of Chaucer's English: A Study of Words* reassesses Chaucer's contributions to the English language and shows Chaucer to be more traditional than radical in his use of language.

Stephen Barney's *Chaucer's Troilus: Essays in Criticism* provides attention to the technical craft of Chaucer's poetry through an examination of text, meter, and diction, working with both traditional and modern approaches. As an editor of the poem, Barney brings up many issues that may not prove useful for undergraduate students, although they may prove fruitful in graduate courses if students or instructors have an interest in scholarly editing. Alan T. Gaylord's *Essays on the Art of Chaucer's Verse* addresses Chaucer's poetic forms, his rhythms, his rhyming, his versification, and his prosody. This collection is useful for instructors interested in identifying, explaining, and bringing to life the patterns of sound and sense in Chaucer's verse. Its general essays, offered in two sections, "Historical and Theoretical Essays" and "Essays Combining History, Theory, and Close Reading," provide valuable information on Chaucer's prosody.

Critical Works

Studies of *Troilus and Criseyde* and the shorter poems engage in an ongoing dialogue about the themes and meanings of the texts, a dialogue that students should be invited to join. Ian Bishop's *Chaucer's* Troilus and Criseyde: *A Critical Study* offers an engaging overview of the poem. Beginning with "the actors," he considers the "lovers and their histories," "the epiphanies of the beloved," and "the operators." He then shifts to "the action," and, after discussing "the fortunes of love," he looks at the poem first as a "comedye" and then as a "tragedye" through the dialectical force of love. He also focuses on the poem's ending, considering "the flight from love" and "from prologue to epilogue." Bishop's accessible style makes this a useful book for instructors new to the poem, as well as for students seeking to ground themselves in the poem's issues.

Ida Gordon's *The Double Sorrow of Troilus: A Study of Ambiguities in* Troilus and Criseyde addresses a key challenge in reading *Troilus and Criseyde*—its insistent ambiguity. It goes without saying that this topic could easily generate class discussion of the poem at any level. The appendix "Kynde and Unkynde" takes a specific look at a pair of words in the poem and offers a model for an interesting assignment on the poem's language. Donald Rowe's *O Love, O Charite! Contraries Harmonized in Chaucer's* Troilus complements Gordon's reading by focusing on the text's unities.

A question that frequently arises in teaching *Troilus and Criseyde* concerns the poem's genre. Monica McAlpine, in *The Genre of* Troilus and Criseyde, addresses genre in a variety of ways, suggesting that the poem operates in accordance with such coordinated generic hermeneutics as a Boethian comedy in its treatment of Troilus and a Boethian tragedy in its treatment of Criseyde. Henry Ansgar Kelly's *Chaucerian Tragedy* looks at how Boccaccio is the ancestor of and John Lydgate and Robert Henryson are the descendents of *Troilus*. In the process, Kelly articulates Chaucer's theory of tragedy as a narrative genre. In *Conquering the Reign of Femeny: Gender and Genre in Chaucer's Romance*, Angela Jane Weisl examines the conflict of romance and epic in *Troilus and Criseyde*, considering the effect of one on the formation of the other in Chaucer's text.

John M. Steadman's *Disembodied Laughter:* Troilus *and the Apotheosis Tradition* explores several intriguing questions about the narrative of *Troilus and Criseyde*, particularly its complex ending. He focuses on specific narrative sites in the poem in such chapters as "The Eighth Sphere: Lunar Concave or Stellar Vault?" and " 'Feld of Pite': Elysium and Purgatory." Steadman provides a useful approach to the poem's conclusion: given that Chaucer's ending is likely to vex students and instructors alike, this book outlines provocative answers to the difficult questions it raises. Chauncey Wood's *The Elements of Chaucer's* Troilus analyzes the tone of Boccaccio's *Il Filostrato*, the intersection of love and will, the ennoblement of Troilus, the fickleness of Venus, and the text's recurrent imagery. Each of these chapters could serve as the basis of enlightening class discussions.

Another useful source providing critical background to the poem is C. David Benson's *Chaucer's* Troilus and Criseyde. In the sections "Boccaccio," "Readers," "Troy," "Character," "Love," "Fortune," and "Christianity," Benson examines key elements of the poem that inevitably arise as subjects for discussion in a course that considers *Troilus and Criseyde*. Balancing between background information and critique, he begins the introduction by acknowledging how infrequently the poem is taught and then provides a helpful apparatus to teach this work. C. David Benson's *The History of Troy in Middle English Literature* provides additional background and context, focusing on the city's central place in the narrative of *Troilus and Criseyde*.

Winthrop P. Wetherbee's *Chaucer and the Poets: An Essay on* Troilus and Criseyde approaches the poem in the context of its forebears, showing it to be primarily concerned with the poetic tradition. As such, it considers Chaucer's poetics of key importance in reading the work. Wetherbee's book begins with the chapter "The Narrator, Troilus, and the Poetic Agenda" and moves on to "Love's Psychology: The *Troilus* and the *Roman de la Rose*," "History versus the Individual: Vergil and Ovid in the *Troilus*," "Thebes and Troy: Statius and Dante's Statius," "Dante and the *Troilus*," "Character and Action: Criseyde and the Narrator," "Troilus Alone," and "The Ending of the *Troilus*." The material on Ovid, Vergil, and Dante can be useful in teaching undergraduates, particularly those at colleges that include a "great books" program.

Allen Frantzen's Troilus and Criseyde*: The Poem and the Frame* is a work useful for both students and instructors. After a chronology of Chaucer's life and works, it addresses the text's literary and historical context and then offers sections on "Social Text, Historical Context," "The Importance of the Work," and the "Critical Reception and the History of the Work." For those seeking to teach graduate students to write an introduction to a text, Frantzen provides an exceptionally thorough and useful example. He then offers a reading of the poem that provides an excellent model and structure for discussing the poem in an undergraduate course. The chapters each take up a different key issue and are titled "Past and Present: Book 1 and the Narrator," "Coming Together: Book 2 and Pandarus," "Falling in Place: Book 3 and Boethius," "Coming Apart: Book 4 and the War," and "Lost in Space: Book 5 and Fate." For instructors who devote one class period to each book, these concerns provide a fine framework for discussion and focus.

In *Chaucer: The Earlier Poetry: A Study in Poetic Development*, Derek Traversi traces Chaucer's work from its earliest examples to *Troilus and Criseyde*. He includes a chapter on each major dream vision as well as one titled "Language and Poetics in Chaucer's Early Poetry." Traversi concerns himself with "the development of Chaucer's understanding of the potentialities and limitations of his art" (7). With an eye on the later major works as the apex of this development, Traversi nonetheless seeks to bring Chaucer's lesser-known works to the attention of students and instructors, considering them alongside Chaucer's understanding of the poetic tradition, which Chaucer inhabits and from which he departs.

Critical anthologies are often useful because they provide an instructor with an accessible overview of a key area of criticism. Barney's *Chaucer's* Troilus offers a series of classic essays, showcasing important readings of the poem from 1915 to 1979. Mary Salu's *Essays on* Troilus and Criseyde follows neatly on Barney (literally, being published in 1980); the articles in Salu's volume showcase shifting paradigms for reading Chaucer. Such an approach also structures R. A. Shoaf and Catherine Cox's *Chaucer's* Troilus and Criseyde: "Subgit to Alle Poesye," which is virtually a "greatest hits" collection of theoretically oriented criticism. Cindy Vitto and Marcia Smith Marzec's *New Perspectives on Criseyde* outlines a series of new assessments of Chaucer's enigmatic heroine. Thomas C. Stillinger's *Critical Essays on Geoffrey Chaucer* offers some helpful selections for readers of *Troilus and Criseyde* but focuses primarily on *The Canterbury Tales*.

Critical overviews of Chaucer's dream visions include Michael St. John's *Chaucer's Dream Visions: Courtliness and Individual Identity*; Robert R. Edward's *The Dream of Chaucer: Representation and Reflection in the Early Narratives*; and James Winny's *Chaucer's Dream-Poems*. St. John's thesis is that "a reading of Chaucer's dream visions . . . forces us to rethink the distinction between medieval and early modern subjects, especially the idea that self-reflexive subjectivity is in some sense the product of the Renaissance" (2). Edwards, focusing on *The Book of the Duchess*, *The House of Fame*, and *The Parliament of Fowls*, argues that these poems balance the demands between mimetic art and the narrators' self-referentiality. Winny suggests that *The Book of the Duchess*, *The House of Fame*, and *The Parliament of Fowls* insistently embody "the writer's inward experience" (43) and that reading these works as romans à clef reduces Chaucer's artistic achievement.

William A. Quinn's anthology *Chaucer's Dream Visions and Shorter Poems* reveals a critical history of the reception of Chaucer's lesser-taught works. To quote Quinn's introduction, this work "is meant to provide advanced undergraduates and graduate students with a common core of exemplary and influential studies" (3). So, too, does it enable instructors new to this material to approach it in their classes in ways both traditional and contemporary.

Several studies focus on a particular Chaucerian dream vision. J. A. W. Bennett's *Chaucer's* Book of Fame seeks to redeem the work from critical dismissal; B. G. Koonce's *Chaucer and the Tradition of Fame: Symbolism in* The House of Fame focuses on the traditions of fame and prophecy that influence the work and on Chaucer's response to Dante's *Commedia*. Looking at the scriptural, Boethian, and literary traditions of Fame, Koonce sets the poem's literary context; he then considers its dream symbolism, its symbolic date, and Chaucer's access to "Dante in Inglissh." Sheila Delany's *Chaucer's* House of Fame*: The Poetics of Skeptical Fideism* views the poem as an example of skeptical fideism, which Delany examines in the Middle Ages both historically and poetically. Looking at the poem's engagement with the problem of choice among various conflicting traditions, Delany sees this work as establishing the "literary virtues of necessity" (113) in Chaucer's works that follow. Boitani's *Chaucer and the Imaginary World of Fame* views the poem in relation to its past, present, and future, paying particular attention to its classical and medieval predecessors.

A number of recent works act as an antidote to the assumption that *The Legend of Good Women* itself is essentially an unfinished draft, dwarfed by the works that precede and follow it. Studies include Florence Percival's *Chaucer's Legendary Good Women*, Delany's *The Naked Text: Chaucer's* Legend of Good Women, Lisa Kiser's *Telling Classical Tales: Chaucer and* The Legend of Good Women, Quinn's *Chaucer's Rehersynges: The Performability of* The Legend of Good Women, Rowe's *Through Nature to Eternity: Chaucer's* Legend of Good Women, and Robert Worth Frank's *Chaucer and* The Legend of Good Women. See Calabrese's essay in this volume, "A Guide to Teaching *The Legend of Good Women*," for descriptions of these critical studies.

Few monographs focus exclusively on *The Parliament of Fowls*. In The Parliament of Foules*: An Interpretation*, Bennett reads the text as a definition and exploration of love in its poetic and aesthetic contexts, eschewing a historical reading of the poem. In *Chaucer and the Cult of Saint Valentine*, Kelly's analysis of *The Parliament of Fowls* argues that Chaucer " 'invented' St. Valentine as the patron of matchmaking" (xi).

Several critical anthologies address both *Troilus and Criseyde* and the shorter poems. Corinne Saunders's *Chaucer*, a new addition to the Blackwell Guides to Criticism series, focuses on the development of Chaucerian criticism. Other helpful sources include Richard Schoeck and Jerome Taylor, *Chaucer Criticism:* Troilus and Criseyde *and the Minor Poems*; Julian N. Wasserman and Robert J. Blanch, *Chaucer in the Eighties*; C. David Benson, *Critical Essays on Chaucer's* Troilus and Criseyde *and His Major Early Poems*; and Leigh A. Arrathoon's collection, *Chaucer and the Craft of Fiction*.

Reference Works

Separate volumes of the Oxford Guides to Chaucer that address *Troilus and Criseyde* and the shorter poems offer a fount of background material and thematic discussions to instructors wishing to deepen their understanding of the poems' context. The volume on *Troilus and Criseyde*, edited by Barry Windeatt, discusses the poem's date, texts, and manuscripts as a preface to a consideration of the poem's sources (from the fictional Lollius to Boethius to the *Roman de la rose*). The poem's multiple genres, structures, themes, and styles receive due critical attention. Additionally, a section called "Imitation and Illusion" shows the poem's life beyond itself. The guide's comprehensive bibliography covers an excellent range of critical works written before the early 1990s. Alastair J. Minnis, V. J. Scattergood, and J. J. Smith's guide, *The Shorter Poems*, likewise establishes a firm critical foundation for understanding the poems' respective texts. The collection begins with a discussion of the shorter poems' social and cultural contexts and considers "Chaucer and the love-vision form." For each of the major love visions, the guide examines its texts, dates, verse forms, rhetorical devices, and styles. Each section takes up issues germane to the particular poem. A comprehensive look at Chaucer's shorter lyrics and a useful appendix on Chaucer's language round out this helpful volume.

Peter Brown's *A Companion to Chaucer* comprises twenty-nine essays on a variety of Chaucerian topics. Douglas Gray's *Oxford Companion to Chaucer* is a mini-encyclopedia for Chaucerians, and Gillian Rudd's *The Complete Critical Guide to Geoffrey Chaucer* offers quick survey essays on Chaucer's life, literature, and criticism. These three volumes provide succinct references on crucial Chaucerian topics. Historical overviews of critical responses to Chaucer include Derek S. Brewer's two-volume *Chaucer: The Critical Heritage* and Caroline F. E. Spurgeon's three-volume *Five Hundred Years of Chaucerian Criticism and Allusion, 1357–1900*. Jackson Campbell Boswell and Sylvia Wallace Holton have catalogued references to Chaucer during a 165-year period, updating some of Spurgeon's references and adding others in *Chaucer's Fame in England: STC Chauceriana, 1475–1640*. M. C. Seymour's two-volume *A Catalogue of Chaucer Manuscripts* offers essential information about the location and distinctive features of Chaucer's manuscripts.

The *Middle English Dictionary*, essentially the medieval equivalent of the *Oxford English Dictionary*, provides detailed information on Chaucer's words, providing pronunciation, variant spellings, etymology, context, first usage, and textual examples. It is an excellent resource for instructors and can provide the framework for fruitful linguistic assignments on Chaucer's language. Many universities subscribe to the online version. Concordances of Chaucer's works include Akio Oizumi's *A Complete Concordance to the Works of Geoffrey Chaucer*; John Tatlock and Arthur Kennedy's *A Concordance to the Complete Works of Geoffrey Chaucer and to the* Romaunt of the Rose; and Larry Benson's *A Glossarial Concordance to* The Riverside Chaucer.

Print bibliographies have been largely superseded by Web searches and computer databases, but scholars may nonetheless find the following bibliographies useful: Bege K. Bowers and Mark Allen's *Annotated Chaucer Bibliography, 1986–1996*; John Leyerle and Anne Quick's *Chaucer: A Bibliographic Introduction*; Lorrayne Baird Lange and Hildegard Schnuttgen's *A Bibliography of Chaucer, 1974–1985*; Lorrayne Baird's *A Bibliography of Chaucer, 1964–1973*; William Crawford's *Bibliography of Chaucer, 1954–1963*; and Eleanor P. Hammond's *Chaucer: A Bibliographical Manual.*

The Chaucer industry continues to publish energetically, and this introduction to the necessary scholarly materials to teach Chaucer faces its own unavoidable obsolescence in the future. Maintaining one's reference library creates a never-ending challenge for every Chaucerian, but it is one that keeps our profession vibrant and illuminating.

Part Two

APPROACHES

Introduction: A Survey of Pedagogical Approaches to *Troilus and Criseyde* and the Shorter Poems

Our survey of instructors and our research into Chaucerian pedagogical practices confirm that *Troilus and Criseyde* and the shorter poems receive less attention in the classroom than *The Canterbury Tales* does. The "Materials" section describes the resources available to ameliorate this problem, we now offer twenty-nine essays and an appendix that detail teaching strategies designed to incorporate Chaucer's lesser-taught works into the classroom.

The first ten essays, collected under the heading "Teaching the Backgrounds," consider the literary, historical, and cultural contexts of these works. William A. Quinn's "The Short Poems: Sources, Genres, and Contexts" addresses Chaucer's use of genre, since genre offers an excellent means of introducing students to Chaucerian criticism. Quinn's essay on the shorter poems ponders the multivalent uses and interpretative paradigms of such genres as envoys, prayers, and complaints. Chaucer's authorial brilliance is nowhere more apparent than in his deployment of multiple generic tropes in a single text. When students are introduced to the range of medieval genres, they are allowed to discover for themselves Chaucer's deft exploitation of genre as a tool for playing with readerly expectations, and they are thus able to generate their own interpretations of the texts.

The following three essays—Karla Taylor's "Chaucer and the French Tradition," Warren Ginsberg's "Boccaccio's *Il Filostrato*, Chaucer's *Troilus and Criseyde*, and Translating the Italian Tradition," and Noel Harold Kaylor, Jr.'s "Boethius, Dante, and Teaching Aspects of Chaucer's Tragedy"—consider Chaucer's relation to his continental literary heritage. Exposure to the world and the literary traditions outside England made lasting impressions on Chaucer's literature, and Taylor, Ginsburg, and Kaylor explore how the European world influenced Chaucer's understanding of himself as a writer working in and against various traditions. These approaches introduce students to Chaucer's literary and social context and show him to be a poet steeped in multiple traditions.

The growth of the English vernacular into a literary language also greatly influenced Chaucer's literature, and Susannah Mary Chewning examines the pedagogical implications of these developments in her essay, "Chaucer and Vernacular Writing." Julia Boffey's "*Troilus and Criseyde* and Chaucer's Shorter Poems: Palaeography and Codicology" approaches manuscript study and research as a reconstructive and interpretive exercise crucial to creating meaning from the historical record.

Since *Troilus and Criseyde* and the shorter poems share the marks of Continental and vernacular literary traditions, and they also evince Chaucer's participation in and concerns about history, both classical and English. Scott Lightsey's essay, "The Pagan Past and Chaucer's Christian Present," tackles the intersection of pagan texts and Chaucer's Christianity by pondering the meaning of the pagan golden age to Chaucer's literature. Lightsey considers the conflicted medieval reaction to past authorities—esteemed for their great wisdom and learning but rebuked for their inevitable failure to participate in salvation as promised by Christianity. Alison A. Baker's "Contemporary English Politics and the Ricardian Court: Chaucer's London and the Myth of New Troy" looks at Chaucer's historicity through the mythology of *Troynovant*, or New Troy, and its connection to contemporary English politics and national identity.

The final essays in this section, Lynn Arner's "Trust No Man but Me: Women and Chaucer's Shorter Poetry" and Holly A. Crocker's "Teaching Masculinities in Chaucer's Shorter Poems: Historical Myths and Brian Helgeland's *A Knight's Tale*," demonstrate how ideological constructions of gender influenced Chaucer's literature and continue to influence today's readers. The question of Chaucer's relation to women is vexed and must receive critical attention, especially because it has been argued that Chaucer makes Criseyde responsible for Troilus's death and because Chaucer offers an apology to women for doing so in *The Legend of Good Women*. Arner discusses ways of teaching students how Chaucer's narratives reflect tropes of medieval misogyny and how he reifies and subverts this misogyny. Recent scholarship on Chaucer and gender also asks readers to examine constructions of masculinity in the Chaucerian canon, such as the homosocial friendships in *Troilus and Criseyde*, knightly identity as a construction of masculinity in *The Book of the Duchess*, and the masculinity of authorial identity in *The Legend of Good Women*. Crocker suggests ways to enlighten students' conceptions of medieval masculinities as a complex arena of male privilege and power that is often under duress, and she does so through an intriguing analysis of male homosociality in Chaucer's "envoy" poems and in Brian Helgeland's recent film, *A Knight's Tale*.

The next section, "Approaches to Teaching the Poems," opens with Quinn's second essay, "Suggestions for Rehearsing the Short Poems in Class," which complements his first by providing professors with ways to introduce unfamiliar genres to today's students. Glenn A. Steinberg's essay, "Chaucer and the Critical Tradition," explores how readers and scholars have created different visions of Chaucer over the centuries; he suggests how to engage students in analyzing these visions and their ideological ramifications.

Carolynn Van Dyke's "Small Texts, Large Questions: Entering Chaucerian Poetics through the 'Miscellaneous' Poems" uses a series of exercises centered on Chaucer's shorter verses to explore the poetic forms and traditions with which Chaucer engages. In "Teaching Chaucer's Postmodern Dream Visions," Myra Seaman focuses on the pedagogical challenges of Chaucer's dream visions, as well as the ways in which postmodern literary theories enlighten these texts. Michael Calabrese's "A Guide to Teaching *The Legend of Good Women*" makes practical suggestions for teaching this notoriously tricky work.

The next two essays—Clare R. Kinney's "Chaucer's Dialogic Imagination:

Teaching the Multiple Discourses of *Troilus and Criseyde*" and Peggy A. Knapp's "Philology, History, and Cultural Persistence: *Troilus and Criseyde* as Medieval and Contemporary"—consider how dialogic perspectives, both Chaucer's and the reader's, structure our understanding of the Chaucerian canon. Kinney's essay on Chaucer and narrative addresses how genre and generic expectations influence interpretations of *Troilus and Criseyde*, and Knapp's essay investigates the complex relation between philology, history, and the ways in which disparate cultures contend with similar issues.

The following essays explore the pedagogical ramifications of recent trends in literary theory that have created new perspectives on the Chaucerian world. Angela Jane Weisl and Tison Pugh's "Chaucer and Gender Theory" illustrates how gender theory productively complicates our students' understanding of gender roles, both medieval and modern. Roger Apfelbaum's " 'Made and Molded of Things Past': Intertexuality and the Study of Chaucer, Henryson, and Shakespeare," through a hermeneutic of intertexuality, considers the historical trajectory of the Troilus legend after Chaucer, notably in the works of Robert Henryson and William Shakespeare. James J. Paxson's "Triform Chaucer: Deconstruction, Historicism, Psychoanalysis, and *Troilus and Criseyde*" assesses the benefits of using multiple theoretical approaches in teaching Chaucer. The questions posed in these essays can help professors formulate assignments that challenge their students to build on the close-reading skills developed in their years as English majors and create sophisticated and complex personal interpretations of Chaucer's words.

The next three essays—Martha Rust's "A Primer for Fourteenth-Century English and Late Medieval English Manuscript Culture: Glossing Chaucer's 'An ABC,' " Alan T. Gaylord's "Two Forms, Two Poetic Stages, Developing Voices: *The Romaunt of the Rose* and *The Parliament of Fowls*," and Barbara Stevenson's " 'In Forme of Speche Is Chaunge': Introducing Students to Chaucer's Middle English"—address methods of assisting students to overcome lexical difficulties in reading, hearing, and comprehending Middle English for the first time. Through the different perspectives of these three essays—Rust on reading, Gaylord on speaking, and Stevenson on translation—professors will discover a wide array of techniques for helping their students meet the challenge of reading an unfamiliar form of English.

Just as students should experience Chaucer on an auditory and textual level, so they should experience the pleasures of the visual iconography of Chaucer's medieval world. Glenn Davis's "Visual Approaches to Chaucer" suggests myriad ways to bring Chaucerian images into the classroom to facilitate student interest in the author and his cultural milieu. Jean-François Kosta-Théfaine's "Teaching Chaucer without (or with) Translations: An Introduction to Othon de Grandson's 'Les Cinq balades ensuivans' and Chaucer's 'The Complaint of Venus' " argues for using nontranslated texts in the Chaucer classroom, a practice that more closely approximates Chaucer's own polyglot literary milieu.

In the final section, "Course Contexts," we include essays on teaching Chaucer in courses, including those other than the traditional undergraduate Chaucer course. Jenifer Sutherland's "Notes on a Journey: Teaching Chaucer's Shorter Poems and *Troilus and Criseyde* for the First Time" details her personal experiences and offers practical suggestions to the first-time professor for pedagogical success. Subsequent essays cover teaching *Troilus and Criseyde* to freshmen and sophomores. Marcia Smith Marzec's "Overcoming Resistance to 'That Old Stuff': Teaching *Troilus and Criseyde* through Journaling and Debate" and Adam Brooke Davis's " 'Diverse Folk Diversely They Seyde': Teaching Chaucer to Nonmajors" look at teaching Chaucer to non-English majors. These essays present strategies for engaging students who are unfamiliar with medieval literature. The essays focus on combining close-reading techniques with dynamic thematic interpretations, as well as on helping students engage with reading as an active experience in which they involve themselves with the construction of a text's meaning.

In the last essay of this section, "Chaucer's Early Poetry in Graduate Seminars: Opportunities for Training Future Chaucer Teachers and Molding 'Yonge, Fresshe Folkes' into Publishing Scholars," Lorraine Kochanske Stock suggests how professors can use *Troilus and Criseyde* and the shorter poems to train the next generation of medievalists. She focuses on the philological, theoretical, historical, and cultural perspectives that are essential for graduate students to engage while studying these texts as part of their preprofessional training. In addition, she offers practical suggestions for helping students bring their work on Chaucer into a professional context.

Alan T. Gaylord's appendix, "Suggestions for Reading Chaucer Out Loud in the Teaching of Chaucer's Poetry," completes our volume by providing contextual information for teaching the aural quality of Chaucer's poetry, which his earlier essay demonstrates in practice. The essay considers the necessary resources for effectively capturing the experiential nature of Chaucer's literature and explains how such practices enlighten and illuminate the classroom.

If all these essays share a common thread beyond Chaucer himself, it is the belief that an invested and concerned teacher can overcome any challenge in teaching Chaucer's literature and open up these complex yet rewarding texts to students at all levels. The challenges for instructors are manifold, but the rewards are endless.

The Short Poems:
Sources, Genres, and Contexts
William A. Quinn

Twenty-two lyrics plus *Anelida and Arcite* make up a miscellany of minor pieces attributed, with varying degrees of confidence, to Geoffrey Chaucer. Though seldom taught as a unit, this incohesive grouping is occasionally sifted for biographical information. These short poems may also be taught as significant moments in the progress of Chaucer's career, as exemplars of medieval genres, as interpretive complements to Chaucer's major works, or as formal innovations in the history of English prosody.

Reputedly Chaucer's earliest surviving lyric, "An ABC," or "La Priere de Nostre Dame," illuminates The Prioress's Tale and The Second Nun's Tale. This prayer, sui generis among Chaucer's short poems, was presumably composed for Blanche, the Duchess of Lancaster. It can be taught, therefore, as a complement to *The Book of the Duchess* and so as a key item in any discussion of Chaucer's orthodoxy or Lollardy. As an abecedarius, it can also be taught as an example of the popularity of Middle English acrostic verse. This remarkably faithful translation of an *écrit* by Guillaume de Deguilleville offers an opportunity to assess formal equivalence between a French twelve-line stanza and the English eight-line stanza. Chaucer apparently invented what is now conventionally called "the Monk's Tale stanza" (used in several lyrics). The pentameter line of this stanzaic pattern exemplifies Chaucer's early and extraordinary success as a formal experimenter.

If prayer is now the least represented type of Chaucerian lyric, complaint is the most common. Like "An ABC," Chaucer's "Complaint unto Pity" is thought to be a sincere, artificial, and immature exercise—a sensibility that owes more to Guillaume de Lorris than to Statius, and a fashion that shows the influence of *il dolce stil nuovo*. This complaint is generally considered to be Chaucer's first composition in "sevins," or rhyme royal, a modification of the French *ballade royale*. Chaucer subsequently favors this pattern in narratives that focus on suffering women. The "Bill of Complaint" in "Pity" begins with a hyperbolic apostrophe that echoes Marian oxymora: "Humblest of herte, highest of reverence" (57). Frustration converts Chaucer's prosopopoeia into a legal petition. His clever use of legal terminology anticipates Harry Bailly's parroting of court patois (*CT* 2.33–38). In "Pity," the poet-petitioner argues a typically impossible case. He must beg Cruelty, queen of Furies, for mercy (92). What he wants most, he has least; what he abhors, he has in plenty (99–105). Pity is dead; so Chaucer's complaint might as readily be labeled a dirge (118).

Chaucer sounds every bit as sincerely abject in "A Complaint to His Lady" (67, 87, 89). His only worth is his persistence. To be surpassed by another servant-suitor would prove fatal (110–12). These two complaints offer an excellent chance to learn the language of service and humility, of truth and ruth as dictated by *fin'amors* (without a dizzying array of more typically Chaucerian subversions). Since courtly love lyrics often appropriate religious diction (e.g., 125–26), prayer may also be considered a generic influence on Chaucer's rhetoric. The poem's catalog of virtues belonging to Lady "Bountee" (24) sounds clichéd, but very promising, until her surname, "Faire Rewtheless" (27), is disclosed. Chaucer shifts his complaint about lady "Bountee" (1–49) into a petition addressed directly to her. In section 4, there is a curious pronominal shift from "she" (last used in line 49) to direct address; but, insofar as Chaucer uses "you" forms (53, 56, 59, etc.), his petition sounds less than optimistic. His final, simplest appeal to her as "swete" (124) remains desperately hopeful. Formally, this particular complaint reflects Italian influences. Since the extant text of Chaucer's short poem may be a scribal composite, it is difficult to affirm that the poet deliberately constructed its extraordinary conjunction of different stanzaic patterns. Nevertheless, "A Complaint to His Lady" may be used in class to provoke discussion of prosodic experimentation and the resulting destabilizing of regularity in English verse.

In "Womanly Noblesse," Chaucer begs his lady "auctour" (27) to nurture the author's love. Formally, this complaint is identified as a ballade. Chaucer compensates for the omission of a conventional refrain by using only two rhymes. The juxtaposition of this particular ballade to the French norm allows a class to discuss both the perceived effects and the putative motives for Chaucer's formal changes.

Besides these complaints firmly identified as Chaucer's own, a set of "Poems Not Ascribed to Chaucer in the Manuscripts" compose a sequence of monologues lamenting the poet's own "double sorwe" (*TC* 1.1). "Against Women Unconstant," "Complaynt D'Amours," "Merciles Beaute," and "A Balade of

Complaint" also represent an exercise in editorial intuition. In direct contrast to the omission of a refrain in "Womanly Noblesse," the rhyme royal "Against Women Unconstant" uses an incrementally more bitter refrain that was probably familiar as a translated echo of Guillaume de Machaut. Notorious for its castigation of Criseyde, this complaint may be Chaucer's most misogynistic lyric. It pairs well with "Womanly Noblesse" and may indeed be read as Chaucer's disappointment regarding his prior petition.

"Complaynt D'Amours," "Merciles Beaute," and "A Balade of Complaint" are no more (and no less) interesting to teach than "A Complaint to His Lady." Indeed, "A Balade of Complaint" is a three-stanza reprise of the same themes, also in rhyme-royal format. "Complaynt D'Amours" imitates Othon de Grandson's "Complainte amoureuse de saint Valentin" and echoes Machaut's poems as well. Its closing reference to Saint Valentine's Day (85) complements *The Parliament of Fowls*. Though similarly conventional in sentiment, "Merciles Beaute" survives as a more formally intriguing tour de force. A pastiche of French allusions, "Merciles Beaute" may be taught as a mélange of correspondences to Chaucer's other works. For example, the lady's penetrating eyes may be compared with Troilus's first sighting of Criseyde. Though pitiless, the "quene" (9; cf. "The Complaint unto Pity" 92) may be compared with Alceste in the prologue to *The Legend of Good Women*; likewise, the sarcastic reference to the God of Love in stanza 3 may be compared with the portrayal of Love in the prologue to the *Legend*. The image of Chaucer's name being stricken from the book (or less permanent "sclat") of Love in "Beaute" (34–35) may be compared with the melted names on "A roche of yse" (*HF* 1130); the poet threatens to erase Love's name from his own books in retaliation. Chaucer's happy escape from love in stanza 3 may be compared with the "Lenvoy de Chaucer a Bukton." So too the lean-versus-fat refrain reiterates Chaucer's self-caricature as a "popet" in Sir Thopas (7.700–01) and echoes Chaucer's primary conceit in "The Complaint of Chaucer to His Purse."

Three lyrico-narrative complaints demonstrate—perhaps in extremis—Chaucer's creative habit of synthetic experimentation and inventive imitation. All three are set in "The Matter of Rome the Great" (cf. *TC* 5.1849). *Anelida and Arcite* is generally considered Chaucer's most unsuccessful single poem, and it is perhaps most interesting to teach as such. Its form is rhyme royal, but the nine-line stanzas of Anelida's complaint proper achieve a symmetry comparable to that of Greek odes. This poem also has quasi-epic features—for example, the invocation (1–21; cf. *CT* 1.2383–93 and *TC* 3.724–25) and proem (211–19; cf. *CT* 4.41–43). The prelude to Anelida's complaint may be compared with The Squire's Tale as an aborted overture. Particular lines are lifted from a choir of French poets—two names (Arcite and Emily) are from Boccaccio. But the most prestigious and familiar paradigms of Chaucer's plaintive impersonation of a jilted woman (as in his *Legend of Good Women*) are book 4 of Vergil's *Aeneid* and all of Ovid's *Heroides*.

The so-called complaints of Mars and Venus seem forever conjoined—

thanks to John Shirley—as a teachable diptych, but this pairing is largely illusory. Teaching "The Complaint of Mars," or "broche of Thebes" (245), works better with *Anelida and Arcite*. It begins with a rhyme-royal prelude (1–154). The initial apostrophe to the mourning birds (1) and Saint Valentine their healer (13) also harmonizes well with *The Parliament of Fowls*. Chaucer claims Statius (21; cf. *TC* 5.1498a–l) and the elusive Corinna as his classical authorities. Passages translate Statius, Boccaccio, and especially Ovid; but, since Chaucer's real source seems to have been court gossip, this complaint may be taught as Chaucer's most pure example of a rather dirty roman à clef. "The Complaint of Venus," which is also designated a "lai" (71), translates three discrete ballades by Grandson, flower of French poets (82) and admirer of Chaucer. There is no textual indication (except perhaps line 2 of "The Complaint of Mars") that this complaint belongs to Venus herself, but it is clear that the speaker of Chaucer's first ballade is female. Chaucer's closing comments about "remembraunce" (78) and writing as penance (79) complement his themes in the prologue to *The Legend of Good Women*.

The intensity of a sincere complaint is easy to ridicule, and Chaucer's mock complaints are more fun to teach precisely because their subversive playfulness seems typically "Chaucerian." The humor of "The Complaint of Chaucer to His Purse" depends initially on the discrepancy of identifying such a "supplicacion" (26) as a wooing complaint (2; cf. *CT* 1.3141). Chaucer addresses his purse with epithets appropriate to Mary (13, 15; cf. "An ABC") or Christ (16). The joke's premise is sustained by several playfully obvious puns (heaviness, sound, color)—precedents for which may be readily found, notably in Machaut and Eustache Deschamps—and concludes with outrageous analogies (between the savior and savings, a courtier's bankruptcy and a mendicant's poverty).

Until 1891, "To Rosemounde" was unknown. This complaint seems a burlesque-ballade in which "daliaunce" signals the poet's hoped-for reward (16). The opening formality of addressing a not-undergrown bar girl as "Madame" sounds hilarious if not tipsy (1). It is easier to footnote a tearful allusion than to convey to a class the humor of imagining "tregentil" Chaucer himself as "trewe Tristam the secounde" (20; cf. *TC* 2.651). Troilus languishes; Chaucer wallows like a fish in wine. His hot love needs no reheating. The double entendre of the silly *senhal* "Rosemounde" (Rosey mouth / Rose of the World) plays against both an idol of Guillaume de Lorris's amour and an icon of Marian devotion.

"Adam Scriveyn" is a fascinating triviality, a complaint contra proofreading. This verse Post-It note is most often cited as indicative of Chaucer's anxiety regarding scribal transmission. Since the poem is a single stanza of rhyme royal, it might be annexed as yet another envoy to the conclusion of *Troilus and Criseyde* (5.1856–58).

A grouping of five short poems is usually identified as Chaucer's "Boethian poems"; they may as readily be termed his metra. "The Former Age" is essentially a Juvenalian jeremiad. The idea of a golden "Etas Prima" is traceable to both Hesiod and Genesis. But Chaucer's three most at-hand maestros seem to be Boethius, Ovid, and Jean de Meun. No mere *ubi sunt?* elegy, only the first stanza of "The Former Age" recalls "[a] blisful lyf" (1). The rest damns the present *lapsus*. Chaucer's outrage is distilled in the negative anaphora that composes the third stanza (17–24). The text of "The Former Age" reports a *vox clamantis* against the counterfeit cupidity and lecherous tyranny of "oure dayes" (61). The final note of "The Former Age" sounds like despair, and so does the last line of the third (originally final?) stanza of "Lak of Stedfastnesse." But there is an annexed hope of reform in the ballade's envoy. "Fortune" conjoins three ballades into a debate. Section 1 offers a first-person complaint against Lady Fortune (cf. Lady Fame); like Socrates (17), the plaintiff "that over himself hath the maystrye" (14) defies this two-faced, painted woman (but see *CT* 3.729). Section 2 presents Fortune's rebuttal; section 3 contains the uneven closing arguments. Fortune wins the debate, but in the envoy she bribes the court to reward her friend (75). Chaucer's initially philosophical complaint thus ends as a mock *quête*. This ballade-debate may also be compared with "The Complaint of Mars" as a disguising. "Truth," Chaucer's most frequently copied ballade, anticipates Thomas Wyatt's renunciation of the "tikelnesse" (3) of worldly ambition; it consists of sententiae attributable to Boethius or Seneca or John Gower, conjoined with a biblical refrain. "Hold the heye wey" (20) echoes the meditation that heads The Parson's Tale, an association enhanced by the address to the "pilgrim" reader (18). "Gentilesse," or "Moral Balade," may be Chaucer's most egalitarian manifesto. This ballade invokes the first order of things (1, 8, 19) to rebuke the current state of affairs. The poem borrows from Boethius, Dante, Jean de Meun, and Boccaccio, but Chaucer's most compelling inspiration may have been a chant attributed to John Ball: "When Adam dalf and Eve span, / Wo was then a gentilman?" (see "John Ball's Sermon"). Chaucer's ballade is most often taught as a corollary to the loathly lady's apologia in The Wife of Bath's Tale (*CT* 3.1162–67; cf. The Franklin's Tale [*CT* 5.686–95]), but its implicit threat to succession (12–13) and the iterative scorn of its refrain sounds much more threatening as an echo of the Peasants' Revolt of 1381.

Both the "Lenvoy de Chaucer a Scogan" and the "Lenvoy de Chaucer a Bukton" are similar in spirit to the verse epistles of Horace or Machaut yet contrary to each other. Bits and pieces of these poems have been attributed to Dante, Alain de Lille, and Ovid, among other *auctores*—all "common domain" allusions among collegial, protohumanist bookmen. Chaucer, as a chubby, gray-haired companion (31), feels comfortable enough to jest about his impotence (39)—poetic, that is (cf. *PF* 1–4). He even blames the plague on his much younger (43) friend's recklessness in love (14). Such homosocial jocularity claims the fructifying authority of Cicero's *amicitia*, or "kyndenesse" (47; cf. *CT* 5.761–90). Unlike other still-hopeful "Grisels," Chaucer just wants a nap (38). The Jerome-like advice of "Lenvoy de Chaucer a Bukton" seems straightforward enough, but not its motivation. The poem's explicit reference to "[t]he Wyf of Bathe" (29) suggests that *The Canterbury Tales* may have been circulating in manuscript segments. Like Alison (*CT* 3.154–60), this bourgeois male readership had its way with Saint Paul (17–18).

Last and least among Chaucer's short poems are the "Proverbs." Aphorisms permeate Chaucer's poetry. These twin quatrains are among his least inspiring. Since teaching any text by Chaucer affirms, however, that "out of olde feldes, as men seyth, / Cometh al this newe corn" (*PF* 22–23), don't throw away your winter coat in summer; don't grasp more than you can hold; and don't dismiss the short poems from class.

Chaucer and the French Tradition

Karla Taylor

Chaucer was immersed in French literary culture throughout his writing life. As unavoidable as air, it defined the international literature of court, chivalry, and love (see Muscatine; Nolan; Braddy, "French Influence"; Wimsatt, *French Love Poets*, "French Poetry," and *French Contemporaries*; Scattergood, "Short Poems"). But Chaucer classes can rarely include even chief sources, let alone his entire pervasively French literary milieu. My solution for advanced undergraduate and graduate students is to prompt and enrich discussion of Chaucer's poems with brief lectures on selected French intertexts, which students have not read. These intertexts help them see literary history not as static and already given but as constituted by dynamic reading relationships from which central aspects of Chaucer's poetry emerge. Two examples show how the French tradition can decisively affect students' understanding: Chaucer's narrative persona in *The Book of the Duchess* and the ethical critique of literary love ideology in *Troilus and Criseyde*.

French literary fashions and writers shaped the reading expectations of Chaucer's audiences through the mid-1380s (Minnis, *Shorter Poems* 9–35). Most important were the *Roman de la rose*, the thirteenth-century love allegory so fundamental to courtly erotic literature, and the fourteenth-century *dits amoureux* of Guillaume de Machaut, Jean Froissart, and others (Wimsatt, "French Poetry" and *French Contemporaries*). From them Chaucer learned the ideology and conventions of literary love—both the behavior of lovers and the allegorical mode in which it was represented. These works offered Chaucer an extended narrative form capable of great interiority, as well as a genre—the secular love vision—that framed such interiority in first-person experience.

The minilecture on *The Book of the Duchess* sketches in the social contexts of mid-fourteenth-century court literature in order to focus on what Chaucer learned from Machaut: how to negotiate the relations between contemporary vernacular court writing and classical literature and between the poet's own middling status and that of his highborn patrons and audiences. I briefly describe Chaucer's pervasively French milieu during the 1360s, when Jean de Berry (Machaut's patron) and Froissart were present in London. *The Book of the Duchess* transposes French *dits* into English (Minnis, *Shorter Poems* 91–112; Phillips, "Fortune"; and Palmer; for excerpts from the French *dits*, see Windeatt, *Dream Poetry*). Machaut's *Dit de la fonteinne amoureuse*, written for Jean on his departure into English captivity, is especially instructive. My synopsis stresses the intimacy, born of shared poetic experience, between poet and patron. The *Fonteinne*'s narrator overhears a knight (a stand-in for Jean) singing a complaint in which the Ceyx and Alcione story parallels the knight's own separation from his beloved. Impressed, the narrator transcribes the complaint and praises its artistry. Machaut thus compliments his patron even as he draws attention to his own poetic accomplishment. Poetic exchange forges intimacy when the narrator, asked by the knight to write a complaint, produces the transcription. Falling asleep, both then share the same dream, just as they earlier shared the complaint.

Reworking Machaut's synthesis of classical literary tradition and courtly culture, Chaucer not only fashions the first English *dit* but also discovers the lineaments of his own classicism. Perhaps more surprising, as students infer, he also re-creates the characteristically Chaucerian narrator of *The Book of the Duchess* from Machaut (Minnis, *Shorter Poems* 105–11; Butterfield). Machaut's self-deprecating, subservient narrator—a means of negotiating his social position as a cleric writing for princes—allows Machaut to give advice and correction without offense and to achieve a fictive intimacy with his socially elevated patrons. I ask students to compare this intimacy with exchanges in *The Book of the Duchess*, such as the dreamer's response to the Man in Black's overheard song (443–538) and the chess game with Fortune (652–748). They recognize Machaut's diffidence in the dreamer's slowness to grasp why the Man in Black should be stricken by his loss of a queen. Literal mindedness, they discover, allows the dreamer to elicit the eulogy to White without ever presuming the intimacy or shared knowledge so remarkable in the *Fonteinne*. Because the Man in Black instructs the dreamer, Chaucer does not appear to instruct or correct his patron John of Gaunt.

Once students recognize the social purposes of the poem's deftly handled narrator, I sketch in some historical implications of Chaucer's appropriation of Machaut. By inviting condescension from readers, Chaucer's narrator negotiates the divergent purposes of elite court audiences and poets. However ambitious the French vernacular tradition, social prestige belonged to the patronizing audience. Court writers, who provided graceful occasional entertainment affirming aristocratic values and self-esteem, had no correspondingly lofty role (Olson, "Deschamps" and "Making"; Middleton). By registering a social tension alien to Machaut, the relationship between dreamer and Man in Black reworks—and works around—the constraints of court literary culture, which shaped the voice of both poets.

An older French tradition illuminates the amatory ethics of *Troilus and Criseyde*. What Chaucer really did to *Il Filostrato* (to use C. S. Lewis's phrase) was to adapt it to the ideology of court culture defined, above all, by the *Roman de la rose*: the *Troilus* thus appropriates from the *Roman* not only the conventions of love service, with its feudally defined relationships and rituals, but also many specific echoes (Lewis, "What Chaucer"; R. Edwards, "Pandarus's 'Unthrift'"; Windeatt, *Troilus* [1992] 228–30). More realistic than the *Roman*, *Troilus and Criseyde* nevertheless is also shaped by that poem's allegorical agency, facets of which Chaucer builds into his characters in order to invent an ethical critique of amatory discourse from within. The French tradition can render this critique visible, not as a twenty-first-century imposition but as integral to the poem, and indeed as one of its central discoveries.

We begin with discussion. As my students consider the developing love affair in books 1–2, they become restive with its artifice. With interspersed comparisons to passages from the *Roman*, I encourage them to regard the French tradition as a repertoire of scripts for Troilus and Criseyde to follow, as when Troilus imitates Amant in falling victim to Love's arrow (*TC* 1.204–329; *Roman* 1681–1880) and then (like Amant in the face of Dongier, the lady's resistance or reserve) lapses into demoralized passivity (Windeatt, *Troilus* [1992] 115). Troilus's paralysis, Criseyde's reluctance, the elevated intensity of love—all are indebted to the exploration of the lover's experience in the *Roman*. Considering the language and conventions of idealized romantic love as roles inhabited by Troilus and Criseyde, students collectively arrive at a more complex understanding both of the lovers' agency and of their tactical appropriations of convention.

Pandarus introduces much of the poem's conventional love discourse as he teaches Troilus how to conduct a courtship and imposes on Criseyde the roles scripted for romance women (Taylor, "*Inferno*" 245–54). My students are invariably troubled by Pandarus's role, which results in an unsettling account of amatory mediation—of how, that is, the love affair comes about at all. I try to deepen their disquiet by asking them to look at the conversations that frame book 3. Starting with Pandarus's conversation with Criseyde on the morning after the consummation (*TC* 3.1555–82), students identify and struggle to account for the scene's suggestive evasions, which provoke (but do not confirm) suspicion of an erotic relationship between Criseyde and Pandarus. As Louise O. Fradenburg suggests, "the undecidability of Chaucer's text is designed not just to occlude violence but to make us 'see' its occlusion" ("Our Owen Wo" 101). My goal is to help students find a different source for their discomfiture, not in a literal erotic liaison but in Pandarus's vicarious involvement (Taylor, *Chaucer* 78–84).

We then look at the conversation between Troilus and Pandarus (3.232–420), which suggests Pandarus's vicarious entanglements with *both* lovers. To explore this scene's astonishing examination of the ethics of amatory mediation, I ask my students to consider the pattern of substitutions thus far. Pandarus has already threatened to join Troilus in death if Criseyde persists in her pitiless disdain (2.323–25). When Criseyde first kisses Troilus, it is Pandarus who is gratified: he falls on his knees, raises eyes and hands to heaven, and thanks Cupid and Venus (3.176–89). Now, when Pandarus assumes the place of the merciful lady, Troilus responds with inexpressible joy, so that "His olde wo, that made his herte swelte, / Gan tho for joie wasten and tomelte" (3.347–48). I ask my students to account for the unmistakably erotic language. Since a literal sexual liaison between Pandarus and Troilus would be as damaging to the poem's ethical concerns as one between Pandarus and Criseyde (for Pandarus's "polymorphous" erotic involvements, see Pugh; Dinshaw 48), this line of questioning intensifies their discomfiture.

Here a minilecture on the role of the *Roman de la rose*'s allegorical agency in constituting Pandarus's character provides a background against which his desire becomes more unsettling than even literal erotic acts. My broader purposes are to suggest that, since literary tradition is made up of acts of appropriation, intertextual comparisons have interpretative consequences and to show that Chaucer's appropriation of allegory results in an ethical critique of amatory discourses. The critique arises because Chaucer reworks the *Roman*'s allegorical characters Amis, or Friend (*Roman* 3099–246) and Bel Acueil, or Fair Welcoming (*Roman* 2765–822) as elements of Pandarus's realistic social character. In essence, Chaucer reverses the *Roman*'s allegorical strategy of turning human interiority inside out. By representing the complex currents of human thought and desire as separate, autonomous agents, the *Roman* rendered subjectivity itself visible and susceptible to precise analysis. When Chaucer reintegrates these allegorical figures into a single complex character—Pandarus—he prompts the ethical questions occluded by allegorical representation.

As a descendant of Amis, Pandarus translates Troilus's deeply felt experience into action (Lewis, "What Chaucer" 68–73; Muscatine 137–53; Wetherbee, *Chaucer* 54–76; Windeatt, *Troilus* [1992] 116). In distributing love's action and passion to two separate characters, Chaucer appropriates the *Roman*'s representational fiction whereby the erotic overtures to the Rose emanate not from Amant directly but from a third autonomous agent, Amis. This separation shields Troilus's idealized innocence from the love affair's sometimes coercive manipulations; these belong only to Pandarus.

Even more troubling, Pandarus's mediation encroaches on Criseyde's autonomy, usurping her capacity to be the subject of her own desires. In a critical reworking of the *Roman*, Chaucer renders this usurpation visible by adding Bel Acueil (the lady's erotic reciprocation) to Pandarus's character. His entanglements, knottier than any literal sexual liaison, are problematic instead because they are vicarious. The vicar of the love affair, Pandarus substitutes for both lovers as he represents each to the other. Such mediation is built into the French ideology of love, first as a means to maintain the secrecy and discretion enjoined on lovers, and second as a means to overcome the resistance (*dongier*) that defines female virtue. Thus Bel Acueil—the counterforce to Dongier in the female beloved's delicate negotiation between virtuous resistance and erotic response—is a pivotal mediator (*Roman* 2823–970). Because interior conflict is represented as a battle among autonomous allegorical agents, the lady can be both virtuous and responsive; interior conflict also displaces social coercions. The grammatically masculine Bel Acueil's responsiveness carries little or no homoerotic charge since he represents an aspect of the female object of male desire. Allegory attenuates "natural" gender reference even as it obscures the ethical problem of agency in a mediated love affair.

Not so with Pandarus's vicarious place-holding. Integrating the analytic fictions of allegory into a realistic human social agent, Chaucer renders these ethical difficulties visible. His appropriation also subjects allegorical discourse itself to scrutiny. Despite its complex analysis of human subjectivity, allegory tends to occlude what Chaucer exposes by appropriating it: the coercion to which Criseyde is subjected, the usurpation entailed by Pandarus's mediation, and the extent to which the ideality of romantic love depends on both. Returning to discussion, students can now confront the erotic entanglements caused by Pandarus's mediation, neither erasing them nor simplifying them into literal sexual attachments. Instead, they can discover Chaucer's searching ethical critique both of amatory ideology and of the allegorical representation that idealizes it.

Boccaccio's *Il Filostrato*, Chaucer's *Troilus and Criseyde*, and Translating the Italian Tradition

Warren Ginsberg

> Love renders a body into history.
> —Sara Suleri

Among the many beguiling sentences of *Meatless Days,* Sara Suleri's memoir of life in Pakistan, this essay's epigraph will intrigue teachers of *Troilus and Criseyde.* Through the outreach of affection, Suleri suggests, love weaves flesh and bone into the texture of the day and turns our yesterdays into warp and woof of a design this moment's touch completes. Yet the baldness of her statement sits oddly with the raveling in time and circumstance she claims love brings about; no matter when or where, our bodies in love undergo a reconfiguration that ushers their entrance into the contingencies of history. Even those who believe such a process always occurs will agree that each word in Suleri's expression of it asks for clarification. Certainly *love, body, renders,* and *history* meant something different to Boccaccio and Chaucer than to Suleri or us. Yet to judge from *Il Filostrato* and *Troilus and Criseyde*, poems in which love is aleatory and overdetermined, carnal and ideal, neither poet would have taken it amiss if Suleri's thought stood as his epigraph as well.

The manner in which love, bodies, and history operate in the Italian work, however, differs from how they operate in the English. I want to discuss a way to approach the differences that sidesteps the tendentiousness of inquiries that answer, in one form or another, C. S. Lewis's famous question, What did Chaucer do to *Il Filostrato*? We can avoid the inevitable reduction of Boccaccio's poem to inert backdrop for *Troilus and Criseyde* by examining how the "mode of meaning" of each follows and disrupts the other.

Mode of meaning is a phrase I adopt from Walter Benjamin's "The Task of the Translator" to indicate those linguistic, literary, and cultural traditions that shape the events of a text and make them understandable to its audience (see my *Chaucer's Italian Tradition* 8–10, 148–89). According to Benjamin, the translator's task is to express "the central reciprocal relationship between languages" (72). This relationship is revealed through the disclosure of the intention that underlies each language as a whole. The differences in sound and letter that distinguish *bread*, for example, from the French equivalent *pain* underwrite discrete chains of associations; when the words are substituted for each other, the morphological and cultural logic that connects the English word with, say, *bled* on the one hand and *wine* on the other (a loaf of bread, a jug of wine) disarticulates and is disarticulated by the logic that connects *pain* with *vin* (either in phonic terms or as the fare one once received in bistros for the cover charge). Since all philological and social incompatibilities arise from different combinations of vowels and consonants before they have acquired a meaning in language, Benjamin calls the aggregation of these divergences "pure speech" (74). The orientation of any language to this collective pure speech determines its intentional mode, and it is a language's mode of intention that Benjamin says translations should seek to translate. When a corresponding manner is found, the original and the translation second and undo each other's claim to be the first or final word.

In *Il Filostrato*, the mode of meaning from which character and event derive their bearing and coherence is the "the orality of writing" as an ethical element in verbal mediation. To a great extent, everything in Boccaccio's poem depends on writing's success or failure to vocalize itself; behind his decision to cast his work as a form of "visible speech" (a phrase Dante invented to characterize God's art in the *Purgatorio* [10.95]), a particular version of Italian literary and cultural history has preconditioned the meanings writing itself had.[1] In *Troilus and Criseyde*, the corresponding mode is recitation per se. Instead of writing that scripts its own utterance, English conventions and ideologies prompt Chaucer to present a narrator and characters who speak the texts they write or read. It is precisely in this difference, the difference, that is, between the manner in which the textual and the oral are related to each other, that Chaucer's and Boccaccio's works become translations.

Since most readers of this volume know *Troilus and Criseyde* better than *Il Filostrato*, I devote the rest of this essay mostly to Boccaccio's *proemio*; by examining the ways in which pen and ink are related to intentionality in this prologue, I hope to suggest how writing becomes a mode of meaning. For comparable passages in Chaucer, I would turn first to the narrator's prologues and intrusions and to the many scenes of reading in the poem. While I will not be able to examine these textual examples, I end with a word on how oral rehearsal gives them their intentional carriage.

In the widest sense, Troiolo, Criseida, and Pandaro are direct responses to the idea of means and mediation in those late medieval philosophies of mind and action that formed the context of the *dolce stil novo*. This "sweet new style" enabled thirteenth-century northern Italian poets to celebrate love as an intellectual and ethical virtue by describing its operations in the scholastic languages of pneumatology and faculty psychology. More specifically, *Il Filostrato* revises Dante's attempt to make the agency of words an act of faith. To warrant the sanctity of his "poema sacro," as he calls it (*Par.* 25.1), Dante describes himself as both its scribe and author. He is Love's amanuensis, who notes when Amor breathes in him; he is also a poet who fashions his own way of being in the world, in that he says he then "goes signifying" not the inexpressible inspiration he noted but "in the mode in which Love had dictated within" (*Purg.* 24.52, 53–54). In *Il Filostrato*, Boccaccio in essence replies that creative language can never be so transparent; it always takes on the rhetorical opaqueness of personal motives. Writing or speech not only derives its value from the use it is put to but gives value to the end it is used for as well.

The prologue of *Il Filostrato*, which purports to account for its genesis, establishes the work's textual and intertextual dynamics. Besides locating the narrator's entire experience within the confines of a rhetorical love debate, the particular question the speaker contemplates invites us to read *Il Filostrato* in conjunction with another of Boccaccio's works, *Il Filocolo*, where the same question appears. In this prose romance, Graziosa asks whether seeing one's beloved or thinking about her provides greater delight. Fiammetta, the debate's judge, holds that thinking gives more joy; the learned terminology she uses is very much in the style of the *stil novo*. In *Il Filostrato*, the narrator acknowledges that he once thought as Fiammetta did. But the "bitter experience" of his lover Filomena's relocation has taught him, as Criseida's removal to the Greek camp taught Troiolo, that thought's ability to "make a loved one kind and responsive according to one's desires" (*proemio* 5) dissolves into nothing in the face of not being able to see her.

The differing responses to the repeated question encourage us to invent a history of Boccaccio's literary development. No longer can recourse to the idealized fancies of romance or the airy dialectics of love disputations offer consolation; only the temporal distance of sad historical events stands as an adequate analogue to the despair that Filomena's absence causes her paramour.

Yet how far, one wonders, is *Il Filocolo*'s psychology of love from the rhetoric of desolation in *Il Filostrato*? To make the heart's grief resolve itself as the recantation of an argument in a debate seems inappropriately bloodless. Because he no longer can see Filomena, the narrator tells her that his heart was forced to cry out in Jeremiah's anguished words: "how solitary sits the city, which was once full of people and mistress among nations" (*Filostrato*, line 12). This lamentation from Lamentations is shocking not merely for the borrowed articulation of the narrator's sorrow but for the passage's two-facedness. Readers of the *Vita nuova,* including Boccaccio, would recall that Dante used these same words to herald Beatrice's death. The invitation to equate her parting from Florence and Filomena's departure is outrageous. The allusion is meant to express the magnitude of the narrator's despair. But there is an insidious side to his quotation. In the light of the story he is soon to tell, Filomena's debouchment makes Naples not only Jeremiah's widowed city but also a latter-day Troy. If we remember how Troy was brought low, we remember a series of betrayals. By granting himself the author's privilege of future-perfect retrospection, the narrator conceals in his compliment to his lady a warning that his love will have its vengeance if she proves to be a treacherous Criseida. Filostrato wants to persuade Filomena to return, yet he also seems ready to condemn her for not returning. Indeed, he says his life depends on his poem's ability to induce her to return, but his anger peeps through his supplication, and anger has no desire to persuade. Rather, we suspect that under the guise of persuasion, Filostrato wants to upbraid Filomena, not for not having returned, but for having left in the first place.

The narrator accordingly frames his experience as a love debate because he is unable to judge the truth or falseness of his lady. It may turn out that Filomena remains faithful, just as events proved Criseida did not. But Filostrato is not motivated by fairness to hold his hopes and doubts in unbiased balance; his seeming evenhandedness actually masks his hijacking of the protocols of rhetorical argumentation to accuse Filomena of betrayal at the same time that he swears he believes in her fidelity. Instead of determining the sincerity of Filomena's love by arguing both sides of the case, Filostrato prosecutes the divided urgings of his soul. For him, truth is the "manner of meaning" he fashions to determine her truthfulness, so that he can say to Filomena "odi et amo," which he would translate as "I hate, I love, it depends on you."

For all Filostrato's idealization of Filomena, his own identification with Troiolo makes us suspect that her return is not his ultimate goal but only a means to it: he wants to sleep with her, just as Troiolo slept with Criseida. The persuasiveness of the story he will tell, from which Filomena can infer her goodness by the extent of his ardor for her, is a blind for his own exercise in salacious wish fulfillment. The moral of the story, which would argue that false women like Criseida must be avoided, becomes similarly self-serving. We know that Criseida was untrue because history has told us she was. But in Filostrato's hands, history is not an uninflected recitation of what was; it becomes instead an excuse to tell the story backwards. By positing Criseida's guilt from the start, the narrator can vilify Filomena for leaving or hector her into rejoining him.

Boccaccio, however, did not merely make this double-voiced, translational revision of the impartiality of means and ends in rhetorical disputation the theme of *Il Filostrato*, he lent it flesh and gave it a name: Pandaro. If we compare the *quistione* of *Il Filostrato* with that of *Il Filocolo*, we notice that the former proposes a third possibility in addition to sight and thought as the greatest delight in love: speaking to the lady. This is the very function the narrator gives his poem; he hopes its words will prove as effective with Filomena as Pandaro's are with Criseida. In Troy, though, Pandaro panders by speaking to his cousin face-to-face. Because Filomena has left Naples, *Il Filostrato* is able to act as go-between only by addressing her indirectly, not in speech but in the written pleadings of an absent suitor. But, in the end, there is no difference between Pandaro's mediation and the poem's because Pandaro is the performance of *Il Filostrato*'s mode of meaning: he is the orality of its writing. In the poem, Pandaro is the figure through whom Filostrato vocalizes his absence and presence so that Filomena might calculate the loss of staying away against the gain of returning. Beyond the poem, Pandaro is the figure through whom Boccaccio argues that writing, because of its simultaneous embrace of presence and absence, is the only medium capable of representing simultaneously divided desires.

In Italian cities, where aristocratic families commonly needed to keep commercial records, that writing is a mode of meaning in *Il Filostrato* may have caused less surprise than the meaning and character Boccaccio ascribed to it. After all, by the mid–fourteenth century, Troy's fall had long since been baptized as a moment in salvation history. A Christian audience of Troiolo's story would assume that it, no less than the events Saint Paul said "happened to [the Israelites] in figure," was "written for [its] correction" (1 Cor. 10.11 [see *Holy Bible*]). What the Italian merchant-nobleman who read Boccaccio's Troy chronicle would not have anticipated was the narrator's demonstration that the same means of figuration could be used to script a history not intent on common profit but on his own.

Chaucer quotes Paul's doctrine twice in *The Canterbury Tales*, underlining its importance to his storytelling (7.3441–42 and 10.1083); in *Troilus and Criseyde*, the final stanzas that suggest Paul's view of historiography suggest as well Chaucer's response to Boccaccio's insinuation that even Christian teleology has ulterior motives. From my perspective, it is not the presence of the saint's ideas that makes Chaucer's tragedy a translation of *Il Filostrato*; it is the absence of writing as a mode of meaning. I do not mean to say the English work is less textual than its Italian counterpart; writing is everywhere, from the love letters to the narrator's sources to the poem itself. But in each instance writing is folded into an act of recitation. In *Il Filostrato*, the narrator composes an epistle-poem that speaks to Filomena through Troiolo, Criseida, and Pandaro, who are made ventriloquists of the double-purposed message he wants his lady to hear. By contrast, Chaucer's narrator announces that he will read *Troilus and Criseyde* to his audience for everyone's benefit, yet, as he does this, he reads himself into and out of all the characters. Instead of providing lessons in the art of self-aggrandizement, however, the Chaucerian narrator's Trojan entanglements, which are no less driven by his needs than Filostrato's are driven by his, become a model of unselfish impartiality. The narrator's sympathetic, critical voicings of Criseyde, of Troilus, of Pandarus perform as a mode of meaning that corresponds to and disarticulates the dubious divisions that writing enables in *Il Filostrato*. In the end, reading texts aloud in Chaucer and the orality of writing in Boccaccio are both ways of figuring the love that renders bodies into history; diverse cultural and ideological commitments cause each work to calculate its ratios of distance and investment differently. By attending to these poems' dialogue between past and present, in which writing and speech are modes that follow and undo each other's meaning, we can teach *Il Filostrato* and *Troilus and Criseyde* as the translations they are.

NOTE

[1]Citations to Dante's *Divine Comedy* are from Durling and Martinez's edition.

Boethius, Dante, and
Teaching Aspects of Chaucer's Tragedy

Noel Harold Kaylor, Jr.

Near the end of *Troilus and Criseyde*, Chaucer's narrator refers to the work as his little "tragedye" (5.1786). To help students read the work as a Chaucerian tragedy, the theoretical framework implicit in the text should be introduced into classroom discussion. Aristotle's *Poetics* was unknown to Chaucer, since he did not read Greek and seems to have been unaware of an obscure Latin translation of 1256 (Preminger), so he had to seek his understanding of tragedy as a literary genre in sources that were available to him. Textual evidence points to Dante and Boethius as two of those sources, and it appears that Chaucer proceeded to reinvent tragedy as a narrative genre (for a Boethian reading of *Troilus and Criseyde*, see McCall, "Five-Book Structure"; for Chaucer's reading of Dante, see Taylor, *Chaucer*).

In *The Canterbury Tales*, a simple *de casibus* (or "downfall of great men") framework is suggested by the Monk for the tragedies he narrates (7.1990–94). The descriptive rubric *de casibus tragedy* comes from Boccaccio's *De casibus virorum illustrium*; the stories in this work bear superficial similarity to those narrated by the Monk, but Boccaccio never refers to his stories as tragedies (Kelly, *Chaucerian Tragedy* 7–8; see also his *Ideas* and *Tragedy and Comedy*). Elements of the simplistic framework delineated and illustrated by the Monk appear in Chaucer's gloss on a passage in his translation of the *Consolation of Philosophy*, the *Boece* ("Tragedye is to seyn a dite of a prosperite for a tyme, that endeth in wrecchidness" [bk. 2, prose 2, lines 70–72]); interestingly, no reference is made in the gloss to tragedy specifically as a dramatic genre. The framework implicit in *Troilus and Criseyde* is much more complex than the Monk's many downfalls, so reference to a simple *de casibus* scheme of tragedy alone does little justice to Chaucer's masterpiece (see Wetherbee, *Chaucer*, for the complexity of influences on Chaucer). Consideration of a larger context of Chaucer's understanding of tragedy increases students' appreciation of *Troilus and Criseyde*. A plan for introducing the interrelated aspects of Dante's *Commedia* and Boethius's *Consolation of Philosophy* is outlined in the paragraphs below.

Chaucer is credited with using the word *tragedy* in English for the first time (Kaylor, "Chaucer's Use"). It appears at the end of *Troilus and Criseyde* in contrast to the word *comedye*: "Go, litel bok, go litel myn tragedye, / Ther God thi makere yet, er that he dye, / So sende myght to make in som comedye!" (5.1786–88). The first occurrence of the word in Chaucer's works is found in the gloss, cited earlier, on a line in the *Boece*, which appears without reference to any contrasting concept. It also appears in the prologue to The Monk's Tale in similar isolation, except for the notable comedy of The Nun's

Priest's Tale that follows it immediately in fragment 7 of *The Canterbury Tales* (Kaylor, "Nun's Priest's Tale"). The word *tragedy* then appears in the end of the tragedy of Troilus, written in about the year 1386. We do not know exactly when Chaucer may first have encountered the word, but the mixture of elements in *Troilus and Criseyde* indicates that by about 1382 he had synthesized his own concept of the genre.

From his reading of the *Commedia*, Chaucer extrapolated a five-unit tragic structure for *Troilus and Criseyde* out of Dante's three-unit *Commedia*: Chaucer follows the initial rising fortunes of Troilus's adventures through his falling fortunes in the second half of the work. From his reading of the *Consolation of Philosophy*, Chaucer adopted the image of the Wheel of Fortuna (the "executrice of wierdes" [*TC* 3.617]) to include the rising and falling structure of his tragic plot. From Boethius, Chaucer also developed his understanding of the operations of free will and predestination, which add important thematic dimensions to Troilus's tragedy.

Because an introduction to teaching the Dantean and Boethian aspects of Chaucer's *Troilus and Criseyde* can present only the outline of a complex issue, the sections below touch on the blending of material from these sources at three key points in the text: the opening verses, the middle stanzas of book 3, and the closing verses. (See figs. 1 and 2.)

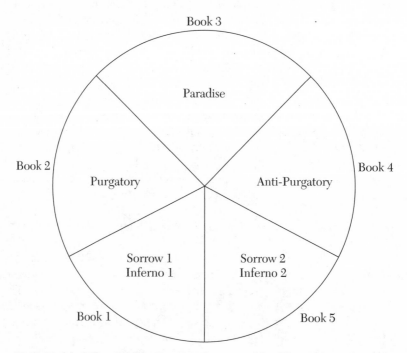

Fig. 1. Model of Chaucer's Five-Unit Tragedy, as Extrapolated from Dante's Three-Unit *Commedia*

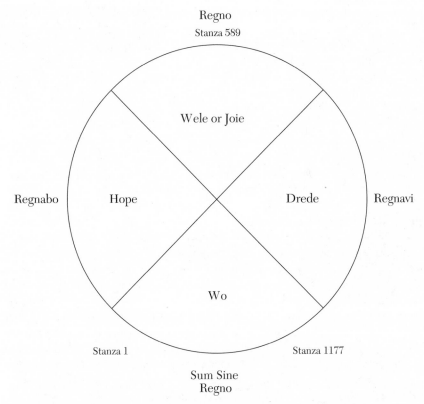

Fig. 2. Model of Fortune's Turning Wheel from Boethius, with the Appropriate Emotion Assigned to Each Position

The opening lines of *Troilus and Criseyde* meld Dantean and Boethian tragic elements:

> The double sorwe of Troilus to tellen,
> That was the kyng Priamus sone of Troye,
> In lovynge, how his aventures fellen
> Fro wo to wele, and after out of joie.   (1.1–4)

The general shape of the tragedy is clearly sketched out in these lines. First, reference to Dante's *Commedia* is implied: Troilus progresses from book 1 to book 3 of his story, from *wo* to *wele*, as does Dante the pilgrim through the three books of his journey, from hell (the locus of woe), via purgatory, to heaven (the locus of joy). Also, reference to Boethius's imagery is suggested: Troilus progresses from book 3 to book 5 in a descent that recalls the downward turning of Fortuna's wheel. In the *Boece*, Lady Fortuna discusses her

withdrawal of favor in these words: "What other thynge bywaylen the cryinges
of tragedyes but only the dedes of Fortune, that with an unwar strook over-
turneth the realmes of greet nobleye?" (bk. 2, prose 2, lines 7–10). This line
carries Chaucer's gloss on the word *tragedy*. The first stanza of Troilus's story
concludes with the following two verses: "Tesiphone, thow help me for t'endite
/ Thise woful vers, that wepen as I write" (1.6–7). The first verse recalls
Dante's woeful netherworld because Tesiphone is one of the three Fury
guardians of the lower infernal regions (Dante, *Inf.* 9.48).[1] The phrasing of
the second verse then recalls the opening lines of the *Boece*: "Allas! I wepynge,
am constreyned to bygynnen vers of sorwful matere, that whilom in florys-
schyng studie made delitable ditees" (bk. 1, metrum 1, lines 1–3). Thus, Chau-
cer's opening stanza establishes a complex mixture of concepts and motifs
from both Dante and Boethius as it lays out the conditions of tragedy for the
story of Troilus that will follow.

Dante opens his *Commedia* with a stanza that calls attention to itself, since
each word demands a reader's consideration: "Midway along the journey of
our life / . . . I had wandered off from the straight path" (*Inf.* 1.1, 3). Imme-
diately, a reader must consider what the word *midway* refers to. Most often,
students are asked to note Dante's age of thirty-five in the year 1300, but
since the journey taken by Dante the pilgrim through the three-volume *Com-
media* represents, at least on the textual level, the journey through the work
itself, students should also look at *Purgatory* 16 and 17 (which are also cantos
50 and 51 of the entire three-volume journey) to discover what the word refers
to at the textual level. *Purgatory* 16 initiates a discussion of free will versus
predestination and canto 17 presents a discourse on the nature of love, which
become two major themes in Chaucer's *Troilus and Criseyde*. Dante's dis-
cussion in *Purgatory* 16, along with certain passages from the *Consolation of
Philosophy* that are noted below, has bearing on Troilus's Boethian monologue
on free will, predestination, and necessity, delivered in the famous temple
scene (4.958–1078). Dante's discourse on love in canto 17 distinguishes nat-
ural love from rational love. Natural love causes human beings to love, and
love springs forth naturally and spontaneously; however, it is how we choose
to love through rational love that makes our loving either noble or ignoble.
Dante's discourse on the two types of love should help students interpret
Troilus's unwavering love for Criseyde as it contrasts with Criseyde's less en-
during love for Troilus: in Dante's *Commedia*, how one chooses to love ulti-
mately determines one's character and fate. This is also true, in a more secular
sense, in Chaucer's tragedy. Concerning his fidelity to the love he pledged to
Criseyde, Troilus says, for example:

> I se that clene out of youre mynde
> Ye han me cast—and I kan nor may,
> For al this world, withinne myn herte fynde
> To unloven yow a quarter of a day!   (5.1695–98)

Troilus remains faithful to the *trouthe* he pledged to Criseyde; Criseyde, however, abandons the *trouthe* she pledged to Troilus and enters into a liaison with Diomede. Interestingly, Dante's Adam requires only six hours (a quarter of a day) to betray the *trouthe* that he owed to his creator (*Par.* 26.139–42); Troilus's otherwise cryptic time factor thus reveals a subtle inversion of Adam's quick infidelity, which also contextualizes Troilus's positive decision in the moral construct of Dante's feudal vision.

Of the 1177 stanzas that *Troilus and Criseyde* contains, the central stanza is 589, and in the fourth line of this seven-line stanza, Criseyde shows Troilus mercy: "And [him] bistowed in so heigh a place" (3.1271). In response, he praises her "bounte" and "excellence" (3.1274). The phrasing of the central verse of *Troilus and Criseyde* echoes words in the opening stanza of The Monk's Tale to describe the high point on Fortune's wheel, from which a tragic descent begins. The Monk's opening stanza contains a two-verse sentence that applies here: "For certein, whan that Fortune list to flee, / Ther may no man the cours of hire withholde" (7.1995–96). From Troilus's highest point of fulfillment, attained exactly midway through the text, descends his *aventures in lovynge* and, from that place of *joie*, develops the dichotomy between how Troilus and Criseyde each chooses to respond to forced separation (1.3, 4). From this highest point, at the very apex of the work itself, the comic, rising structure borrowed from Dante yields to Chaucer's extrapolated, descending structure, which composes the second half of the tragedy. In this central stanza of Chaucer's *Troilus and Criseyde*, Dantean and Boethian structuring elements operate subtly but significantly.

Chaucer structures his five-unit story of Troilus as a complete Chaucerian tragedy by rounding the three-unit structure of Dante's *Commedia* and then adding two further units (or books) to complete one full turn of Fortune's wheel. Thus Chaucer presents an earthly, sublunar tragedy in which Fortuna's "unwar strook" (*Boece* bk. 2, prose 2, line 69) forces the departure of his protagonists from their paradise of earthly love. In the concluding stanza of *Troilus and Criseyde*, the Dantean and Boethian elements converge in a closing prayer:

> Thow oon, and two, and thre, eterne on lyve,
> That regnest ay in thre, and two, and oon,
> Uncircumscript, and al maist circumscrive,
> Us from visible and invisible foon
> Defend, and to thy mercy, everichon,
> So, make us Jesus, for thi mercy, digne,
> For love of mayde and moder thyn benigne.
> Amen.   (5.1863–69)

The first three verses of this stanza are translated by Chaucer from a passage in the *Commedia* (*Par.* 14.28–30), where the verses appear in a song sung by the soul of Boethius, in the fourth heaven, the heaven of the sun, where the philosophers and doctors of the church are stationed. In this hymn, the tragedy of Troilus is closed by Chaucer in a final, harmonious blending of Dantean and Boethian voices.

The closing line of this stanza ultimately recalls the final canto of Dante's *Commedia*, which begins: "Oh Virgin Mother, daughter of your son" *(Par.* 33.1). In canto 100, Dante concludes his themes amid paradox, in the face of which all human words fail. In his final prayer, Chaucer concludes his themes amid ambiguities, in the face of which all human resolutions seem to fail.

To be sure, other scattered passages in *Troilus and Criseyde* underline the structuring significance of the Dantean and Boethian elements contained in the three key passages discussed above, and students should give appropriate attention to them as well. For example, Chaucer begins book 2 with three verses, which nearly translate the three verses that open Dante's *Purgatory*. In similar fashion, Chaucer opens book 3 of his tragedy with reference to Venus, the goddess of love as well as the name of Dante's third sphere in paradise. Interestingly, Chaucer also refers here to Mars, the god of war as well as the name of Dante's fifth sphere in paradise.

Furthermore, Chaucer also assigns to Troilus three monologues that students of *Troilus and Criseyde* must consider. In its content, the last of these three monologues is probably the most notably Boethian. In the monologue, which occupies 125 verses (4.957–1082), Troilus echoes Boethian arguments on the nature of free will, predestination, and necessity to indicate that he considers himself destined to be "lorn" (4.959). Students should note the discussion on this significant passage in the explanatory notes in *The Riverside Chaucer* (1048).

Another monologue, the second "Canticus Troili" (3.1744–71) adapts book 2, meter 8, of the *Consolation of Philosophy*. Again, I refer students to the excellent consideration given this passage in the explanatory notes in *The Riverside Chaucer* (1044). It may be noted, however, that the attractive force of love (Venus) in this passage stands in ironic distinction to the force of war (Mars), alluded to in the opening verses of book 3.

The first monologue assigned to Troilus is a bit less obviously Boethian than the others; it is composed of the first of the two "Cantici Troili," and it occupies three stanzas in book 1 (400–20). It is a hymn to romantic love. As *The Riverside Chaucer* notes, it is "a fairly close rendering of Petrarch's Sonnet 88" (1028). I would also draw students' attention to the *Boece*, book 1 (prose 4, lines 198–201; see Kaylor, "Boethian Resonance"). Even this monologue seems to derive ultimately from Chaucerian synthesizing of Boethian elements.

Troilus and Criseyde is structured and shaped as tragedy in large measure by Chaucer's use of elements drawn from Dante's *Commedia* and Boethius's *Consolation of Philosophy* (see Robertson, "Chaucerian Tragedy," for an alternative interpretation of Chaucerian tragedy). If students read Dante and Boethius in English translation, they should be able to discover many further

elements that derive from these sources. They should also be able to under-
stand the complexities encountered in dealing with the problem of Chaucer's
non-Aristotelian reinvention of tragedy as a narrative genre for his age, and
they should grow in appreciation of Chaucer's extraordinary ability to synthe-
size ideas from his sources. Students might even identify themselves with the
tragedy of Troilus, seeing it as the tragedy of all postlapsarian human beings,
whose nature it is to love but whose fate it sometimes is to lose too soon the
object of that love.

NOTE

[1]Citations to Dante's *Divine Comedy* are from Musa's edition.

Chaucer and Vernacular Writing

Susannah Mary Chewning

In *The Regiment of Princes*, Thomas Hoccleve makes the following statement about Chaucer:

> The first findere of our fayre langage
> Hath seyde in caas semblable, and othyr moo,
> So hyly wel that yt ys my dotage
> For to expresse or touche ony of thoo.
> Allas! My fader fro the world ys goo,
> My worthy mayster Chaucer, hym I mene.
> Be thow advokett for hym, hevenes queen.   ([ed. Pearsall] 333)

This statement, important to medievalists and students of medieval English literature for many reasons, is especially relevant for teaching medieval English poetry, for in it Hoccleve comments on the anxiety of Chaucer's poetic influence. As Harold Bloom points out in *The Anxiety of Influence*, those who follow "great" writers must "clear imaginative space" (5) for themselves to deal with the presence of those other poets, the father-poets from whom their poetry must evolve. The contemporaries of Chaucer must have felt the anxiety of their relationship to such a great and influential writer; their work looks back at his work and forward to the role and power of vernacular English itself, their own works included, as an authoritative poetic presence.

Teachers of Chaucer must not ignore the importance of Chaucer's contemporaries, although it is often difficult to include them in courses devoted to Chaucer or to Middle English literature. One reason is time: in a one-semester course it is difficult to include as much Chaucer as one wishes, let alone such authors as Nicholas Love and William Thorpe.[1] Given the choice between adding another excerpt from *The Canterbury Tales* or from *The Legend of Good Women* or wading through *The Regiment of Princes* or *Confessio Amantis*, many of us would err on the side of more Chaucer since we know from experience that students find meaning in his works and since many instructors have not experimented in the classroom with his less-well-known contemporaries. The other issue is good editions. Neither of the standard survey editions (*The Norton Anthology of English Literature* and *The Longman Anthology of British Literature*) includes Hoccleve, John Gower, or John Trevisa, and so instructors, should they wish to teach these works, must rely on photocopying, library copies, or asking students to purchase editions of these works. None of these options is without its problems, but thankfully The Consortium for the Teaching of the Middle Ages (TEAMS) has made many of these works available in affordable editions and online.[2]

An instructor who wishes to include Chaucer's contemporaries in a course must struggle for a balance between her or his students' needs in the classroom and the cost of providing good Middle English editions of these works. And it is crucial that the works of these authors be provided in Middle English, not in translation. Students must come to know these authors in Middle English, specifically because they, with Chaucer, invent the use of Middle English as a language of poetry and literature. Their poems should therefore be read as they were written.

In a survey course, students can read excerpts of Trevisa's translation of Ranulf Higden's *Polychronicon*, a discussion of the varieties of spoken English in Britain since "the furste moreyn" (230)—approximately 1348, when the black death arrived in England. Higden discusses the difference in education since "Johan Cornwal, a mayster gramere, chayngede the lore in gramer-scole and construccion of Freynsch into Englysh" (230) and described the "scharp, slyttyng and frotyng and unschape" English of the northern counties (231). The usefulness of calling students' attention to this excerpt is threefold. First, it is a powerful example of the developing authority of English, not only in its own representation of Middle English (Trevisa is translating from Higden's Latin, after all) but also in its explanation of the sociological and cultural change from French to English in England as the language of both education and courtly communication from the mid–fourteenth century on.[3] Second, as an artifact of anthropological study, this text—and its statement that everything, even the language spoken, changed in 1348 as a direct consequence of the black death—demonstrates the connection for students between cultural change and literary development. Finally, this excerpt offers contemporary support for Chaucer's mission to write in English because it implies that by 1387 there was a generation of readers that was literate in the language and hungry for new texts and authors.

Each of Chaucer's poetic contemporaries serves as an example of the development of English authorship, representing different genres but participating nonetheless in the flowering of English as a literary language in the latter half of the fourteenth century. Nicholas Love, for example, writes in a direct line of inheritance from the early Middle English mystical works associated with the *Ancrene Wisse* and the Katherine Group, and his influence is clear on the works of Julian of Norwich and Margery Kempe, the two most-often anthologized mystical writers in English. And to omit Gower from any discussion of Chaucer is to omit the most powerful literary voice of the fourteenth-century court. Gower was, after all, part of Chaucer's audience (Brewer, *New Introduction* 279), and often, certainly in *The Legend of Good Women*, Chaucer seems to be imitating instead of seeking to surpass Gower.

Thus, a study of Middle English must include an examination of Gower, and, although his *Confessio Amantis* is represented in Derek Pearsall's anthology, *Chaucer to Spenser*, it is not represented adequately there or in any other anthology.[4] What is included serves an undergraduate seminar on medieval English literature well. It does not duplicate the tales covered in Chaucer to use Gower as a foil for illuminating Chaucer but rather introduces students who may wish to read more of Gower to different tales, told in his style; format; and, most important, use of the English language. In Pearsall's anthology, students can read segments of book 4 (on idleness) and from book 5, the tale of Tereus and Procne. This tale can be used effectively, for example, in a discussion of the motif of the nightingale in British poetry, beginning with Gower and Chaucer and following through to, among others, Walter Raleigh's "Nymph's Reply to the Shepherd" and John Keats's "To a Nightingale."

In the context of medieval English literature as a whole, *Confessio Amantis* reminds students that medieval writers use classical writers as both source and authority while making the works their own. Gower thus provides an excellent comparison with Chaucer, and the two should be examined together. Although Pearsall's edition does not include *The Legend of Good Women*, good editions of the poem are available, beginning with *The Riverside Chaucer*. There are also many excellent translations of Ovid, and students can find much in seeing the development of the story from Ovid's book 6 of the *Metamorphoses* to Gower's book 5 of *Confessio Amantis* to Chaucer's "Legend of Philomela" in *The Legend of Good Women*. Chaucer, who tells the tale mostly from Philomela's perspective, does not dwell on Tereus's inner thoughts and says simply of the moments leading up to the rape:

> And therwithal she wepte tenderly
> And quok for fere, pale and pitously,
> Ryght as the lamb that of the wolf is biten;
> Or as the culver that of the egle is smiten
> . . . so sat she.   (2316–22).

Ovid and Gower, however, weave into the tale the motivation and lack of consciousness in Tereus's rape of Philomela. Ovid writes:

> Fondly he [Tereus] wishes for the father's place,
> To feel, and to return the warm embrace;
> Since not the nearest ties of filial blood
> Would damp his flame, and force him to be good.   (*Met.* 6)

Gower continues with this metaphor of heat:

> And with the sihte he gan desire
> And sette his oghne herte on fyre;
> And fyr, whan it to tow aprocheth,
> To him anon the strengthe acrocheth,
> Til with his hete it be devoured—
> The tow ne mai noght be socoured.   (*Tale* 5.5621–26)

Comparing Ovid and Chaucer with the literary achievement of Gower, who was an interpreter of classical imagery and myth, is extremely helpful in an undergraduate classroom and serves not to dim Chaucer's light but to explain his connection to his contemporaries.

Much has been said about Chaucer's indebtedness to Gower (and Gower's to Chaucer), and each instructor who takes on a semester-length course on Chaucer decides on her or his own how much of Gower to include. Obvious and fruitful comparisons can be made between Gower's "Tale of Florent" (*Confessio* 1.1407–1975) and Chaucer's Wife of Bath's Tale, Gower's "Tale of Constance" (*Confessio* 2.587–1612) and Chaucer's Man of Law's Tale, Gower's "Tale of Phebus and Cornide" (*Confessio* 3.783–817) and Chaucer's Manciple's Tale, as well as parallel tales and motifs in the *Confessio* and other works, specifically Chaucer's *Legend of Good Women*.

Understanding Chaucer—his relation to his time and his relationship to women—is an immense task, but it is one that can be aided by reading beyond the more frequently anthologized tales of the Miller and the Wife of Bath and by looking at the one text that Chaucer himself described as being about (and thus for) women. In discussing Chaucer and his contemporaries, a useful comparison can be drawn between Gower's "Tale of Aeneas and Dido" (*Confessio* 4.77–146) and Chaucer's "Legend of Dido" (*LGW* 924–1367). Chaucer uses Vergil and Ovid as his sources, and his tale expands on Gower's, exceeding it by nearly four hundred lines. However, because of his indebtedness to and use of Gower as a source in other poems, reading the two together demonstrates to students how authors of equal ability and background tell and retell the same story in different ways. Just as Chaucer's Tereus has no sense of self-awareness or morality, so too does Gower's Aeneas seem without any sense of himself or his humanity. Gower creates in the tale a study in "[l]achesce in loves cas" ([ed. Peck, 2003] 4.77), delay in love's pursuit, and that delay's tragic outcome. For Chaucer, however, the story is not about Aeneas's delay but about Dido's grief at her loss in love, and he demonstrates in the poem how worthy she was to be loved by a great knight:

> This fresshe lady, of the cite queene,
> Stod in the temple in hire estat real,
> So rychely and ek so fayr withal,
> So yong, so lusty, with hire eyen glade,
> That, if that God, that hevene and erthe made,
> Wolde han a love, for beaute and goodnesse,
> And womanhod, and trouthe, and semelynesse,
> Whom shulde he loven but this lady swete?   (1035–42).

F. N. Robinson once cited this passage for its audacity—in describing Dido as beautiful enough to be God's choice of a mistress—and it still shocks readers with its boldness (*Riverside* 1068 [2.1039–43]). It stands as a powerful example of Chaucer's originality and creativity. Class discussions can then proceed on the topics of hyperbolic descriptions in Chaucer; of descriptions of

the Virgin compared with those of other women; of the position of women—
and Dido is here a pagan woman—in the mind (and therefore world) of
Chaucer as a poet and a Christian; of Chaucer's use of his sources; of his
originality compared with his contemporaries, none of whom are so daring as
to suggest that someone like Dido, whom Dante places in the *Inferno* for sins
of lust, is a likely paramour for the Judeo-Christian God.[5]

As Pearsall argues, "Chaucer is in danger of being read and learnt about in
a vacuum, away from the structures of linguistics and cultural meaning that
provide the architecture for the understanding of his poetry" (Introd. xv–xvi).
Chaucer's contemporaries are thus more than just touchstones for evaluating
Chaucer's greatness. Although Hoccleve, whose *The Regiment of Princes* is
difficult for most undergraduates to follow, may well be saddled with the unfair
label of the first "poetic follower" of Chaucer (Brewer, *New Introduction* 10),
his other contemporaries remind us of the context of Chaucer's works and
intellectual development. Hoccleve's great description of "fadir, Chaucer"
(*Regiment* [ed. Pearsall] 2078) sets the stage for the role that Chaucer will
take in later generations. Scholars who have examined, for example, John
Lydgate's and Edmund Spenser's influences on William Shakespeare always
return to the linguistic authority of Chaucer as the central precursor to Mod-
ern English (Steinberg). Instructors who seek to make Chaucer available to a
new generation of students can achieve this by presenting him not as the sole
parent of the British literary tradition but as part of a larger continuum, be-
ginning perhaps as far back as Vergil and including Chaucer's contemporaries,
English vernacular poets who sought successfully to make English the lan-
guage of poetic authority in Europe.

NOTES

[1]In the space allotted here, there is insufficient time to discuss all Chaucer's ver-
nacular contemporaries. I thus limit my comments to his poetic contemporaries, al-
though it is important to acknowledge the need for additional resources on Middle
English prose that might be used in conjunction with Chaucer's work in an under-
graduate classroom.

[2]One solution for current instructors is Derek Pearsall's *Chaucer to Spenser: An
Anthology*, which includes many of Chaucer's contemporaries—Gower, Trevisa,
Thorpe, Hoccleve, Love, and Lydgate—in well-annotated, accessible Middle English
excerpts.

[3]Trevisa's translation of Higden was completed in 1397, whereas Higden's own work,
the *Polychronicon*, ends in 1364. Trevisa's edition shows both the impact and meaning
of Higden's work to a later generation of English authors and proves Higden's case
that English, for his generation, was becoming the language of authorship in England.
That he wrote in Latin in the 1360s and that a translation of this Latin work is necessary
by 1397 demonstrates for students the shift from Latin and French to English.

[4]TEAMS now has excellent student editions of the complete *Confessio Amantis* in
three volumes, edited by Russell Peck (2003).

⁵There is a connection here between Chaucer, in his vision of Dido as a suitable partner for God, and his contemporary, Nicholas Love, who refers to Christ as a lover of humanity. Love follows the English mystical tradition begun in *Ancrene Wisse* in his *Mirror of the Blessed Life of Jesus Christ* (c. 1410), describing Christ as a "kyng" and "floure of alle mankynde" (314 [ed. Pearsall]), which provides another opportunity to discuss Chaucer in the context of his lesser-known contemporaries.

Troilus and Criseyde and Chaucer's Shorter Poems: Paleography and Codicology

Julia Boffey

The frontispiece to the copy of *Troilus and Criseyde* in Cambridge, Corpus Christi College MS 61 (reproduced in *Troilus*) offers to students of medieval culture not just a potent evocation of an author's relationship with his audience but also material evidence of the enhancement of a valuable book. It is an excellent starting point for exploring both the characteristics of textual production in a manuscript culture and the ways in which the material forms of medieval book production illuminate these characteristics. Learning about the early material survivals of Chaucer's writings opens the way to thinking about textual analysis and literary theory and introduces a number of transferable bibliographical skills as well.[1] The tasks involved can take various forms: students can investigate the transmission of particular texts; pursue the activities of specific scribes; or explore the contents, makeup, and early readers of individual books.

Comparing the numbers of surviving witnesses of each of Chaucer's works is another instructive starting point: against just over fifty complete copies of *The Canterbury Tales* there are around sixteen of *Troilus and Criseyde*;[2] fourteen of *The Parliament of Fowls*; ten of *The Legend of Good Women*; three each of *The House of Fame* and *The Book of the Duchess*; and varying numbers of the shorter poems, from twenty-two manuscripts of "Truth" to only one of "To Rosemounde."[3] Investigating these statistics means learning about such matters as the "occasional" nature of some of Chaucer's works, the possibility that particular texts were transmitted by scribes working commercially, and, above all, registering Chaucer's apparent casualness about the circulation of his works and the random nature of their survival.

A number of the manuscripts in which *Troilus and Criseyde* and the shorter poems survive can be consulted in facsimile editions, and the full range of manuscripts offers considerable potential for the teaching of paleography.[4] All the facsimiles contain information about manuscript design and layout, scribes and scripts, annotation, and provenance. In addition, there are photographic reproductions of sample folios from most of the manuscripts in Robert Kilburn Root's important early study (*Manuscripts*).[5] Several scribes command special attention: the single scribe of San Marino, Huntington Library MS HM 114 copied part of another *Troilus and Criseyde* manuscript (British Library MS Harley 3943) and part of an anthology that is now London, Lambeth Palace MS 491 (Hanna, "Scribe");[6] British Library MS Harley 2392, unusually, is signed by a named scribe, called "Style"; the copying of Oxford, Bodleian Library MS Arch. Selden. Supra 56, unusually, is dated—to 1441. There is undoubtedly further scope for study of the activities of all the scribes involved in copying *Troilus and Criseyde* and the minor poems.[7]

The early manuscripts of *Troilus and Criseyde* display a consistency of layout unusual among the witnesses to Chaucer's poems. New York, Pierpont Morgan Library MS M. 817 (possibly the earliest surviving copy); Cambridge, St. John's College MS L. 1; and Corpus Christi 61 are all imposing parchment manuscripts in which the poem is carefully copied in relatively formal scripts. Several manuscripts preserve the same number of ruled lines on each page, accommodating five rhyme-royal stanzas (*Troilus* 3). Certain features of the apparatus, such as book divisions, signaling of proems, and annotations of particular sections or sources, are also replicated across various manuscripts, as if the earliest copies, possibly sanctioned by those close to Chaucer, were unusually influential on the poem's later transmission.

The length of *Troilus and Criseyde* also seems to have dictated that it was often copied as the single item in a manuscript. Cambridge, University Library MS Gg. 4. 27; Bodleian Library MS Digby 181 and MS Arch. Selden. B. 24; British Library MS Harley 1239; and Huntington Library MS HM 114 are unusual in preserving the poem alongside other texts of significant length (although in a few other manuscripts it is accompanied by other material). The shorter poems are more routinely copied with other texts, since few are of sufficient length to fill a conventionally sized gathering. With one or two exceptions, the manuscripts of the shorter poems date from around forty years or more after Chaucer's death, an interval longer than is the case for *The Canterbury Tales* or *Troilus and Criseyde*. The apparent availability of the shorter poems in groups or runs seems to support the hypothesis that they first appeared in single gatherings or booklets with certain non-Chaucerian texts, such as John Clanvowe's *Book of Cupid* and John Lydgate's *Complaint of the Black Knight*, which were to remain their companions during later transmission (Brusendorff).

Studying the conjunction of poems in different manuscripts not only teaches something of the processes by which anthologies came into being but also allows for speculation about the rationale underlying the association of particular texts. The occurrence of copies of "Fortune" and "The Former Age" in the middle of *Boece* in Cambridge, University Library MS Ii. 3. 21, for example, may reflect an exemplar made directly from Chaucer's working papers in which drafts of the Boethian lyrics were interleaved with the translation that inspired them (Pace, "True Text"). Other hypotheses might be constructed about the collocation of the unique surviving copy of "To Rosemounde" with *Troilus and Criseyde* in Bodleian Library MS Rawlinson poet. 163, where it can perhaps be construed as a wry extension of the characterization of the *Troilus and Criseyde* narrator, or about the conjunction of a partial text of *The Parliament of Fowls* with Lydgate's *Churl and Bird* and *Horse, Goose, and Sheep* in Cambridge, University Library MS Hh. 4. 12.

Examining the contexts in which Chaucer's shorter poems were transmitted gives a good idea of fifteenth-century literary trends. The companion pieces to *The Legend of Good Women*, for example, confirm that it contributed to a wider debate about the concerns of women in love (Meale), whereas the lyrics circulated with a much more varied range of material, occasionally even appearing as parts of other works: the envoy to "Lak of Stedfastnesse" is incorporated into a copy of Lydgate's "Prayer for Henry VI, Queen and People" (Boffey, "Reputation" 32), and "Gentilesse" is incorporated into a copy of "Moral Balade," attributed to Chaucer's friend Henry Scogan (Connolly 159). Investigation of context can start quite productively with manuscript descriptions published in catalogs of individual collections.[8]

Facsimiles have the edge on descriptions in making visible the range of textual problems relating to the shorter poems and *Troilus and Criseyde*. Large-scale difficulties in the shorter poems include the survival of *The Legend of Good Women* in two distinctly different versions (the G text of the prologue is preserved only in the early Cambridge, University Library MS Gg. 4. 27), the uncertainty over the words of the song that concludes *The Parliament of Fowls* (Hanna, "Authorial Versions"), and mysterious gaps in the text of *The Book of the Duchess* (*Riverside* 1136). The collection of responses by scribes and editors to the end of *The House of Fame* is a small study on its own (Burrow). Among the lyrics, "Truth" survives in two distinct states and (like "Fortune" and "The Complaint of Chaucer to His Purse") apparently circulated both with and without an envoy, whereas "The Complaint of Venus," "A Complaint to His Lady," and *Anelida and Arcite* may each have been put together from originally unrelated component parts (A. S. G. Edwards, "Unity"; *Riverside* 1078–89).

Tracking the hypotheses advanced about the genesis and transmission of the text of *Troilus and Criseyde* is a large study, taking in Root's identification of "early," "revised," and "final" states of the poem (Root, Introd. lxx–lxxxi; *Textual Tradition*) and Barry Windeatt's elucidation of more subtle processes of composition and dissemination ("Text" and *New Edition*). The presence or absence in witnesses of certain significant episodes or sections of the poem— notably Troilus's Boethian song in book 3 and his predestination soliloquy in book 4—contributes to Windeatt's compelling argument about the complex processes by which the work took shape. At a more detailed level, study of the minutiae of textual variation can fuel discussion of scribal habits and procedures (Windeatt, "Text"; see further the bibliography concerning "textual criticism and manuscript culture" and "the text of *Troilus*" in Windeatt, *New Edition* 569–73).

Reception and response are topics that give the chance to combine the study of Chaucer's works with consideration of theoretical issues of broader kinds (Lerer, *Chaucer*, demonstrates these possibilities). One way into these areas is through the study of scribal interventions and annotations, along with the comments of later readers. In manuscripts of the minor poems, scribal annotation consists mostly of Latin glosses to parts of *The House of Fame*. However, *Troilus and Criseyde* seems to have attracted more concerted attempts at commentary, including attempts not only to signal source material but also to clarify the poem's structure, by the marking of book divisions and proems, the flagging of significant passages such as letters and songs, and in a few manuscripts the categorizing of different forms of utterance (Benson and Windeatt; Boffey, "Annotation"). Identifying early readers of the poems offers another way of thinking about reception. Owners of considerable means and social status must have commissioned and read the lavish early copies of *Troilus and Criseyde,* but the Londoner Thomas Usk also had access to it at the time of its composition (*Riverside* 1020). Women's names occur in at least two copies (Harley 4912 and Corpus Christi 61), and the poem is mentioned in a treatise directed at nuns (Patterson, "Ambiguity"). Readers of the minor poems encompassed Chaucer's own friends (Scogan and Bukton, who were recipients of envoys, and Vache, who received a version of "Truth") and probably included members of aristocratic and gentry families with the means to commission or purchase large, well-produced collections. But a number of the manuscripts in which these poems survive are workaday in that they are not especially carefully or expensively produced and preserve texts for instruction, household needs, or general social purposes. *The Parliament of Fowls,* which survives in notably more copies than the other dream visions, made its way into a several such anthologies. There remains scope for much further work on reception and on the social, cultural, and political affiliations of the milieus in which Chaucer's works circulated.

The posterity of Chaucer's writings—their dissemination through the course of the fifteenth century and their transmission into printed forms from 1476 onward (A. S. G. Edwards, "Chaucer" and Forni, *Chaucerian Apocrypha* 44–87)—offers many openings for further study. Some of the minor poems were among the earliest texts that Caxton chose to print in England, fairly closely followed by *Troilus and Criseyde.* The minor poems also figured in Richard Pynson's three-volume edition of Chaucer's works, printed in 1526, and in William Thynne's imposing collected works of 1532. But the poems continued to circulate in manuscript as well and to offer themselves to new forms of use as readers chose to copy whole texts or favorite extracts for their own particular purposes (Lerer, *Courtly Letters*). From the indications of the dissemination of *Troilus and Criseyde* and the shorter poems in Chaucer's lifetime to the evidence of sixteenth-century witnesses, what we can learn of the transmission of these works suggests an ongoing process characterized by dynamism and variety.

NOTES

[1] The annual bibliographies in *Studies in the Age of Chaucer* now incorporate sections titled "Manuscripts and Textual Studies."

[2]The approximate numbers take account of fragmentary copies.

[3]These figures are derived from the textual notes to each poem in *The Riverside Chaucer* and the information in Brown and Robbins and Robbins and Cutler. The survival of extracted tales from *The Canterbury Tales* and of extracted single stories from *The Legend of Good Women* warrants separate study. Printed editions are recorded in Pollard and Redgrave 1976–91; details about and reproductions of some of these editions can be consulted online through *Early English Books Online*.

[4]For facsimiles of *Troilus and Criseyde* see *Troilus*; *St. John's College*; *Pierpont*. For *Troilus* together with some of the minor poems, see *Poetical Works*; *Works*. For the minor poems, see *Findern Manuscript*; *Bodleian Library*; *Manuscript Bodley*; *Manuscript Tanner*; *Manuscript Pepys*; and *Manuscript Trinity*.

[5]Palaeographic features of the work of two *Troilus and Criseyde* scribes are discussed in Parkes (plates 3 and 13).

[6]Hands in parts of Oxford, Bodleian Library MS Digby 181 and Cambridge, Trinity College MS R. 3. 19 also appear elsewhere: see Mosser; Fletcher xxvi–xxix.

[7]Further comparisons to the hands can be found in facsimiles of other Middle English manuscripts (for a list of which see Beadle) and in reproductions of manuscripts made available on CD-ROM by *The Canterbury Tales* Project and The *Piers Plowman Electronic Archive* or online through Web sites such as the *Digital Scriptorium*.

[8]Those relating to the Huntington Library collections (Dutschke); to the Pepys manuscripts at Magdalene College, Cambridge (Beadle and McKitterick); or to the manuscripts in St. John's College, Oxford (Hanna, *Descriptive Catalogue*) contain detailed information about texts and codicological matters. The information in older catalogs sometimes needs to be supplemented with details from Root, *Manuscripts*; Windeatt, *New Edition*; and Seymour; and in some cases from works like Manly and Rickert.

The Pagan Past and Chaucer's Christian Present

Scott Lightsey

For Geoffrey Chaucer and his contemporaries, pagan antiquity was a fountainhead of knowledge, a cultural reservoir of ethical, moral, scientific, and political truth. The medieval moderns, or *moderni*, could look back to the pagan philosophers, the *antiqui*, as their intellectual precursors. The *moderni* could overlook the *antiqui*'s errors—explained as unknowing precursors to Christian faith—in order to access their wealth of authoritative information and poetic virtuosity. Medieval authors reworked classical pagan images such as the idyllic golden age and the capricious goddess Fortuna to express ideas about their own culture and views of history. Observations about this mechanism of rewriting can be a teaching tool, demonstrating the value of Chaucer's negotiations with pagan antiquity for students, whose own sense of history and engagement with the world can be harnessed to inform their work in English literature.

Taking advantage of students' interest in medieval syncretism or assimilation of the pagan past has helped me develop ways to introduce students to Chaucer and to ease them into his major poetry. The shorter, so-called minor poems offer the obvious advantage of brevity, so that students can begin gently, through poetry that enforces a Middle English–only policy but that does not have an overwhelming scope. Further, the relative unity of Chaucer's Boethian laments in works such as "The Former Age," "Fortune," "Truth," "Lak of Stedfastnesse," and "Gentilesse" functions as an introduction to the poet's historical perspective—a good jumping-off point for opening modern critical debates.

Teachers often find themselves teaching Chaucer's relation to the *antiqui* piecemeal, since new readers find themselves surprised to discover apparently pagan sentiment. Students seem most likely to perceive independently the pagan elements in Chaucer's minor poetry through the personification of Fortuna and through Chaucer's references to a pre-Christian golden age, for example, in the capricious movements that belie trust in Fortuna, who "turneth as a bal" ("Truth" 9); in the fallen morality that has turned the modern medieval world "up so doun" ("Lak" 5); or in comparisons between fallen modernity and the antique morality before Christ ("Former Age" 1–2). By exploiting these references to pagan antiquity in the minor poems, we can enlarge students' understanding of pagan sentiments such as Troilus's fatalism in *Troilus and Criseyde*.

An effective strategy for easing students through the shock of finding pagan elements in medieval Christian writing is to acquaint them with some general medieval attitudes toward pagan ideas. By Chaucer's time it was becoming common practice to isolate pagan thinking through a historical perspective that transmitted pagan authorities without implicating the Christian author in pagan errors of faith. Thirteenth- and fourteenth-century encyclopedists and compilators maintained a distinction between the transmission of pagan ideas on the one hand and belief in pagan ideas on the other. Transmission was credited to the medieval writer as *recitatio*, or the rehearsal of others' ideas, whereas belief was attributable only to the pagan authority, whose *assertio*, or assertion of truth, was outside the medieval writer's control and responsibility.

Chaucer's most sustained representations of pagan belief are found in *Troilus and Criseyde* and in *The Canterbury Tales*' stories of the Knight and the Franklin (Minnis, *Chaucer*, esp. ch. 1–3). There, Chaucer explicitly follows the encyclopedists in accepting "neither thank ne blame" (2.15), for example in the pagan matter of *Troilus and Criseyde*, which he explicitly rejects as "payens corsed olde rites" (5.1849). In the minor poetry, he is at pains to employ these classical ideas through medieval topoi without subscribing to the pagan errors of his models in Ovid, Juvenal, and others.

Given the limitations of a survey, in which students may come to know Chaucer through the lens of an anthology, core curriculum, or some more-anxious form of reduction (what can I fit on that syllabus!?), one rarely has more than The General Prologue and a few tales to work with. Even if circumstance puts the pagan-infused Knight's Tale or Franklin's Tale before students, I prefer to invite them into Chaucer's works through the brief poem "The Former Age," which they can acquire easily without expense or difficulty. In this poem, Chaucer's analysis of his modern age is explicitly rendered in the context of a pre-Christian past. Here, Chaucer engages in a form of poetic historiography, looking back on antiquity from his position as a jaded modern invested in luxuries such as the "quern and eke the mill" (6). He employs the notion of the *senectus mundi*, the aging world against which the tapestry of life in the pagan golden age appears as a Christian primitivist paradise (Dean 94–98).

Students confronted with "The Former Age" immediately identify the negative formula ("No man yit knew"; "Unkorven and ungrobbed lay the vyne," [12, 14] that Chaucer uses to express the positive qualities of the past as a normative moral center that has been lost in the wake of Nimrod's depredations. Conversely, the golden age lies idealized, passive, sufficient yet austere of luxuries, lost in both time and space. I ask students to characterize these modern methods and conveniences—spicery, winemaking, culinary art, shipbuilding, mining—and to use them to find the moral center of the work. They find ideas of loss, self-implication, even irony—familiar sentiments that help them identify with the author's sense of history.

The overlapping perceptions of the past that students share with Chaucer form an avenue for many explorations of Chaucer's contemporary scene, and the parallel can be exploited to familiarize students with Chaucer's views of pagan antiquity. Chaucer's use of the classical golden age and the *senectus mundi* demonstrates the kind of assimilation that allows medieval Christian authors to deal comfortably with philosophical matters rooted in pagan perspectives. Chaucer's "The Former Age" is expressed in terms of biblical history, since the pristine environs of the age are interrupted by the ravages of Nimrod's legacy of strife and urbanization. But it also finds its origins in the classical pagan idea of the golden age, a period of primitive innocence characterized by Juvenal in the *Satires* as a stringent moral existence, and in Ovid's *Metamorphoses* as a somewhat softer time of earthly abundance. Chaucer combines these hard and soft approaches to the golden age with the biblical paradise to offer a negative analysis of his contemporary scene: its political and moral turpitude is served up with a solid dose of wry personal implication. Chaucer's observation here serves as an excellent introduction to the authorial views behind *The Canterbury Tales*.

To better illustrate the place of this syncretized classical golden age in Christian history, I use images of maps such as the elaborately illuminated Hereford Map, available in an excellent recent edition (Westrem lx–lxxxiv; includes a foldout map). Electronic slides of similar maps are easily obtained online, adding a visual hook for engaging students' understanding through a spatial representation of medieval history. On these early maps, the Garden of Eden is often pictured at the top, in the farthest east, at the point where earthly time begins after the Creation. By tracing the movement of mankind from the expulsion from Eden, we literally move through time, from pre-Christian history down through the aging temporal world and into the fallen modern Europe of Chaucer's fourteenth century. Another helpful image comes in the form of the familiar statue from Nebuchadnezzar's dream (Dan. 2.31–45), whose head of gold represents the pagan golden age but whose feet of clay remind *moderni* of their present, degraded state. The passage on this dream, elaborated in the prologue of John Gower's *Confessio Amantis* (lines 585–624), helps illuminate the late-fourteenth-century approach to antiquity. Russell Peck's TEAMS edition includes the Oxford, Bodleian Library MS Fairfax 3 illumination of the statue (1: 63), making it easy to provide students with this telling visual allegory.

Another exercise on the author and his contemporaries turns on the students' sense of the dual historiography they negotiate as they read Chaucer's history of the world. I begin by asking students to compare their sense of connection to their own past with what they are able to derive about Chaucer's portrayals and uses of the pagan past. Of course, all students are familiar with some form of the "good old days" vision of the present. Each era has its better past against which it measures with proximate clarity its contemporary ills and concerns. Students have their own personal good old days, or a sense of them based on culturally constructed golden ages such as the "expansive" 1950s, the "radical, freewheeling" 1960s, or the "booming" 1990s. This familiar notion of past greatness forms a template for situating Chaucer's views of his own past. The purity and simplicity of the antique in "The Former Age" or "Lak of Stedfastnesse" provide for Chaucer a restorative vision to guide his contemporaries' negotiations with a jaded and corrupt medieval present. The entire movement of "Gentilesse" can be characterized as a historicization of the medieval present in which the "first stok, fader of gentilesse" (1) has bequeathed a rich inheritance that lies squandered by the paucity of modern virtue. The author's contempt for this fallen world is expressed in the sentiment that characterizes moderns as beasts "wrestling" for a world that "nis but wyldernesse" (16–19). Similar is the golden age behind "Lak of Stedfastnesse," which begins with a lament for a time when "the world was so stedfast and stable" (1). In Chaucer's time, modern life has "mad a permutacioun" (19) from the moral high ground of earlier days, and the universality of this sentiment alone can generate discussion.

This mutability is often paired in Chaucer's work with the classical image of Fortuna—depicted as the goddess of luck, good and ill fortune, chance or formulated in any number of ways that correspond to human incomprehension of the world's mutability. Fortuna appears so often in Chaucer's poetry that students cannot help but notice her. That students detect Fortuna's high profile in Chaucer's poetry offers teachers another opportunity to exploit his uses of pagan antiquity. What Chaucer instructor has never been asked whether Chaucer's representations of Fortuna amount, in some way, to non-Christian belief?

The brief poem "Fortune," in which Fortuna reminds her defiant addressor that "Thou born art in my regne of variaunce" (45), invites students to examine how the goddess Fortuna endures—but as a secular allegory. Fortuna thus exemplifies the capricious vestiges of pagan deities, who fit into the medieval Christian perspective of a fallen world that offered only a limited understanding of God's will. Although no longer a goddess, the explanatory power of Fortuna's allegorical figure guaranteed her survival (Patch, ch.1). The inexorable cycles and fickle mutability of classical paganism had, by Chaucer's time, become assimilated into Christian belief as the idea that the Fall and expulsion from paradise had drawn a veil between humankind's perception and the movements of God.

Images of Lady Fortuna turning her wheel are easy to obtain in books (e.g., see Thomson's catalog of the Folger Shakespeare Library's exhibit of Fortuna imagery) and provide students with opportunities to examine their preconceptions about more-familiar allegories, such as Blind Justice and the ubiquitous Lady Luck (although with my students, game-show parallels frequently emerge before associations with allegorical figures). Through these images, with their blindfolded women, scales, and wheels, students realize that they subscribe to notions of personal fortune in much the same way Chaucer and his contemporaries did over six-hundred years ago. I usually get a laugh by asking students if that makes them pagans too.

Pointing out that Chaucer's historiography uses pagan images and thus evinces his ambivalent modernity, I find it easier to guide students through concepts like the trifunctional model, estates satire, and Chaucerian irony in The General Prologue. Once students have internalized the idea that, like them, Chaucer was looking back through overlapping historical lenses or frameworks, it becomes easier to draw them into discussions of contemporary issues in Chaucer's poetry. The comparative histories and class distinctions evident in the minor poems also provide a jumping-off point for more in-depth conversations about current critical debates and approaches. The benefit is in the opportunity to contrast the collapsed distance between students' and Chaucer's perceptions of the past with the estrangement that emerges in investigating that collapse.

Few of our students will go on to become medievalists, but they all must be taught to come to terms with complicated forms of representation, often presented in overlapping historical frames with competing intellectual interests. By engaging Chaucer's shorter poetry and *Troilus and Criseyde* as part of the wider diachronic relation between the antique, medieval, and modern, instructors can engage the interpretive mechanisms students bring to bear not only on Chaucer but also on a range of critical situations.

Contemporary English Politics and the Ricardian Court: Chaucer's London and the Myth of New Troy

Alison A. Baker

In an age of siege warfare, social revolt, and factional struggles among the civic leaders of London and the royalty, identification of London with "New Troy" stirred imaginations and steeled nerves. Geoffrey of Monmouth explains that the founder of Britain was Brutus, descendant of Aeneas, the Trojan prince who fled Troy as it crumbled. This literary legend persisted well into the fourteenth century and gave Chaucer's London a link to a mythic past and to a heroic culture that helped develop and explain English national identity. But this identity proved problematic because the myth was not entirely glorious. In a recent book entitled *New Troy: Fantasies of Empire in the Late Middle Ages*, Sylvia Federico states:

> The Trojans were considered a noble society, but they also were considered lecherous and traitorous. . . . The troubling implication of this aspect of the Trojan legacy was that London, too, was full of deviant rulers whose passions would lead to the destruction of the city. (2)

The myth of Troy and the desire for London to be New Troy, then, informs a reading of *Troilus and Criseyde*, where the siege of old Troy is depicted in minute detail, and the fall of Troy in the poem presages the fall of New Troy and Richard II.

In teaching *Troilus and Criseyde*, I begin by providing an introduction to the Hundred Years' War, Richard II's conflicts with the Lords Appellant, and the Peasants' Revolt. This generally takes the form of a brief history lecture to orient students. Into that setting, I place the Ricardian court's chivalric code and its love of reading romances. This pedagogical strategy parallels Chaucer's poem, where he begins with a vision of a war-torn society and then focuses on love letters and the individuals who produced them.[1]

With the historical context established, students break up into small groups to discuss possible allegorical connections to the court at the time Chaucer wrote the poem. Do we want, for instance, to see Richard II in Troilus? If we do, who is unfaithful to him? While I do not see *Troilus and Criseyde* as a true roman à clef, one can complicate the reading of the poem by searching for connections to contemporary life. Such strategies allow students to recognize what Christine Chism asserts about alliterative texts contemporary to *Troilus and Criseyde*: that "[t]hese poems are simultaneously curious about the past as other, delighted by the particularities of historic re-creation, and anxious to assimilate or overwrite the unfamiliar, to make the past theirs" (6). I invite students to investigate the ways in which Chaucer's ostensibly historical poem also reflects the contemporary political landscape of Ricardian England.

Contemporary History

During the whole of Chaucer's lifetime, England was at war with France. Beginning in 1337 and lasting until 1453, the Hundred Years' War was fought with siege tactics over territory and identity. Did France belong to the French or to the English? And how was that confounded when "the imperative to conquer and humiliate the enemy, the French, was at odds with the fact that the English house of Plantagenet was, itself, French" (Federico 69)? When the history and genealogy of the current kings were too difficult to reconcile, Troy provided an external source of identity for the English, removing them from the present mayhem to a time and place of perceived honor and order.

While the wars with France were chronic and the battles more distant, there were acute flare-ups of violence closer to Chaucer's home, such as the Peasants' Revolt in 1381. In fact, the rebels marched by Chaucer's house on Aldgate as they entered London. With Jack Straw leading a slaughter of Flemings in London and Wat Tyler marshalling the rebels and negotiating with the king for an end to serfdom (among other things), the revolt was a brutal explosion of temper on the part of the laborers. The poll tax of 1380—a flat tax of one shilling for every adult—was a desperate attempt to raise funds to pay the soldiers fighting in France and was seen as the final in a series of abuses. Because John of Gaunt, duke of Lancaster and uncle to the king, was targeted as a key offender, his palace, the Savoy, burned to the ground.

Part of the fallout from these dramatic events returns us to New Troy: Nicholas Brembre, a lord mayor of London, was ultimately charged with treason by the Lords Appellant and executed. Among his alleged crimes were that "he had thought to destroy the name of the Londoners by renaming the city 'Little Troy' and that he further had thought to style himself duke of London" (Federico 1). The Trojan image was fine in literature but too tainted for application in real life.

The Court of Love

After establishing the political backdrop, I continue the history lesson by introducing the French affinities and tastes of the courts of Edward III and his queen, Phillippa of Hainault, and of Richard II. I explain the practice of reading romances as court entertainment (drawing attention to the beginning of book 2, where Criseyde and her ladies are reading a romance), the games of courtship, and the literature of courts of love.

Jean Froissart, the chronicler of events in the Hundred Years' War, reports his evening readings of romances and songs in the court of the count of Foix (Froissart, *Chronicles* 264), and there are many other accounts of public readings, in the works of Christine de Pisan, for instance. The frontispiece of the Cambridge, Corpus Christi College MS 61 manuscript of *Troilus and Criseyde*, in fact, boasts an illustration of Chaucer presenting his work to a courtly audience. Indeed, Richard Firth Green, in his *Poets and Princepleasers*, asserts, "It is quite clear that not only kings but also their courtiers regarded the public reading of such things as moralized histories and improving stories as an enjoyable and worthwhile pastime" (100). Joyce Coleman, too, confirms that "public reading was and remained popular because people enjoyed listening to books in company; these aural audiences included the sort of literate upper-middle- and upper-class readers for whom Chaucer wrote" (xi). So where Froissart read his Arthurian romance *Meliador*, Chaucer could also have read his *Troilus and Criseyde*. I always ask students to read a few stanzas aloud to sense how it sounded and how long it would have taken to perform (a feat that has been admirably performed by readers for the Chaucer Studio in a recording I highly recommend).

Chaucer's other minor works can be seen as figuring into this discussion as well. *The Legend of Good Women* presents a court where offenses to Love are punished, including the poet's own work in *Troilus and Criseyde*. *The Parliament of Fowls* depicts a court whose agenda is filled with the process of courtship. *The House of Fame* is a vision of all the source material for love poems presented as a reward for true service to the God of Love in creating his earlier works. Each of these poems appeals to an audience who was enamored of "playing out [a] generally mock-serious game of courtship which involved literary stereotypes" (Green 119). *Troilus and Criseyde* provides a narrative working out of these conventions, from the stereotypical swooning lover to the verse love letter.

And in this romance, through this love affair, the image of Troy and the identification of London as New Troy carry their most profound meaning. The poem takes place in a prefall Troy, just as London was in its prefall state. In the poem, though, the lovers act on good faith. Federico claims that this is one of the strengths of the poem, that, from inside the poem, history and current events seem fluid; Troy teeters, but tragedy is held at bay. In her words, "*Troilus and Criseyde* considers how individuals and empires might be able to move around in, or even transcend, the apparent fixity of the past" (65). It is as if the fall is not inevitable, as if Criseyde is not fated to be unfaithful, as if Richard is not doomed to be foolish.

Troilus is a man fighting against fate to maintain the status quo of his relationship. Criseyde is a pawn in a political game, trying to make the best of what she is given. Pandarus is a manipulator who takes advantage of people and situations for his own ends. Calkas is a traitor, a man living in a foreign society who claws his way high enough in that new hierarchy to bargain for the trade of his daughter. Helen is a captive, a catalyst and a perpetuator of the discord around her. I invite students to make parallels between these character types and fourteenth-century Londoners and courtiers, as well as between parallel crises and scenes.[2]

In this light, *Troilus and Criseyde* can be seen as deeply politically engaged. As he does in The Nun's Priest's Tale, Chaucer issues a warning to Richard II (see Astell 109–16). But he issues the warning in the *Troilus* by showing how glorious England could be; by identifying it with the pride of Troy; and by suggesting that Richard's kingdom is in danger of collapse, because its citizens exhibit a faithlessness like that of Calkas and Criseyde.

So my presentation of the backgrounds works from the macrocosm to the microcosm: from war between nations to battles between classes of people in London society to mock battles on the field of love as presented in public readings to the individuals making love through letters. This kind of background helps students interpret and create meaning for themselves from what they read. As we move through the text, then, we put their skills to work by breaking into groups and trying to connect the text to the society it reflects.

Once students have a general overview of the period and its concerns, they are asked to get specific. Given the four levels of social structure (nation, city, court, individual), I ask which elements of Chaucer's depiction of the old Troy might be commenting on aspects of New Troy? How have Chaucer's hopes and fears for his own country been grafted onto the irresistibly turbulent matter of Troy?

Inevitably, students begin by trying to place Richard II in the poem. If he is Troilus, then they can see him as the noble but misguided hero. If Pandarus leads Troilus into sin and away from what should be his priorities, then the flattering friends of Richard do the same—Robert de Vere, Simon Burley maybe. Or students can see Troilus as the idealistic lover, too easily given to his feelings to the point that he becomes self-absorbed. The cynics, usually women, in the class like to take this route, claiming that just as Troilus's relationship with Criseyde is more about him than love, so Richard is too narcissistic to take note of the societal crises raging about him. This division among interpretations should not, probably, come as a surprise. As Paul Strohm points out, division is implicit in the text, where the narrator variously seems to encourage sympathy with Troilus and then, a few lines later, "[implies] that his sorrows might be overblown or partially self-inflicted" (60).

In exploring this potential for multiple readings of a character, some students always want to claim that Richard is Criseyde. They see Richard as unfaithful to the peasants. They are quick to see traditionally feminine traits in him, from vanity and superficiality to fickleness—the perpetually damning changeability of Criseyde.

It gets more interesting when students branch out. Is Pandarus a depiction of John of Gaunt, the one who really pulls the strings behind the whole operation? Someone sees Tyler in Calkas, the traitor, or sometimes Brembre, and at this point it is important that we make distinctions between archetypes and allegories. Just because Chaucer paints a traitor does not mean he intends a characterization of a contemporary traitor; indeed, the lines of allegiance shifted so often that many people were considered traitorous at various times (see Hanrahan for a fine discussion of the definitions of *treason*). Again, my point is not that this poem is a roman à clef but that the context can add depth to our reading of the poem.

This historical approach to *Troilus and Criseyde* works in my senior-level Chaucer class and in the graduate medieval survey. I have never chosen to teach the poem in the lower-division survey, because I think it would take too much time for such a survey. If I could, however, I imagine it would appeal to some members of the nonmajor audience those classes attract. By focusing on such a combination of history, politics, and detective work, this pedagogical strategy dispels the illusion that English majors only care about comma splices and literary devices.

NOTES

[1]A very accessible book for this historical material is Brewer's *Chaucer and His World*. Also see Astell's *Political Allegory in Late Medieval England* for an illuminating reading of Chaucer's political messages—including other uses of the Trojan myth.
[2]Hicks's *Who's Who in Late Medieval England, 1272–1485* is very helpful here.

Trust No Man but Me:
Women and Chaucer's Shorter Poetry

Lynn Arner

Chaucer's Medea demonstrates unusual restraint. Instead of slitting a king's throat, dismembering her brother, and murdering her sons, in *The Legend of Good Women* Medea is one of several hapless victims ruined by callous men who seduce and abandon women. The hypercastrated femininity of Medea and of other women in *The Legend of Good Women* is one of many gendered issues worthy of study in a Chaucer course. This essay offers a feminist approach to teaching *The Legend of Good Women* as well as *Troilus and Criseyde*, *The Book of the Duchess*, and *The House of Fame*.

Professors who discuss Chaucer's shorter poems in relation to gender routinely encounter two problems. The most common difficulty is students' erroneous assumptions about women in the Middle Ages. Since hegemonic ideologies in contemporary America insist that there has been a teleological history of progress in terms of women's rights—with contemporary America at the apex—most undergraduates believe that women in medieval England were relentlessly oppressed. To counter this construction, one can expose and critique the social-Darwinist premise that, over time, women have incrementally gained more rights. Ways to demonstrate the fallacy of this belief include pointing out that rights are not irrevocable but may later be lost; explaining that comparing rights across time often resembles comparing apples and oranges; and demonstrating that different groups of women have disparate rights, determined by class, race, ethnicity, age, or marital status. (For example, among medieval Englishwomen, the ability to write was largely confined to the ruling ranks.) Emphasizing variations in rights among diverse groups of women thwarts totalizing statements about female agency in medieval England.

The best strategy for countering misconceptions is to provide as much information as possible about medieval Englishwomen. Excellent resources for students include Eileen Power's *Medieval Women*; Mavis E. Mate's *Women in Medieval English Society*; Caroline M. Barron's "The Education and Training of Girls in Fifteenth-Century London"; and Maryanne Kowaleski and Judith M. Bennett's "Crafts, Gilds, and Women in the Middle Ages." The following Web sites are also useful: *Monastic Matrix* (http://monasticmatrix.org); and *Feminae: Medieval Women and Gender Index* (www.haverford.edu/library/reference/mschaus/mfi/mfi.html).

A second problem is the accusation that Chaucer raped a woman. As Carolyn Dinshaw observes, there is no consensus about the rape ("raptus") charge from which Cecilia Chaumpaigne released Chaucer in 1380 (10–11).[1] Each professor must decide whether or not to mention the charge, weighing the stakes of disclosure versus not telling. If one decides to disclose the charge, timing is important, since every new piece of biographical information alters students' readings of Chaucer's poetry. If students know of the accusation, a few of them will read Chaucer's works through the incident in a reductive way: when a poem exhibits suspect gender politics, some students pose the rape charge as proof of the inevitability of misogyny in Chaucer's work. One can counter this understanding by emphasizing that medieval tales were communally produced and that ideologies of gender in late-fourteenth-century England speak through the text; thus, constructions of femininity in Chaucer's poems do not simply evidence his misogyny (or enlightenment). If one decides not to mention Chaumpaigne's charge, a student may raise the issue and even articulate resentment toward the professor for "withholding" information.

Topics for Lower-Level Undergraduate Courses

Acceptable versus abject femininity is an accessible topic for undergraduate students. *The Book of the Duchess* lists qualities that good women in late medieval English literature conventionally possess. A woman must be beautiful, and Blanche is described at length as very beautiful of face and body.[2] The good woman does not try to control her husband, and Blanche did not chide (937). Acceptable femininity is associated with stasis. Female characters frequently arrest narrative action through ample descriptions of their physical attributes. Accordingly, instead of recollections of her activities, Blanche's presence is largely composed of prolonged, static descriptions of her character and body, with her body described in fetishistic detail. Because Blanche is dead, she produces the occasion for mourning and reflections of loss by male characters; thus, her stasis pervades the poem. Being a faithful wife is of utmost importance, and Blanche was as loyal as Penelope and Lucrece (1080–82). Similarly, *The Legend of Good Women* argues that chastity is of utmost importance for women. The poem revolves obsessively around female sexuality, with most tales centering on a woman's affair with a man. Most female protagonists articulate desire and are punished for desiring: their partners abandon them; the women are thrust into misery; and several of the women perish.

On intersections of gender and class in Chaucer's shorter poems, Karl Marx and Friedrich Engels's observation in *The German Ideology* is applicable: history is the drama of princes. History is typically told from the perspectives of the ruling classes and revolves around their lives. In late medieval England, ruling groups consisted of royalty, aristocracy, high-ranking clergy, and wealthy merchants. Chaucer's shorter poems are the dramas of these ranks. *Troilus and Criseyde* centers on a prince and his royal family; on Greek princes; and on a high priest and his property-owning, leisured daughter. *The Book of the Duchess* focuses on a dead duchess and her duke; the praiseworthy woman whose death is worth lamenting is from privileged echelons. In *The Legend of Good Women,* tales feature royalty and nobility. By implication, a woman (good or not) worth remembering requires noble birth. In all three poems, members of nonruling ranks rarely appear, and, when they do, they are name-less characters who provide mise-en-scène. Chaucer foregrounds the ruling ranks, in part, because he was from the protobourgeoisie and because his patrons and audiences were primarily from ruling groups.

The racialization of women in Chaucer's shorter poems is striking.[3] In *The Book of the Duchess,* the beautiful Blanche—as her name attests—is em-phatically white. Her hands (955), neck (939), and hue (905) are white, while her hair resembles gold (858). Blanche's shoulders are fair (952), and "Hyr throte . . . / Semed a round tour of yvoyre" (945–46). Her whiteness is em-phasized and fetishized. Blanche is also described by the related word "fair" (e.g., 909, 950, 1079, 1180). Her nickname—"goode faire White" (948)—encapsulates her racialization. "Goode faire White" is fair in three Middle English senses of the word: beautiful, light skinned, and good or virtuous. *The Book of the Duchess* reinscribes the alignment of beauty, virtue, and whiteness.

Beautiful women in Chaucer's shorter poems are frequently white and blond—even women who, given their geographic locations, one might expect to appear otherwise. Although Troy was located in what is now Turkey, Cri-seyde has "mighty tresses of . . . sonnysshe heeris" (4.816). During the con-summation scene, the narrator reveals Criseyde's "sydes . . . white" (3.1248) and "snowissh throte" (3.1250). *The Legend of Good Women* similarly angli-cizes some of its characters. The beautiful Lucrece—an ancient Roman woman—is blond (1747). Dido, another character whose beauty is empha-sized, possesses "bryghte gilte her" (1315), despite ruling a northern African city. Jason, "a semely man withalle" (1603), has "yelwe her" (1672), although he is from Thessaly. Chaucer's shorter poems frequently equate beauty with whiteness and blondness.

Despite this privileging of whiteness, Chaucer intermittently does count non-European women—including Cleopatra, Hypsipyle, and Thisbe—among the beautiful in *The Legend of Good Women* without making them pale. More-over, Chaucer spins stories of ancient Babylon, Persia, and Troy and occa-sionally recounts tales from Asia. Unlike contemporary Americans, late me-dieval Englishmen and women were willing to view Babylon, Persia, and Troy as part of their heritage, as Nebuchadnezzar's dream in John Gower's *Con-fessio Amantis* attests (prologue 585–1052). Chaucer represents the lives of women of color and the histories of non-European countries as worthy of consideration.[4]

Topics for Upper-Level Undergraduate and Master's-Level Courses

Female agency is a provocative topic. In *The Legend of Good Women,* most leading ladies initially show considerable agency, flouting paternal and societal restrictions. However, once men betray them, these women are largely sapped of the ability to act. Although Dido, Hypsipyle, and Phyllis rule kingdoms, once their lovers abandon them, they are capable only of writing to their betrayers and of dying. Traditional representations of Medea, Philomela, and Procne argue that when a woman has been done an injustice, she may exact vengeance. Conventional portrayals of Cleopatra and Hypsipyle contend that, even without provocation, a woman can be vicious. Chaucer strips female characters of this power: Medea merely writes Jason a grievance; Philomela and Procne are simply reunited and left in an embrace; and Cleopatra is reduced to a simplistic, lovesick wreck. Chaucer has rendered these women no longer threatening to men. These tales repeatedly enact the fantasy that a man can do anything he wishes to a woman, and she will seek no vengeance. Instead of being castrating, "good women" punish themselves for men's misdeeds. Moreover, the tales testify that women who act on their desires destroy their own happiness.

Another suitable topic is the commonplace medieval association of femininity with mutability, orality, babbling, and deception, whereas masculinity is aligned with stability, steadfastness, writing, and truth—a convention replicated in most of Chaucer's shorter poems. In *The Book of the Duchess*, Fortune is female and bears her typical traits: instability, unpredictability, and guile (618–54). In *The House of Fame*, femininity's association with fickleness is emphatic in Lady Fame (Fortune's sister [1547]), whose gifts of fame, notoriety, or oblivion are arbitrary. Lady Fame is also connected to linguistic instability and orality, for she bears as many tongues and ears as there are hairs on a beast (1388–90). The cliché that women are unfaithful structures *Troilus and Criseyde*: witness Helen and Criseyde. At the poem's close, there is a warning for women to beware of men (5.1779–85), but the inversion of gender roles in one stanza cannot negate the preceding tale. Replicating this inversion on a grander scale, *The Legend of Good Women* features male characters who, sporting the deceit typical of female characters, seduce and betray women, while the women are unflinchingly faithful, some to the point of committing suicide when abandoned. Students benefit from Michele Wallace's introduction to *Invisibility Blues*, which outlines the implications of the type of inversion strategy Chaucer employs. Wallace explains why substituting terms aligned with the dominant group for those associated with the subordinate group (and vice versa) is politically ineffectual and why understanding texts as negative or positive representations of a group is not productive. Students could also discuss how the narrator's warning "[a]nd trusteth, as in love, no man but me" (2561) functions in this text and in *Troilus and Criseyde*, a poem for which Chaucer's persona in *The Legend of Good Women* claims to be making amends.

A final topic is Chaucer's construction of tradition. Chaucer legitimates his vernacular poetry by positioning his work as continuous with prestigious texts of the past. Not only are his shorter poems typically structured by Greco-

Roman texts, but Chaucer bids his "litel bok" on Troy to "kis the steppes where as thow seest pace / Virgile, Ovide, Omer, Lucan, and Stace" (5.1789–92), thereby appending his name to a list of revered male authors. In *The House of Fame*, the narrator/Chaucer envisions himself immersed in and inheriting an impressive textual legacy. Again, this tradition is phallocentric, as the gender of the great hall's statues of celebrated writers attests (1419–519). These homages constitute Chaucer's construction of a canon, one without women. Fortunately, when the surrounding poem discusses cultural producers, a few mythological women are mentioned, notably Calliope and her sisters (1399–1406) and Marcia the satyr (1229–32). Nevertheless, most cultural producers are male, including Boethius (972), Plato (759; 931), Aristotle (759), Orpheus (1203), Arion (1205), Martianus Capella (985), Chiron the centaur (1206), and others (e.g., 1208, 1227, 1228, 1243). Chaucer erects a predominantly male tradition as his legacy to inherit and to bequeath. To illuminate the politics of Chaucer's knowledge production, students could read Michele Wallace's *Invisibility Blues*, the title chapter from Raymond Williams's "Traditions, Institutions, and Formations," and selections from Michel Foucault's *Archeology of Knowledge*. As an alternative to Chaucer's masculinist canon, students could consider Christine de Pisan's gynocentric intellectual heritage in *The Book of the City of Ladies*.

There are many more topics to pursue when teaching Chaucer's *Troilus and Crisedye*, *The Legend of Good Women*, and shorter poems in relation to gender. At the diegetic level, these topics include the absence of mothers, exchanges of women between men, and constructions of female subjectivity. At the discursive level, these issues include voyeurism, identifications facilitated for readers, the alignment of femininity with death, and the prevalence of upper-class male subjectivities.

NOTES

[1] Compare Cannon, "Chaucer" 266; Pearsall, *Life* 137; and Delany, *Medieval Literary Politics* 128.

[2] Although the dead woman is named only "White," in *The Book of the Duchess*, it is generally assumed that Chaucer wrote the poem as a memorial to Blanche, duchess of Lancaster, first wife of John of Gaunt.

[3] On medieval white-black binaries, see Loomba 57–58; Hahn 1–37; and Cohen 114–24.

[4] Albeit some of Chaucer's considerations are unkind. See Delany, *Naked Text* 153–86.

Teaching Masculinities in Chaucer's Shorter Poems: Historical Myths and Brian Helgeland's *A Knight's Tale*

Holly A. Crocker

When Geoffrey Chaucer (as played by Paul Bettany) trudges into Brian Helgeland's *A Knight's Tale*, a historical personage breaks into the fictional frame of a film—but not really. Helgeland's Chaucer introduces himself as a writer, but his pitch for recognition fails because none of the company that rescues Geoff from his destitute condition has read (or can read) his *Book of the Duchess*. Although the film only refers to the historical Geoffrey through distorted winks at the audience, the filmic Chaucer's later success as a herald depends on the poetic persona that he has not yet assumed in a historical context. In other words, the film's audience is meant to see that Geoff Chaucer is good at fashioning the fictional knightly persona that the protagonist William Thatcher (Heath Ledger) will put on, because Chaucer is the father of English poetry just waiting to come into his own.[1]

Helgeland's dramatization of Chaucer is useful for teaching the construction of masculinities in many of Chaucer's poems, although I focus only on "Lenvoy de Chaucer a Scogan" and "Lenvoy de Chaucer a Bukton" in this essay. Because *A Knight's Tale* introduces students to the notion that identities are staged combinations of fabrication and fact, discussing the film's strategies in relation to Chaucer's ballads assists students in exploring the collaborative creation of Chaucerian masculinities. Chaucer's "envoy" poems combine literary pose with historical detail, using a mock-epistolary style to give the impression of honest communication between "real" men, when in fact this communication circulates for a wider audience (Horvath 174). And even if we put aside the topics of these poems—love and marriage—we see that they construct male bonds through shared dynamic experience. *A Knight's Tale* is useful, therefore, because it lets students explore the combinations of history and fiction required to make representations of masculinity persuasive.

The primary challenge in teaching Chaucerian masculinities is to get students to engage masculinity as a critical category. For many students, manhood is such a neutral part of human experience that they have a hard time identifying it. Most students are willing to admit that there are different types of men, but many of their distinctions depend on the extent of men's control over fame or fortune. When students try to define masculinity in relation to femininity, most find this task surprisingly difficult: the only relation diverse students can agree on is a division based on biological sex, a pop-psychology Mars-Venus distribution of agency. In a reification of the old active-passive binary, students in one class after another insist that men are actors, agents, individuals. While *some* women can have agency, most women do not lose face and in fact gain more respect when they take up passive roles that reinforce and complement masculine control. If I suggest to my students that these conceptions of gender are old fashioned for persons who invariably profess their self-determining capabilities, many students quickly deploy the myth of history, suggesting that what they are really talking about is a model of gender difference that is primitive, or, as they put it, "medieval."

The first obstacle to teaching masculinities in the "Lenvoy de Chaucer a Scogan," then, is history itself. It is relatively easy to identify Henry Scogan as Chaucer's younger associate, a member of the king's household who also wrote poetry and became tutor to the sons of Henry IV (Pearsall, *Life* 183–84). It is comparatively difficult to convince students that this historical personage is relevant to the portrait of masculine friendship that Chaucer paints in his poem. Because students already see Chaucer as a more significant historical and literary figure, they have a hard time accepting the shared masculine perspective that Chaucer constructs in the poem. It is only when we demystify Chaucer's literary position through his historical relation to what has become known in criticism as his "literary circle" that students can more fully appreciate the kind of masculine friendship the "Lenvoy de Chaucer a Scogan" explores (Strohm 46, 75–76; Lenaghan).

It is in this demystifying function, I submit, that Helgeland's *A Knight's Tale* is useful. In Helgeland's film, Chaucer is not a member of a group of "Lollard knights" or even a group of men in royal service (McFarlane 139–226). His company is a provisional formation, a ragtag set of commoners whose interdependent desire to excel in an arena constricted by the certifications of birth unite them in a collaborative fiction of masquerade. Yet in its membership this band shows the multiplicities of masculine identity as they function even in cross-gendered arrangements. From its accomplished but pragmatic Kate (Laura Fraser) to its maternal but burly Roland (Mark Addy) to its violent but loyal Wat (Alan Tudyk), Chaucer's party unites through a shared interest in making the noble but common William into a knight. In their shifting attempt to authenticate a fiction of knightly masculine identity, the members of this group show that gender identities are masks that men and women can assume in different contexts to meet common goals.

The collective formation of identities—of knight, squire, armorer, herald—allows students to investigate the ways that Chaucer's address to Scogan fashions both men in a collaborative poetic performance. Masculinity in "Lenvoy de Chaucer a Scogan" is characterized by vulnerability and ineptitude. Chaucer jests that those who "ben hoor and rounde of shap" (31) will be most damaged by Scogan's refusal to serve love, including himself in the group of hapless men whom Cupid will abandon: "He wol nat with his arwes been ywroken / On the, ne me, ne noon of oure figure" (26–27). When Chaucer scolds Scogan for lacking steadfastness in the service of love, however, he also suggests that his friend is a character whose supposed incompetence confers the power of self-determination. Even if Scogan here seems more powerful than Chaucer, the poem's mocking equation of the ability to serve love and to write poetry connects these men through their cross-generational failures. If we look at Chaucer's poem as a deliberate manipulation of history that constructs a myth of masculine unity, we can see that Chaucer's actual relation to Scogan is both important and irrelevant to the poem's focus on male friendship.

Thus, if we can bring ourselves as Chaucer scholars to ignore the title of *A Knight's Tale*, we can use Helgeland's film to engage the literary construction of Chaucer's persona outside *The Canterbury Tales*. While it is true that Helgeland's film has really nothing to do with Chaucer's Boethian romance (Forni, "Reinventing"), its construction of Chaucer as simultaneously sociable and savvy nevertheless fits students' (and scholars') conceptions of Chaucer's authorial presence (Trigg 29–33; Pace and David 141). So the first obstacle to teaching masculinities in "Lenvoy de Chaucer a Bukton" is fiction itself. Because Chaucer refuses to draw a line between his fictional presence in the poetic world inhabited by a woman like Alison of Bath and his relations in the actual historical community occupied by the Robert or Peter Bukton he addresses, it is difficult to keep students from assigning Chaucer's poetic attributes to his real person.

Here, again, is where Helgeland's film becomes a useful pedagogical tool. When students watch the film, I ask them to keep a running list of adjectives that describe the filmic Geoffrey. While their lists begin with terms including *skinny*, *dirty*, even *geeky*, by the film's end they include terms such as *smart*, *clever*, even *hot*. We discuss the attitudinal changes their lists record, and, almost without exception, students agree that the successful fashioning of the knightly Ulrich von Lichtenstein from the lowly William Thatcher results in the construction of Geoffrey Chaucer as successful. They like Geoffrey more and more as the film progresses, and they increasingly believe that his performances are even more important to Ulrich's reputation than William's physical skill in jousting or romantic success with Jocelyn (Shannyn Sossamon). Using these lists to think about the figuration of fictive identity, we turn to Chaucer's "Lenvoy de Chaucer a Bukton" to think again about the ways that the myth of Chaucer is a fiction of male power that makes itself true.

When students compare their lists of Chaucerian attributes with the speaking voice in "Lenvoy de Chaucer a Bukton," they do not find many resemblances. In fact, about the only terms they are willing to apply to both Chaucers are *clever* and *smart*. Instead, students come up with a new set of adjectives, most of which relate to artistic acumen. Including terms like *mature*, *ironic*, *playful*, *wise*, *sincere*, and *manipulative*, their new lists appear to contain contradictory characteristics. While students agree that their varying perceptions of Chaucer are not the product of a progressive shift in "Lenvoy de Chaucer a Bukton" itself, they suggest that the poem constructs a personal history for its speaker, a sense of past that implies Chaucer's changes over time. When I pursue the impression that the poem's Chaucer is a mature man with marital experience, inevitably history will creep into the discussion and color the fiction of Chaucer. If the poem's probable date of 1396 crops up in our conversation, inevitably some students will feel that the past the poem invokes is *really* Chaucer's.

I am certain that most (if not all) of the students have no clue that the date of "Lenvoy de Chaucer a Bukton" reflects Chaucer's widower status (Philippa is believed to have died in 1387), but when this information is introduced— either by a student or by me—many students latch onto it with a fervor that suggests they believe it is the key to unlocking the meaning of this poem. Indeed, if I indulge my desire to see students' reactions to this historical tidbit, I caution myself beforehand because their reactions invariably lead us down the path of "blessed bachelors," making *us* part of the masculine community that George L. Kittredge extolled in his imaginary scenario for the poem (34). When we discuss the relation of Chaucer's poetic persona in "Lenvoy de Chaucer a Bukton" to Chaucer the man's historical circumstances, students quickly divide themselves into groups differentiated by their attitudes toward masculine views of marriage. These attitudes, to be clear, have no grounding in historical fact.

Indeed, students' loyalties are quickly aligned with the manly attitudes that "Lenvoy de Chaucer a Bukton" puts into play. The poem affects men and women equally: about half of my students think that Chaucer must be protesting his own bad marriage, and half believe that Chaucer is mimicking a manly warning that he ridicules. Students agree that Chaucer's use of refusal, such as "I dar not writen" (7) or "I wol nat seyn" (9), marks his poetic control, whether or not the poem's critique of marriage is serious. As students continue to discuss whether the Wife of Bath's presence in the poem is supposed to be an ironic nod to an audience of knowing contemporaries or a sarcastic invocation to undermine antifeminist attitudes, it becomes impossible to determine whether the students' Chaucer is based on historical fact or poetic invention. To use E. Talbot Donaldson's classic distinction, we might say that students have trouble distinguishing between Donaldson's "Chaucer the Pilgrim," "Chaucer the Poet," and Donald R. Howard's "Chaucer the Man," because the envoy to Bukton collapses these distinctions.

The final way that Helgeland's film can be helpful in teaching masculinities in Chaucer, then, applies not just to "Lenvoy de Chaucer a Bukton" but also to "Lenvoy de Chaucer a Scogan" and other works with occasional or historical connections. When students squabble over Chaucer's "true" attitude toward marriage in "Lenvoy de Chaucer a Bukton," they use history in the same way as Helgeland's *A Knight's Tale*. History here becomes a support for fantasy: students use historical circumstances to prop up the fictions of masculinity they perceive. Even if historical facts have only a conjectural relation to the poem, students invest them with the authority of truth, at least for the sake of the manly fiction they seek to keep together. This habit is plainly a case of selective history, but I want to hold off the pejorative connotations that this designation might otherwise carry.

Before we attribute students' confusion of fictional personae and historical circumstances to their lack of literary savvy or historical knowledge, I want to suggest that discussing Helgeland's film in conjunction with Chaucer's poems makes it clear that students intentionally violate these time-honored boundaries, and not just as a "reductive appreciation of [Chaucer's] work" (Ellis 27). While as Chaucerians we may step carefully to avoid confusing literary and historical representations, students run roughshod over this distinction in order to pass off different versions of identity, here masculinity. Students attempt to cobble together bits of history to preserve a unified myth of masculinity, but in the process they end up highlighting their awareness of masculinity's constructed status in Chaucer. Similarly, when I use the film as a way to explore *The Book of the Duchess*, the film's representation of Chaucer as unknown and unheralded gives students a better sense of Chaucer as an anonymous writer working among the powerful personalities of his day (such as John of Gaunt). Helgeland's story of a commoner's rise to knighthood is inaccurate as history and banal as fiction. But because it succeeds through a collaborative performance of players whose shared complicity solidifies bonds of loyalty, *A Knight's Tale* creates a diverse masculine community through its fabrication of a manly type. Similarly, the historical facts behind the masculine figures in Chaucer's "envoy" poems are not their most important features; rather, as critics from Kittredge to Seth Lerer (*Chaucer*) to Stephanie Trigg point out, the appeal of the "envoy" poems is their ability to create a sense of masculine community that includes their audiences. What Helgeland's film demonstrates and my students' discussions confirm is that positions in these manly communities can be taken up by women *or* men, as long as all participants recognize that masculinities are historical fictions that they create in collaboration.

NOTE

[1]Thatcher's knightly persona is dubbed Ulrich von Lichtenstein, itself a nod to literary formations of chivalric masculinity, since the name also refers to a German minnesinger (c. 1200–1275), whose *Fraundienst* (1255) and *Frauenbuch* (1257) trace the intersection of chivalry and courtship in an ideal of manliness.

Suggestions for Rehearsing
the Short Poems in Class

William A. Quinn

In addition to conventional contexts for teaching Chaucer's short poems, each text's original presentation occasions provocative classroom discussion. Although some of Chaucer's short poems survive as mere page fillers in the manuscripts, several significant moments of protopublication or inaugural recitation can be induced from internal and external evidence. The putative dynamics of a poem's first context of reception helps define its apparent "voice." The fundamental questions waiting to be asked about each text are, How did Chaucer intend to publish or send forth each composition? What audience or readership did he anticipate for each? What might have been Chaucer's expectations regarding his direct presence or, conversely, his absence during future readings of these verses?

Chaucer's short poems fall into four different categories of presentation, or rehearsing: commissioned pieces, formal exercises, poetic presents, and laureate poems. Commissioned pieces anticipate the reactions of a specific patron or court on a specific occasion. Chaucer's formal exercises seem more *sua sponte* experiments, often composed in friendly competition with poems by other literati. Poetic presents are gifts that anticipate the author's own presence—either the immediate recognition of "I" by a familiar reader or the author's literal presence as the text's initial reciter. Each of Chaucer's presents was apparently composed with a specific first recipient in mind, but these seemingly impromptu lyrics addressed to readers of comparable social standing sound somewhat comfortable, often jovial. Whereas Chaucer's presents are usually considered his most appealing short poems, his laureate poems offer vatic pronouncements addressed to all. These metra were apparently intended for widespread publication; their mise-en-scène is history, indeed destiny, rather than the court or boudoir or bar.

Each short poem needs to be interpreted dramatically as well as thematically according to its proper context of rehearsing. In certain senses, all medieval poetry was intended for performance. The critical challenge for teachers is to have students determine which conception of performance is most appropriate for each lyric. All of Chaucer's ballades, as well as his *carmen* ("An ABC"), can be sung. But, during the fourteenth century, many such lyric patterns originally designed to be sung (i.e., melic verse) were meant to be recited with much the same voice and metricality as stichic verse, or "natural music." In addition to this fundamental distinction between lyrics intended to be sung and those meant to be said, certain categorically different conceptions of reading may be invoked to distinguish lyrics originally composed for private (solitary, silent) reading from those composed for public entertainment (reading aloud), to distinguish actual recital to a familiar audience from manuscript publication intended for a more general readership (including posterity).

Commissioned Pieces

"An ABC" is Chaucer's most conspicuously artificial poem and thus may readily be taught as a formal exercise and as an occasion for discussion of the alterity of medieval sensibilities. Although a display of technical expertise, a commissioned liturgical piece like "An ABC" requires the almost complete suppression of Chaucer's bourgeois ego in order to express the humble piety of his patroness. Chaucer's anticipated context of presentation is both the primer of Lady Blanche and the heavenly court of Mary. The style satisfies a Lancastrian taste, but the sentiment is catholic.

A completely different esprit is exemplified by "The Complaint of Mars." If commissioned as a "disguising" or "mumming," this roman à clef indicates the ad hoc inspiration required of a courtier-poet. It exemplifies Chaucer's somewhat daring but never presumptuous rapport with his familiar patron audience whom Chaucer addresses as "hardy knyghtes of renoun" (272) and as "ye, my ladyes" (281) and, collectively, as "ye lovers" (5) but whom he first addresses as "ye foules" (1). Given the very debatable wink-wink subtext of this complaint, having the entire class play his protoaudience is a more significant teaching challenge than having one person impersonate the reciting Chaucer.

Formal Exercises

In a post–New Critical profession, these short poems may be the hardest to teach because their delight is almost exclusively formalist. The prosody of "A

Complaint to His Lady" is at once fascinating and baffling. Chaucer's complaint as a whole may simply be a scribal or editorial construct. Yet line 23, "Now sothly what she hight I wol reherce," could preserve a significant key to understanding Chaucer's original intent for this workshop piece; the extant text presents a sampler of Chaucer's makings. "The Complaint of Venus" is most often cited because of Chaucer's (self-serving) claim that it is harder to rhyme in English (80) than in French. But, as a showpiece, Chaucer's triple ballade with ten-line envoy defies the challenge of this relative difficulty by employing only two rhymes. Chaucer's tour de force seems especially addressed to fellow poets and connoisseurs.

Presents

Though there is a natural temptation to read all Chaucer's lyrics addressed directly to women as poetic presents, there are a number of interpretive problems with doing so. Chaucer's complaints seem like confidential rather than secret gifts; they anticipate being shared by more than one recipient but not by everyone. "The Complaint unto Pity" represents how difficult it is to determine whether Chaucer's lyric voice should be played as sincere or ironic. The teacher's own *pronuntiatio* actualizes an unannounced interpretation of Chaucer's authorial intent. This particular complaint is problematic because it may conjoin at least two separate presentation events. The preliminary eight stanzas that refer to "Pite" in the third person specify that "the bill" proper addressing her directly was "writen, in myn hond" (43), presumably for some prior occasion. This missive to "Pite" herself had been private. Chaucer kept the "pleynte stille" (47)—with a possible double entendre on "spille" (46)—stating that "to my foes my bille I dar not shewe" (55). In the extant text's first eight stanzas, Chaucer publicly presents what "seith" this prior text "in wordes few" (56), which is submitted as evidence in a pseudolegal appeal to his courtier friends. Although the tone of Chaucer's "bill" looks straightforward, it is intriguing to consider that Chaucer's subsequent recital of this amorous complaint might have once sounded much more jaundiced. In publishing a dead letter, Chaucer proposes one self-contradiction after another. He wants to beg Pity to take revenge (11) but finds her "buried in an herte" (14). He sees a hearse, and he himself drops dead as a stone (15–16). What Chaucer means when he states that he rose again "with colour ful dyverse" (17) eludes glossing. Does "colour" pun on "colores" (i.e., rhetorical figures)? "Dyverse" on "verse"? He prays for Pity's soul but is lost (damned? [20–21]). Her ladies in waiting, who now serve as pallbearers, show no grief (36–37). After such a prelude, rehearsal of the entire "bill" is vulnerable to self-mocking recitation.

If one does not consider its subsequent subversion by the recital of a rejected lover, the naked text of "Womanly Noblesse" reads like a billet-doux.

This complaint may be taught as the voice of a youthfully passionate Chaucer assuming the role of a squire-suitor. The envoy indicates that this text was actually delivered on time (30) for the lady's private, silent reading. Critical scrutiny finds the missing ninth line of stanza two clumsy (compare the strained rhyme "governeresse" in "Pity" [80]). Such mistakes may be dismissed (i.e., corrected) as scribal contaminations, and such flaws may be overlooked if young Chaucer struggled to finish his poems in a timely fashion. Such poetic presents are not merely occasional but opportunistic. If Chaucer's original addressees scanned these poems, no wonder his love was doomed. Likewise, when Chaucer declares "I am youres" (9) in "A Balade of Complaint," his plan is to hand directly to the poem's recipient a copy of "this litel pore dyte" (16) that he is presently reciting. His suit is to serve (12) and so remain, like her attendant virtues, "ay" in her presence (7). Accepting this text as an amorous present suggests welcoming its author as well.

The text of "Merciles Beaute" now looks like one poem that consists of three different segments held together in a dramatic sequence, primarily by a common *b* rhyme. In the first two installments, Chaucer sounds as if he is pleading in direct sight (1–2) and hearing (4, 8, 18) of one lady. But in the third palinode-like rondel, Chaucer mocks Cupid. This final segment sounds, therefore, more in harmony with the tone of "Lenvoy de Chaucer a Bukton" (and may have been similarly circulated among friends).

Chaucer's complaints about women seek the commiseration of similarly frustrated men. Lines 8–32 and 71–77 of "Complaynt D'Amours" are addressed directly to a single woman (8, 10, 73, 76–77) and compose a wooing poem that can be extracted from the enframing third-person complaint. Chaucer's reference to a six-line song (24–25) does not suggest that the "Complaynt D'Amours" was likewise sung; on the contrary, line 67 suggests that the (final, composite) text was intended first for one lady's silent, solitary reading (and then for others). Chaucer introduces himself as the text's rehearser: "Beginne right thus" (4). The lyric shifts to a complaint about *la belle dame sans merci* when the rejected poet answers his own rhetorical question (33). The tenth stanza (64–70) provides a bridge between the two distinct presentation events by picturing the moment of handing over the text: "That I now dorste . . . / Shewe by word, that ye wolde ones rede / The compleynte of me" (66–68). The last stanza functions more as a colophon than an envoy. The apparent redundancy of "[t]his woful *song* and this *compleynte*" (88, my italics) may in fact signify these two different rehearsal contexts. Whereas "The Complaint unto Pity" may be read as a sort of "take-that" therapy (11) and "Against Women Unconstant" seems an even more bitter catharsis, "Complaynt D'Amours" still waffles between hope and reality.

"Lenvoy de Chaucer a Scogan" and "Lenvoy de Chaucer a Bukton" obviously preserve more jovial letters given to specific male friends. "Bukton" seems the more private ditty; "Scogan" anticipates circulation among a rather small fraternity of readers (30–33). "The Complaint of Chaucer to His Purse" seems comparably familiar with its anticipated audience; it assumes the reader will be readily amused by the contrast between Chaucer's girth and lean income. John Shirley claimed that this begging poem was originally addressed to Richard II—an interpretation that, economically, makes sense (*Riverside* 1088). But it is difficult to imagine Chaucer *in propria persona* kidding this particular king with such quasi-sacrilegious remarks (13, 16, 19). A more receptive audience for this rather meretricious meter would be Chaucer's fellow courtiers in financial distress. It can be argued that the pretentious style of the dubious envoy to Henry IV sounds "un-Chaucerian"; it is sufficient to discuss in class whether it suits the playful tone of the preceding petition.

"Fortune" offers a more plausible demonstration of how Chaucer actually begged money from his betters. In the envoy, Lady Fortune addresses the members of court as a peer. She requests, on Chaucer's behalf, that two or three members of the audience in turn petition "his beste frend" (78) for financial sustenance. One of the most significant observations Lady Fortune makes is that misfortune distinguishes "[f]rend of effect and frend of countenaunce" (34). All of Chaucer's poetic presents were addressed to friends or lovers and inspired by ulterior motives. "Chaucers Wordes unto Adam, His Owne Scriveyn" too preserves only a nonce epigram (or verse curse). For once, Chaucer sounds sincerely annoyed. Yet even this apparently scribbled jibe to a single subordinate had, at some later occasion, to be transcribed and so rehearsed as a caveat to a wider audience.

Laureate Poems

Chaucer's Clerk of Oxford idolizes Petrarch as "the lauriat poete . . . whos rethorike sweete / Enlumyned al Ytaille of poetrie" (*CT* 4.31–33). In turn, John Lydgate eulogized Chaucer as "the noble rethor Poete of bretaine / That worthy was the laurer to have" (Spurgeon 1: 19). With much the same reverence, Shirley praised Chaucer as "our laureal poete" and in British Library MS Harley 7333, Chaucer is also identified as "the Laureall Poete of Albion" (1: 47). Though Chaucer dismissed any claim to such personal prestige, his laureate poems do pronounce inviolate truth. There is no anxious, witty, irascible, or frustrated persona, indeed no "I," who speaks "The Former Age," "Truth," "Gentilesse," or "Lak of Stedfastnesse." All four laureate poems offer public counsel "bon" and "morale" to both Chaucer's contemporaries and posterity—without apology or irony: "That thee is sent, receyve in buxumnesse" ("Truth" 15). The political (i.e., moral) themes that Chaucer clearly affirms in these poems require little explication. But why he spoke in this highly serious and so seemingly "un-Chaucerian" fashion at all deserves class discussion. All four are dated, with unusual confidence, after 1380 because they seem haunted by the troubles that ended the fourteenth century. They speak to immediate historical concerns (an almost explicit relevance that is generally considered "un-Chaucerian"). "The Former Age" is thought to have been addressed specifically to Richard II immediately before his deposition. Shirley suggested that Chaucer composed "Truth" on his deathbed ([Spurgeon 1: 48] though a date c. 1386–89 seems more probable). The advice to Vache concluding "Truth" as well as the admonition to a "prince" (presumably King Richard) ending "Lak of Stedfastnesse" indicate the immediacy of such timeless advice.

Encouraging students to research the circumstances motivating each poem promotes more historicized appreciations of each poem's mise-en-scène. Also commanding class attention is the largely legendary elevation of laureate Chaucer to his status as "Father of *English* Poetry" (Spurgeon 1: 276), a functional fiction that informs much of the future history of English prosody.

Chaucer and the Critical Tradition

Glenn A. Steinberg

G. K. Chesterton once wrote, "[w]hat matters is not books on Chaucer, but Chaucer" (9). I would counter that books on Chaucer *do* matter. Our appreciation of and for Chaucer today cannot be divorced from the critical tradition that has shaped our access and approach to "the Father of *English* Poetry" (Dryden, qtd. in Spurgeon 1: 276). In fact, our reading of Chaucer is always necessarily mediated by the history of Chaucer's reception since the fourteenth century. Without the books on Chaucer that have been written by John Dryden, Frederick James Furnivall, George Lyman Kittredge, and E. Talbot Donaldson, among others, Chaucer might not matter to us at all, and we might not consider him the master of irony and ambiguity that we do.

Perhaps nowhere is the critical tradition of Chaucer's reception more obviously important to our reading of Chaucer today than in the decline in status of *Troilus and Criseyde* and the so-called minor poems over the last three hundred years. As Derek Pearsall has noted of Chaucer's initial imitators and admirers, "the poems to which they turn again and again . . . are *The Parliament*, the *Troilus*, *The Legend of Good Women*, and *The Knight's Tale*. The *Canterbury Tales* in general are less highly regarded" ("English Chaucerians" 202). But in the eighteenth century, regard for *The Canterbury Tales* began to increase dramatically. The trend is perhaps most apparent in terms of the publication history of Chaucer's works. Until 1700, more editions of Chaucer's collected works were published than editions of *The Canterbury Tales*, but since 1700 that balance has shifted increasingly in favor of *The Canterbury Tales*. In fact, *The Canterbury Tales* accounts for only about a third of editions of Chaucer before 1700, just over half the editions of Chaucer in the eighteenth century, almost two-thirds of editions of Chaucer in the nineteenth century, and nearly ninety percent of the editions of Chaucer in the first decade of the twentieth century (Spurgeon 1: lxxi; 3: 22–23, 25–26).

As a result of this shift in priorities, students of Chaucer today read the "minor" poems in the shadow cast by *The Canterbury Tales*. For this reason, readings of Chaucer before the eighteenth century, based as they are on a greater intimacy and affinity with Chaucer's "minor" works, can seem decidedly alien to us. Indeed, readers of Chaucer today are often surprised and perplexed to learn that Chaucer's early critics praise him primarily for his learning, his rhetorical skill, and his alleged proto–Protestant leanings—not for his humor, his realism, or his irony. John Lydgate, in the first decade of the fifteenth century, for example, calls Chaucer "[t]he noble rethor Poete of breteine" (Spurgeon 1: 19). In 1577, Raphael Holinshed characterizes Chaucer as "a man so exquisitely learned in all sciences, that hys matche was not lightly founde anye where in those dayes, and for reducing our Englishe tong to perfect conformitie, hee hath excelled therein all other" (Spurgeon 1: 114).

To William Caxton in the 1480s, Chaucer's *House of Fame* is a worthy text for printing, "[f]or he towchyth in it ryght grete wysedom & subtyll vnderstondyng / . . . [and] he wrytteth no voyde wordes / but alle hys mater is ful of hye and quycke sentence" (Spurgeon 1: 61). Because *The House of Fame* is generally viewed today as a parody of the "hye and quycke sentence" of medieval encyclopedic literature, Caxton's reading of the poem seems to us a gross misreading.

But we must be careful not to make overhasty generalizations about Chaucer's early readers or about the correctness of our own readings of Chaucer. As Seth Lerer observes, "modern readers have traditionally found fifteenth-century scribes and compilers, as well as writers such as Clanvowe, Hoccleve, Lydgate, and Hawes, incapable of understanding Chaucer's literary genius or his cultural milieu" (*Chaucer* 6). But as Lerer continues, "Why, we might ask, are modern editors, [who are] so willing to accept the fifteenth century's attributions of Chaucer's work [in terms of authorship], equally willing to dismiss its readings of his lines [in terms of interpretation]?" (*Chaucer* 6). The seeming incongruities of early Chaucer criticism can serve to challenge and correct the complacent certainties of our own perspective on Chaucer, including our reliance on *The Canterbury Tales* as the principal standard and focus of the Chaucer canon.

In addition, overemphasis on humorless readings of Chaucer in the fifteenth and sixteenth centuries can misrepresent Chaucer's early reception. Early commentators stress Chaucer's "hye and quycke sentence," but they unquestionably recognize and appreciate Chaucer's comic irony as well. As Derek Brewer has noted, Lydgate imitates Chaucer's "self-depreciatory fun" with "elephantine gaiety" in the prologue to *The Siege of Thebes* ("Images" 247). John Skelton, in *Philip Sparrow*, praises Chaucer's "mater" as "delectable / Solacious and commendable" and his "tearmes" as "pleasaunt, easy, and playne" (Spurgeon 1: 69). Gabriel Harvey in the 1580s notes the widespread popularity of Chaucer's "witt, pleasant veine, varietie of poetical discourse, & all humanitie" (Spurgeon 1: 128). Despite the common perception among Chaucer scholars today that fifteenth- and sixteenth-century readers universally misperceive Chaucer as "that *noble grete philosopher*, as he was for Caxton, Skelton, and Spenser" (Miskimin 91), the reality of Chaucer's early reception is far more complex, nuanced, and interesting than such a view supposes.

How, then, can we best teach our students about the long and complex critical tradition that informs—and, on occasion, challenges—our reading of Chaucer today? How can we both teach Chaucer's "minor" poems and unpack the assumptions and the history that led to their becoming minor for us? In answer to these questions, I would like to suggest two potential strategies for incorporating elements of the critical tradition into a Chaucer course for advanced undergraduates.

First Strategy: Teaching History by Example

Alexander Pope's *Temple of Fame* (1711) comes at an important moment in the history of Chaucer criticism and can be used to teach students both about that moment and about its influence on our reading of Chaucer today. Beginning in the sixteenth century, readers repeatedly comment on Chaucer's "auncient phrase" (Thomas Greene, qtd. in Boswell and Holton, "References" 296) and "termes olde" (Robert Copland, qtd. in Spurgeon 1: 77), "which by reason of antiquitie be almost out of vse" (Peter Ashton, qtd. in Spurgeon 1: 87). As the seventeenth century unfolds, the obsolescence of Chaucer's language becomes a greater and greater concern, to such an extent that, in 1635, Francis Kynaston published a translation of the first two books of *Troilus and Criseyde* into Latin, with the purpose, according to William Barker's prefatory poem, of reviving the reputation of a "booke, not tractable to every hand, / And such as few presum'd to vnderstand" (Spurgeon 1: 207–08). By 1700, Chaucer is viewed, at best, as a poet whose "Antiquated Muse / In mouldy Words could solid Sense produce" (Samuel Cobb, qtd. in Spurgeon 1: 271).

The perception that under Chaucer's "mouldy Words" lay "solid Sense" gives rise to what Caroline Spurgeon has characterized as "the period of 'modernizations' " (Spurgeon 1: x), beginning with Dryden's *Fables Ancient and Modern* in 1700 and including Pope's *Temple of Fame* eleven years later. Dryden, in the preface to his *Fables*, lays out his rationale for modernizing Chaucer's language and also provides an influential vision of Chaucer that has continued in many respects to influence our reading of Chaucer to the present day. In place of the fifteenth- and sixteenth-century perception of Chaucer as a skilled rhetor and learned philosopher, Dryden, focusing entirely on *The Canterbury Tales*, proposes an image of Chaucer as a simple poet who "follow'd Nature every where, but was never so bold to go beyond her" (Spurgeon 1: 276). In Chaucer, according to Dryden, we find "God's Plenty" and "have our Fore-fathers and Great Grand–dames all before us, as they were in *Chaucer's Days*," and we take pleasure in Chaucer's judicious portraits of his neighbors, because "their general Characters are still remaining in Mankind" (Spurgeon 1: 279).

Asking students to read Pope's *Temple of Fame* and to research other seventeenth- and eighteenth-century responses to Chaucer is an excellent way to introduce them to this key moment in the history of Chaucer's reception. Pope's 524-line modernization of *The House of Fame* reduces Chaucer's 2,158-line poem to almost exactly a quarter its size. What Pope retains is a significant indication of what eighteenth-century readers of Chaucer perceive as Chaucer's "solid Sense" under his "mouldy Words"—in other words, the elements of "God's Plenty" that Dryden sees portrayed so naturally in Chaucer's *Canterbury* characters. In addition, Pope opens his poem with an imitation of the opening of The General Prologue of *The Canterbury Tales*, situating his modernization of Chaucer's *House of Fame* in the context of what is, in the eighteenth century, increasingly perceived as Chaucer's magnum opus.

What students gain from the experience of reading Pope's poem is an appreciation for the assumptions that the early eighteenth century brought to Chaucer's texts, assumptions that still shape our approach to Chaucer today. In addition, they learn that no response to Chaucer arises in a vacuum. Pope's imitation of Chaucer in *The Temple of Fame* is clearly based on the understanding of Chaucer that was current in Pope's day. At the same time, students gain a better grasp of Chaucer in his medieval context, seeing the conventions, concerns, and images of Chaucer's medieval culture more clearly against the backdrop of Pope's eighteenth-century perception of Chaucer's limitations.

Second Strategy: Teaching the Controversy of History

The tradition of Chaucer criticism changes with Furnivall's foundation of the Chaucer Society in 1868. Before this watershed event, nineteenth-century readers tended to view Chaucer as manly, naive, and sweet—a cheery author of simple poetry with universal appeal (unlike other medieval poets, whose work was of purely antiquarian interest). Samuel Taylor Coleridge sees in Chaucer's works "a chearfulness, a manly hilarity, which makes it almost impossible to doubt a correspondent habit of feeling in the author himself" (Spurgeon 2: 85). Elizabeth Barrett Browning characterizes Chaucer as innocent: "His senses are open and delicate, like a young child's. . . . Child-like, too, his tears and smiles lie at the edge of his eyes, and he is one proof more among the many, that the deepest pathos and the quickest gaieties hide together in the same nature" (Spurgeon 2: 243). According to Henry David Thoreau, Chaucer "is so natural and cheerful, compared to later poets, that we might almost regard him as a personification of spring . . . still the poetry of youth and life rather than of thought" (Spurgeon 2: 250–51).

But with the foundation of the Chaucer Society and the society's publication of such volumes as the *Life Records of Chaucer* (1876–1900), perceptions of Chaucer begin to change. As Larry Benson has observed, "The older idea of a 'naïve,' 'childlike' Chaucer could not be squared with the busy civil servant of the documents. . . . 'Genial' replaced the nineteenth-century 'sweet' in characterizations of Chaucer, and the poet of simple sincerity became instead the master of irony (which became fashionable about the time that the outlines of Chaucer's life became clear)" (Benson "Reader's Guide" 332). In addition, Furnivall's position as founder of both the Chaucer Society and the Early English Text Society "exerted the most profound influence on the unifying of Chaucer with the rest of Middle English" and "re-placed Chaucer firmly back in his time" (Matthews 12), challenging the longstanding perception of Chaucer as a natural, universal poet.

The history of twentieth-century Chaucer criticism can in fact be looked at in terms of the working out of the implications of Chaucer's place in his own era and of the place of Chaucer's era in Chaucer criticism—apparent in, for example, the near-schizophrenic tension between the learned historical annotations and the urbane, ahistorical public lectures of Kittredge (Patterson, *Negotiating* 18), between the New Criticism of Donaldson and the exegetical criticism of D. W. Robertson (Benson, "Reader's Guide" 348–50), between old historicism and new (Pearsall, "Future" 19–21), between historical "totalization" and "anachronistic" literary theory (Fradenburg, " 'Voice' " 172–77). For this reason, assigning students to read polemical twentieth-century criticism in conjunction with Chaucer's works—for example, Louise O. Fradenburg's essay " 'Voice Memorial' " with *The Book of the Duchess*—is a useful, though challenging, way to introduce them to the more recent developments in the critical tradition of Chaucer studies. What students gain from the experience of reading Fradenburg in conjunction with *The Book of the Duchess* is a provocative glimpse at central issues of current Chaucer criticism and a suggestion of the ways in which most Chaucer scholarship has increasingly diverged from "Dryden's 'God's Plenty' theme" (Ellis 26). In this way, students can also be introduced to the questions and issues of historicism that have dominated twentieth-century Chaucer criticism.

Small Texts, Large Questions: Entering Chaucerian Poetics through the "Miscellaneous" Poems

Carolynn Van Dyke

> Of al this world the large compas
> Yt wil not in myn armes tweyne;
> Who so mochel wol embrace,
> Litel therof he shal distreyne.   (Chaucer, "Proverbs," lines 5–8)

Like many of us, I am eager to share so much of Chaucer's "large compas" with students that they may "distreyne" very little. Accepting the counsel of this "proverbe," however, I start small. Early in my undergraduate course, I distribute passages from what F. N. Robinson called the "miscellaneous" short poems (qtd. in *Riverside* 631). Struggling together to translate my minimally glossed handouts, students immediately size up the substantial but finite linguistic difficulties that loom large in their minds. I then guide the class through a discussion of the poems' poetic techniques.

My chief goal in these discussions is to engage the analytic and interpretive skills that students often seem to abandon at the threshold of the Chaucer classroom. Intimidated by linguistic and historical distance, many new readers flee the Scylla of close reading only to meet the Charybdis created by Chaucer's canonicity: even well-prepared English majors resort to plot summaries and prefab interpretations. I try to steer students away from both dangers by demonstrating immediately that they can read Chaucer as they can any other poet.

The short poems themselves deserve far more attention than I give them. "The Complaint unto Pity" brilliantly exposes the reification of women and the obfuscation of agency in erotic allegory. "The Complaint of Mars" refracts profound questions about free will and divine justice through the improbable subjectivity of a lonely planet. "Fortune" and "Lak of Stedfastnesse" epitomize the ambiguous deference to power of The Tale of Melibee. "Lenvoy de Chaucer a Bukton" and "Gentilesse" resonate provocatively with The Wife of Bath's Prologue and Tale. Reluctantly, I limit my "embrace" to excerpts from four short poems that can introduce students to particular aspects of Chaucerian poetics.

The Slippery Bonds of "Truth"

> Her is non hoom, her nis but wildernesse:
> Forth, pilgrim, forth! Forth, beste, out of thy stal!
> Know thy contree, look up, thank God of al;

Hold the heye wey and lat thy gost thee lede,
And trouthe thee shal delivere, it is no drede.   ("Truth" 17–21)

The linguistic and interpretive lessons of this first passage that we discuss are fairly straightforward. Discussion often begins with students' suspicion that "beste" may not mean *best*. After confirming that hunch by referring to nearby words (hoping that students know what a "stal" is), I invite the class to chart the passage's metaphoric network: pilgrim, beast, and soul; home, wilderness, country, and roads; low and high.

The passage also richly illustrates the interplay of meter and rhythm. If asked to scan the lines, students can recognize the variations that convey urgency—trochaic inversions in the first and third lines and spondees in the second and fourth lines—in contrast to the resolving regularity of the fifth line. These effects testify to Chaucer's mastery of the dominant English meter that he was the first to use extensively.

Acknowledging this type of formal sophistication may prepare students for another kind of complexity: the relation between individual poet and culture. With luck, at least one member of the class will recognize the source of the last line (John 8.32); if not, I cite it and ask students to comment on Chaucer's use of a biblical paraphrase as the refrain of a lyric poem. I also ask about the implications of "pilgrim" for our understanding of *The Canterbury Tales*. And I ask how much of the poem's sentiment seems alien to modern readers.

Such reflections reveal the religious doctrines that inform Chaucer's poetics. Equally important, however, are the political pressures revealed in the poem, which I suggest by reading to and translating for them other sections of "Truth," especially lines 1 and 8. After describing the turmoil of the late 1380s, already familiar to students who have studied Shakespeare's history plays, I try to suggest the complex motivations and constraints that shaped his "bon conseyl" ("Truth" subtitle).

An even more interesting complication emerges from a rhetorical device that students may not expect to find in medieval literature: the double entendre in the envoy (22–28), "thou Vache" (22). The apparent allusion to Sir Philip de la Vache, a courtier disfavored by the Lords Appellant, provides a small lesson in Ricardian politics, whereas the bilingual pun illustrates Chaucer's linguistic environment. The relevance of *vache* (*cow*) extends the metaphor with which our discussion of the passage began. Through its wit, the pun also demonstrates what is not beastlike about the human imagination. "Truth" thus exemplifies the sententious tradition in medieval literature, the political uses of that tradition, and the serious playfulness with which Chaucer individualizes it.

Mastering Submission

So hath myn herte caught in remembraunce
Your beaute hoole and stidefast governaunce,

> Your vertues al and yowre hie noblesse,
> That you to serve is set al my plesaunce.   ("Womanly Noblesse" 1–4)

If "Truth" illustrates the poetics of doctrine, "Womanly Noblesse" exemplifies the dynamics of genre and gender. Students' first challenge comes from syntax, but, after they untangle the word order, I ask them to connect the syntactic inversion to other kinds of formal artifice. I read the first stanza aloud, calling attention to the regular meter and the gently end-stopped lines. I ask students to identify the *aabaabbab* rhyme scheme and then demonstrate that the remaining stanzas use the same rhyme sounds. That those sounds remind many students of French words leads to a quick lesson in sociolinguistic history and cultural politics. I cite Chaucer's complaint about the "skarsete" of English rhymes ("The Complaint of Venus" 80) to demonstrate his ironic self-consciousness about translating Continental texts and genres into a humbler idiom.

This discussion prepares students to respond skeptically to my disingenuous suggestion that the poem might express Chaucer's love for a particular woman. Someone who has taken other early-literature courses usually connects the diction and sentiments with Petrarchan conventions. I then try to foreground the relationship inscribed by those conventions: the male speaker's pledge to "serve" an idealized woman whose nobility he equates with her "pity." I also invite students to consider what function the conventions might perform for an aspiring male courtier—or court poet.

Like "Truth," "Womanly Noblesse" also bends its generic constraints; for instance, the speaker idealizes the beloved's character more fully than her beauty. Time permitting, I point students toward Chaucer's gentle sport with the discourse of erotic idealization and submission in "To Rosemounde." But the passage from "Womanly Noblesse" serves mainly to suggest that submission to, and through, formal and cultural conventions can be a means to power, a possibility that I hope they recall when they begin *Troilus and Criseyde*.

The Literal Adam

> Adam scriveyn, if ever it thee bifalle
> Boece or Troylus for to wryten newe,
> Under thy long lokkes thou most have the scalle,
> But after my makyng thow wryte more trewe;
> So ofte adaye I mot thy werk renewe,
> It to correcte and eke to rubbe and scrape,
> And al is thorugh thy negligence and rape.

Of my four short passages, "Chaucers Wordes unto Adam, His Owne Scriveyn," quoted above in its entirety, has been the most difficult for students to translate. My bracketed translations do not remove all the lexical puzzles: recently I have found students oddly slow to process even the most straight-forward glosses. The modestly suspended syntax and the unfamiliar locution "thee bifalle" trip up some new readers, and so does the rough meter, partic-ularly the extra syllables in the third line. But the chief difficulty seems to arise from the coarse diction. Students expect canonical poetry to be elevated in tone, refined or abstract in subject matter, and indifferent to its means of production. They certainly do not expect the "Father of *English* Poetry" (Spur-geon 1: 276) to have wished cooties on the long-haired slacker on whom his reputation depends. More than one student has seen the scribe's name as an allusion to the biblical Adam a kind of overreading that Chaucer invites by casting his colloquial complaint in rhyme royal.

As often happens in teaching, the difficulties that the poem presents are themselves illuminating. Readers' slowness to grasp Chaucer's plain meaning reveals our assumptions about the origins and functions of poetry. More par-ticularly, our amused surprise betrays our habitual disregard of the material determinants of medieval poetics. When I tell students how many Adams have indeed "wryten newe" *Troilus and Criseyde,* not to mention *The Canterbury Tales,* they have good reason both to value modern editing and to regard its products skeptically.

Authoring the Author

> What shul these clothes / thus manyfolde
> Loo / this hoote somers day
> After grete hete / cometh colde
> No man caste / his pilch a way
> Of all this worlde / the large compace
> Yt wil not / in my Armes tweyne
> Whoo so mochel wol / embrace
> Litel therof / he shal distreyne
>
> (Chaucer, "Proverbs," qtd. in Pace and David 199–200)

With the fourth passage, part of which I cite in the opening of this essay, I extend what "Chaucers Wordes unto Adam, His Owne Scriveyn" teaches about material textuality, this time trying to undermine—though ultimately to correct—students' assumptions about authorship. In doing so, I recapitulate my own history as a reader of Chaucer. When I read the second of these quatrains in my undergraduate Chaucer textbook, formatted apparently as one of two "proverbs," I found it unquestionably Chaucerian—a poignant expression of boundless love for a world that would always exceed the poet's grasp. In graduate school, I decided that Chaucer was also professing here the artistic humility that led him to represent a narrower segment of the social and metaphysical "compace" than did, say, William Langland, John Gower, or the *Pearl* poet. Only after having taught "Proverbs" for several years did I take seriously the explanatory note indicating that the quatrain may be neither Chaucerian nor a self-standing poem (*Riverside* 1089).

Initially I give students the passage without reference to its textual uncertainties, entertaining questions primarily about the implicit relationship between the first two lines and the next two. I hope students will notice that the quatrain's form—octosyllabic meter, ballad-stanza rhyme—distinguishes it from Chaucer's other poetry and links it with popular forms. These features take on a fuller meaning, however, when students see the passage in three forms: in Larry Benson's *Riverside* edition, which suggests that Chaucer wrote two "proverbs"; Frederick J. Furnivall's 1871–79 parallel-text edition, which omits modern punctuation but retains Henry Bradshaw's division of each quatrain into "Question" or "Complaint" and "Answer . . . Quod Chaucer"; and John Norton-Smith's facsimile edition of Oxford, Bodleian Library MS Fairfax 16, which includes the eight unseparated lines sandwiched between other quasi-Chaucerian sententious verses (see *Bodleian Library*).

Students can see that the hortatory poems surrounding the quatrain in the facsimile change its meaning, much as reorderings affect individual tales from *The Canterbury Tales*. The facsimile also demonstrates the profound and recursive effects of authorial attribution. I point out that even the Fairfax title "Proverbe of Chaucer" is a scribal addition; I ask where the text might come from if not from Chaucer and why a fifteenth-century compiler might have decided to ascribe anonymous maxims to Chaucer.

The lesson is, in part, that editors and readers sometimes construct the author whose wisdom they may think they are receiving. But I try to move toward a more positive conclusion as well. My early, naive response to the second "proverbe" (or second half of the "Proverbs") was not entirely baseless, for it answered to the self-presentation in Chaucer's other works. More important, that undertone of Chaucerian personality itself achieves its fullest meaning in counterpoint to a collective, anonymous poetic form. That the verses come from an oral vernacular tradition makes them richly appropriate for a highly individualized poet's acknowledgment that his agency is limited. And that we can hear an individual voice through the quatrain's gnomic impersonality confirms what many readers have long sensed: that the chief distinction of Chaucer's poetics is the integrity of his ventriloquism.

Teaching Chaucer's Postmodern Dream Visions

Myra Seaman

Chaucer's dream visions—with their bumpy, nonlinear development; their abrupt shifts from one narrative locus to another; and their extreme inconclusiveness—tend to appear only rarely on our undergraduate syllabi. Since new students of Chaucer are already burdened with learning his Middle English and understanding his distant culture, the dream visions' narrative complexities seem an unnecessary additional load. The very qualities that encourage our neglect, however, make these poems more rather than less familiar to our students. *The House of Fame,* for instance, is "frenetic, almost nightmarish, certainly surreal, full of glittering, witty references to books and authors, consistently undercutting" the central subject of the poem (Saunders 59); such qualities encourage students' fascination by fulfilling many of their expectations of postmodern fiction and, in the process, challenge their assumptions about medieval literature. In our classes, we can use this unanticipated association between the pre- and postmodern to nurture an appreciation of Chaucer's art, applying poststructuralist techniques to these works to help students discern what is quintessentially medieval and Chaucerian about them. Including *The House of Fame, The Legend of Good Women, The Book of the Duchess*, and *The Parliament of Fowls* on our syllabi rewards rather than further burdens our students.

Chaucer in these texts explicitly tackles theoretical questions about the nature and role of poetic art. The result is a metafiction, defined by Patricia Waugh as "fictional writing which self-consciously and systematically draws attention to its status as an artifact in order to pose questions about the relationship between fiction and reality" (2). Chaucer's metafiction, like other metafictions, "explores a theory of writing fiction through the practice of writing fiction" (Waugh 2). Chaucer's dream visions problematize this relationship, emphasizing instead of diminishing the gap between the two, presenting a fiction that makes no consistent claims to be " 'about' an objective reality" (Jordan, "Lost" 101) but is instead about fiction itself. For instance, the ambiguous Dido-Aeneas section in *The House of Fame* is not so much about the actual events of the familiar historical story—events presented by Chaucer in unresolved contradiction—as it is about the implications of the conflicting traditions of telling the story, represented here by both Ovidian and Vergilian accounts. When my students nearly lose themselves in such gaps and contradictions, I do not help them impose order and smooth rough edges but encourage engagement with the ways these gaps force us to consider our roles as readers and writers. Poststructuralist approaches such as Linda Hutcheon's concept of historiographic metafiction help students comprehend and admire Chaucer's theoretical experiment because they are able to view his work from the perspective of their own culturally authorized theory (Hutcheon,

"Pastime"; *Poetics*). They become better readers of literatures medieval and postmodern as a result.

The dream-vision structure offered late medieval writers like Chaucer a forum for debating "the status of poetry, the truth value of artistic representation, and the place of subjective experience as a form of knowledge" (R. Edwards, *Dream* 25). Through a given dreamer-narrator's investigation of the meaning of his dream and of dreams as sources of knowledge and truth, Chaucer the poet investigates poetry's capacity for conveying knowledge and the processes of meaning production. These early poems reveal a developing artist's concerns about the foundations for poetry's and the poet's authority. Students are fascinated by this, attracted to the way the author is thus constructed within and by the text. Here they feel they are seeing the "real" Chaucer—a fantasy I encourage even while reminding them of the metafictional implications. Through the narrator's roles, students observe the author-reader dichotomy being broken down in a way they would expect of a contemporary novelist but not a medieval poet. In his dream visions, through his engagement with *auctores*, Chaucer makes "[t]he 'old' book . . . 'new,' " so that "Ovid [for instance] becomes Chaucer" (Boitani, "Old Books" 44). In the process, Chaucer theorizes the translation and reinvigoration of tradition by readers whose interpretive acts result in new writing. The medieval aesthetic of art as transformation from *auctor* to poet often disturbs students; the dream visions enact it powerfully, demonstrating its capacity for creative expression.

Although all four dream visions engage these issues, *The Book of the Duchess* and *The House of Fame* in their intense self-reflexivity especially invite students' use of poststructuralist interpretive techniques; these two poems are overtly and distinctively book oriented and text replicating, since in them a book inspires a dream that ultimately produces a text. The text that each dream produces swarms with other texts, often reading like a postmodern pastiche and making manifest the traditions by which medieval writers like Chaucer were surrounded, giving students an opportunity to become familiar with classical, vernacular, and theological *auctores* while making tangible the highly textual culture in which Chaucer participated.

Chaucer immerses the student readers in and of these poems in worlds of (inter)textuality where texts abound with the need for interpretation. In *The Book of the Duchess*, for instance, the dreamer-narrator wakes in his dream to find *Le roman de la rose*, complete with glosses, painted on the walls and the story of Troy depicted on the glass, so that the central themes of the courtly tradition (love and war) are presented in the words and images of the literary works that transferred and transformed the icons of the ancient past into the medieval vernaculars (R. Edwards, *Dream* 1–2). The sun shines through the glass, clear and bright (*BD* 336–42), animating the imagery and making the communication of story an organic process. Chaucer himself engages in this process by translating the classical tradition to England through the textual products of other contemporary and classical poets. Similarly, *The*

Book of the Duchess narrator describes the book he reads to entertain himself in his insomnia as containing "fables" that "clerks" and "other poetes" had "put in rime" "in olde tyme" (53–54). In these representations, stories are universal truths given new external form by poets, who build the verse structure around a story that is itself static.

Yet in his own rendition of the classical story he has read, the dreamer does much more than simply give the matter a poetic form that makes the abstract ideal concrete and particular: he changes Alcyone into a weak interpreter and he omits Ovid's happy ending of metamorphosis. Through these modifications, he creates a new story about interpretation, presented in terms of his own interpretation. When the object of interpretation is his dream, the narrator claims that no man "had the wyt / To konne wel my sweven rede" (278–79). Its oddity lies specifically in its hermeneutic difficulty. Students often get stalled at this point in their reading and need to be prodded to see that the source of this difficulty is located by the poem in the inevitable inability of language to communicate experience: the act of reading, of interpreting, is shown to be a matter of individual emotional, not just logical, apprehension, for the narrator cannot distinguish between joy and sorrow and has no feeling (10); as a result, he cannot understand the Black Knight's trauma. For a reader to read well, this encounter suggests, he or she must already have shared the experience about which he or she is reading. In his interpretation of the romance that led to his dream, our narrator can imagine Alcyone only as the kind of literal reader he himself is. Similarly, in his reading of the Black Knight's sorrow in his dream, the narrator can understand the other's experience only in terms of what he himself already knows. The dreamer is unable to move beyond where he began. In a poem focused primarily on interpretation and the potential of art to convey knowledge, those possibilities appear to be severely restricted—not by the weaknesses of the poet's art (whether the poet is the Black Knight or Chaucer) but by the limitations inherent in language. Students appreciate this as a proto-Derridean moment, one that surprises them and invites them to investigate the medieval linguistic theories that support it.

Whereas *The Book of the Duchess* depicts the ways speech does and does not communicate information and experience between individuals, in *The House of Fame* the focus is on the ways texts embody and transfer authority (St. John 116). The *Book of the Duchess* narrator claims that his dream would be difficult for even the best to interpret, foregrounding the act of reading; in contrast, *The House of Fame* narrator says that none of the famous dreamers (Isaiah, Pharaoh, Scipio, Nebuchadnezzar) "mette such a dream as this" (517), focusing on the subject matter of the dream itself, on the truth of the narrative it contains. This narrator's interest lies not in craft but in "o sentence" (1100), in the dream's meaning. At the House of Fame, the truth value of the text itself takes center stage. The dreamer sees each *auctor* visually represented in relation to the subject matter about which that *auctor* wrote (as painted on the pillar on which each stands) rather than in relation to the particular text he produced, his unique version of the familiar story. This image reduces the individual textual representation to the essence of the subject matter, and yet the dreamer-narrator struggles in his dream to recognize the role of the author. Asking who made the images in the Temple of Glass, the dreamer-narrator admits "[b]ut not wot I whoo did hem wirche" (474), emphasizing "work" and directing the reader's gaze to the poet-creator of each. He seeks the answer in the House of Fame, whose structure represents the presumed social power of poetry that confers form and meaning and contributes to the social good (St. John 92). The House of Fame is, on the surface, a reassuring contrast to the House of Rumor, where all was unstable and fluid, with endless pieces of information fluttering randomly, lacking the guiding structure of art. However, in the House of Fame the dreamer "is forced to recognize the gulf that can exist between text and reality" (St. John 29), a gulf produced by the intervention of the communicator of the "reality," the producer of the text. The narrator's concern with sources and the role of the artist leads him not to stability but to the inherent malleability of what appear to be solid facts, matter purely articulated through language.

For even when processed by Fame and given a structure that reveals its truth, this factual information is not naturally revealed. In *The House of Fame*, the dreamer sees Fame's house (students are aided by Michael St. John's definition of this edifice as "the iconic representation of the sum total of what can be known through discourse and tradition" [87]) resting on a block of ice in which names have been cut but are melting away here and there, demonstrating "the impermanence of writing and by extension the fragility of art works as a source of knowledge and memory" (R. Edwards, *Dream* 24). Narratives are omnipresent, often evoking apparent truths and long-dead figures and *auctores*, yet the stability implied by their durability is shown to be illusory. Chaucer's close investigation in this poem of the role of *auctores* and tradition—of Fame—shows them to be, ultimately, necessary and welcoming even as they are themselves unstable and fragile, like the engraved ice supporting the House of Fame, and even as truth itself is impossible to convey wholly. Similarly, *The Book of the Duchess*'s dreamer-narrator's interpretive failures provide a problematic picture of the role of books, of the author and of the reader, and of the influence of tradition and *auctores*.

Chaucer's topics of investigation and his methods of inquiry in the dream visions help us invite students to the world of Chaucer and the later Middle Ages by demonstrating the suitability of our subject of study to twenty-first-century sensibilities. In addition, poststructuralist approaches help bring to the fore recurring Chaucerian themes and medieval concerns with authority and the instability of language. Such approaches need not be loaded with Waugh's conception of metafiction or Derridean deconstruction in order to help students conceptualize ways Chaucer and other medieval artists positioned themselves in relation to the predecessors and their present and future readers, a central focus of all of Chaucer's dream visions.

A Guide to Teaching
The Legend of Good Women
Michael Calabrese

This essay is for those who have not thought much about Hypermnestra lately and have neglected their worship of the daisy, that is, for those who need to dust off *The Legend of Good Women* for classroom presentation. We teach this poem much less frequently than *The Canterbury Tales* or *Troilus and Criseyde* because it is deemed a minor work and because it is difficult enough to get students through the major works of Chaucer in two semesters, much less in two quarters. The following is therefore meant to encourage and enable the teaching of these deceptively conventional narratives about women in love at the advanced undergraduate and beginning graduate levels. Our focus is on teaching, not on research, so my essay is not a critical history or an annotated bibliography. It has, rather, three specific aims: to suggest why and in what courses you might want to teach *The Legend of Good Women*; to bring to your attention primary and secondary books and resources that will help you prepare the poem; and to suggest specific topics for class discussion, student presentations, analytic essays, research papers, and in-class performances and recitations.

The Legend of Good Women demands attention for a number of reasons, particularly since the poem is now fully reclaimed from the poor-stepchild status that has burdened it in classrooms and in critical circles throughout the twentieth century. The work will have wide appeal for students. It is about women, men, love, sex, violence, and death, and students of both sexes are often drawn to these themes, just as audiences, including Chaucer's readers, have been for thousands of years. To use a once-hip but now tired formulation: *The Legend of Good Women* is an important document in the history of the construction of gender. The poem will thus work well not only in its standard place in a course on Chaucer but also in special-topics courses either on love, women, or gender in medieval Europe or on the classical heritage in the Middle Ages and Renaissance.

In a course specifically on Chaucer, teaching *The Legend of Good Women* is a good way to discuss the poet's uses of the classics, particularly Ovid. His *Heroides* is the source of several of the legends and may have served as a model for the collection as a whole. *The Legend of Good Women* also reveals much about poetry, court life, patronage, gender, and authorship in fourteenth-century England, for Chaucer says (whether we believe him or not) that he wrote the poem as penance for his mistreatment of women in his translation of the *Roman de la rose* and in *Troilus and Criseyde*. The poem also represents a tradition of catalog literature, a sort of secular saints' lives of both men and women, that was popular in medieval European literature. This genre includes Giovanni Boccaccio (*On Famous Women*) and Christine de Pisan (*The Book of the City of Ladies*), and one could create assignments comparing Chaucer's narratives with those of these other giants.

Now that you are committed to assigning the text, what editions and resources will help you prepare and teach the poem? Larry Benson's *Riverside Chaucer*, a large and expensive book designed for a single-author course, is still the best book for students to have and for teachers to consult. The short introduction by M. C. E. Shaner and the explanatory notes by Shaner and A. S. G. Edwards discuss the undeservedly low esteem in which the text has been held and outline important issues for its critical study. They examine the possible historical reality of Queen Anne assigning the work to Chaucer, discuss the question of its unfinished state, and explore its relation to other works in Chaucer's canon. The notes compile major critical reaction to *The Legend of Good Women* from Walter W. Skeat to the 1980s and give detailed explanations and citations of the various sources Chaucer used or may have used in the prologue and in the individual legends. The *Riverside*'s bibliography will steer you to the primary editions of these source texts.

After *The Riverside Chaucer*, the next place to go is Helen Phillip's edition of the prologue and the "Legend of Dido" in her and Nicholas R. Havely's anthology, *Chaucer's Dream Poetry*. The introduction to *The Legend of Good Women* is thorough: it surveys critical issues and discusses contemporary analogues to the prologue, including works by Eustache Deschamps, Guillaume de Machaut, and Jean Froissart (see Phillips and Havely's bibliography for citations). The introduction also discusses the pivotal issue of the two prologues, F and G (Phillips edits G for the volume); describes the history of the work's title; explores the poem's possible historical occasion; and analyzes its tone and meaning. The introduction also provides an overview of the doctrines of medieval antifeminism that are essential for an understanding of the gendered drama in the prologue and in the legends themselves. The text is presented with copious notes—literally half of each page in some cases—offering historical, lexical, and literary-critical information. Textual notes, a twenty-page bibliography (for all the dream visions), a selective thirty-page glossary, and a name index round out the book. The glossary cross-references lines in the poems and provides helpful descriptions of parts of speech. In short, Phillips's text is a little pot of gold for both teacher and student.

The Legend of Good Women has inspired a rich critical tradition over the last thirty years. All the texts I suggest here in one way or another survey the critical field, address historical and biographical issues, confront Chaucer's learning and use of sources, and explore the importance of *The Legend of Good Women* in Chaucer's canon and as a medieval work of art. Although this list of critical texts is partial, consulting these works will certainly prepare the teacher to present the poem and to guide students to their first steps in research at any level.

Beginning this wake of critical attention is Robert Worth Frank's *Chaucer and* The Legend of Good Women (1972), which takes on the issue of the poem's worthiness and explores the time of "crisis" and "restlessness" in 1386 that brought Chaucer to compose this poem, which displays a new thirst for "stories, as many of them as possible" (10) and which thus anticipates *The Canterbury Tales*. In a comprehensive study of Chaucer and classical myth, John P. McCall discusses Chaucer's *Legend of Good Women* in relation to classical learning in the fourteenth century and argues that Chaucer "fixed his attention on classical women not in order to portray them as grand and noble ladies, but as spiritually and morally helpless people" (*Chaucer* 112). John Fyler offers a chapter on *The Legend of Good Women* in the context of Chaucer's Ovidianism, particularly his attachment to the *Art of Love* and *Remedies for Love*. See also my own comments in *Chaucer's Ovidian Arts of Love* on *The Legend of Good Women* in relation to Chaucer and his awareness of the medieval vita of Ovid (17–23). Lisa Kiser's *Telling Classical Tales* explores how the Christian poet Chaucer directly confronted pre-Christian, pagan morality and philosophy when he set out to write *The Legend of Good Women*. She argues for Chaucer's ironic presentation:

> By parodying the medieval moral poetry within which the characters of Latin culture are forced to exist, Chaucer shows precisely why art that presents a single moral perspective is finally inadequate to the variety and richness of the "olde appreved stories," the "sondry thynges" which form the basis of the medieval storyteller's art. (152–53)

Donald W. Rowe begins *Through Nature to Eternity* with an overview of the major critical issues in the scholarly history of *The Legend of Good Women*, providing many annotations to the relevant bibliography. He tries to save the text from the charge that it is an ironic exercise in self-conscious failure, but students might want to confront Rowe's conclusion that *The Legend of Good Women* is a kind of sacramental poem. Sheila Delany's *The Naked Text: Chaucer's* Legend of Good Women considers the layers of dressing with which Chaucer adorns his apparently simple subject. Chaucer, she argues, explores "sex, gender, religion, politics, history, interpretation, and writing" and achieves complexity through mimimalism (235). She offers not only a critical history of *The Legend of Good Women* but also a striking history of how the work was received by premodern readers like John Lydgate and others, including the Augustinian friar Osbern Bokenham, whom Delany has studied and translated. Florence Percival's *Chaucer's Legendary Good Women* examines the "literary contexts in which . . . *The Legend of Good Women* locates itself," including the notion of palinode, and focuses specifically on the role that "humorous antifeminism/feminist debate plays in the self-definition of the learned poet" (19). Although Janet Cowen and George Kane's 1995 edition of the text is too advanced and detailed for undergraduates, it contains all the textual information, all the descriptions of the manuscripts, and all the variant readings. Sometimes merely reproducing a page of Cowen and Kane can shock students into seeing how artificial and sanitized most editions are; it also teaches them something about scribal reception, manuscript culture, and the processes of editing.

For those who want to teach the text in translation (or merely to have one on hand for consultation), Ann McMillan translates the entire text and includes useful explanatory notes. She sees the poem as ironic, since "chaste, self sacrificing love is a powerful myth to which our culture has given shape" (5). The introduction is a provocative feminist assessment but also an overview of medieval gender doctrine; it discusses, among others, Ovid, Jerome, Boccaccio, and Christine and thus provides the necessary literary context for approaching Chaucer's contribution to the catalog tradition. It currently appears, however, to be out of print.

The Chaucer Studio has produced selections from *The Legend of Good Women*, read by Andrew Lynch. Students can listen to the recordings to aid their reading and comprehension or can be required to recite or memorize a passage (twenty lines or so) for class performance. By selecting an appropriate tone in performance, the student must interpret the voicing and ultimately the meaning of the selection and of the narrative from which it comes. The rest of the class can critique the student's performative decisions and execution. And if interested in performance, the teacher will have to consider the bold arguments of William A. Quinn (*Chaucer's Rehersynges*), who argues that narratives should be seen not only as texts but also as poems-scripts. Quinn tries to discover the "tonal games" (9) Chaucer played in his own historical "rehersynge" of the poem to its original audience. While this volume was in production, a new study of *The Legend of Good Women* has been published, edited by Carolyn P. Collette.

I end my essay with a list of topics and questions for class discussion, library exercises, longer research papers, and student presentations. I write these based on the critical material surveyed above and on simply reading through the text with an eye to students' and teachers' needs. You will, of course, modify the topics to fit the class's particular focus and level. Some of these are obvious but, I hope, no less useful, and the list could be infinite.

> What is the history of the title of the work? How do Chaucer and other poets refer to the work in contemporary writings? How did it acquire the name *The Legend of Good Women* (a phrase found in the text), and what is implied by this title? Is it, finally, an appropriate name for the poem?
>
> Chaucer is not much like William Langland, but in composing two prologues, F and G, he tries his hand at the game of multiple texts. Students could compare the two (side by side in the *Riverside*) to see what Chaucer discarded (or added) in the second effort and why. How, further, do the legends realize or develop (or fail to develop) the themes of either prologue?

Who is this indignant God of Love that chastises Chaucer in the pro-
logue? Where did Chaucer get his depiction from, and why should a
Christian poet worship such a pagan deity? In a related topic, some
scholars associate the god and his queen, Alceste, with Richard II and
Anne of Bohemia, supporting the notion that Chaucer had to write
The Legend of Good Women to compensate for his past literary crimes
against women. If this is true, or even if Chaucer only wants us to be-
lieve that it is, then what does this tell us about the pressures that the
Ricardian poets faced when composing for a small courtly audience?

Discuss Chaucer and literary learning in the fourteenth century. What
role does the poet's library play in the creation of *The Legend of Good
Women*? How does *The Legend of Good Women* relate to other works
in Chaucer's corpus? Let students choose one legend and compare it
with Chaucer's depiction of Criseyde or of any female character in
The Canterbury Tales.

Using the *Middle English Dictionary*, explore the meaning of the terms
false and *true* in *The Legend of Good Women* as they apply to the
behavior of the heroines. How many different definitions of these
terms can you discern in the poem?

In the poem itself, what unifies the depictions of the women: virtue,
power, tragedy, a commitment to love? How many types of female
power—or, from another perspective, powerlessness—are mani-
fested? Are the depictions reductive and parodic or psychologically
and emotionally real? What sort of feminism, if any, does Chaucer
practice in *The Legend of Good Women*? How can we compare our
culture's feminist goals and doctrines with Chaucer's? One way of
getting at these issues is to ask the class if they found the legends
funny.

Related to this question, what assumptions did Chaucer's culture have
about women? If women needed defending through *The Legend of
Good Women*, what did they need defending from? Alcuin Blamires's
anthology of primary documents is useful here. The students can read
a selection from Saint Jerome or from the *Roman de la rose* and
explore how *The Legend of Good Women* responds to these accusa-
tions and assumptions.

Beyond the specific charge of antifeminism, how has Chaucer adapted
his sources in the individual legends? Encourage students to track
down the specific sources listed in *The Riverside Chaucer* and to write
essays on how Chaucer has adapted his sole or multiple authorities.
For example, how has Chaucer adapted both Vergil and Ovid in the
story of Dido? And, finally, what is Chaucer trying to accomplish as
a medieval Christian poet and as a learned humanist by taking on
such a literary, historical, political project about the depiction of
women?

I hope that these scattered rhymes will help you when you undertake this stately, elusive, allusive poem by our favorite poet, as he embraces all his own favorites and proves once again that he sought little more than to be a worthy servant of the servants of love. You and your students might very well want to debate that.

Chaucer's Dialogic Imagination: Teaching the Multiple Discourses of *Troilus and Criseyde*

Clare R. Kinney

Novice readers of *Troilus and Criseyde* are often confused by the work's diverse and seemingly contradictory voices and generic allegiances. Who's in charge here? Chaucer's narrator (who can't decide whether he's keenly engaged with or historically distanced from his "matere")? Pandarus, the Vinsaufian maker (1.1065–71), who builds such intricate fictions as he shapes the encounters of hero and heroine? Giovanni Boccaccio, Chaucer's never-named "auctor," or the ghostly Lollius? Fickle Fortuna, or Clio, muse of history? Is this an epic or a romance, a *de casibus* "tragedye," or a Boethian comedy—and what should we make of all those lyric passages that complicate the narrative's linear unfolding?

Rather than try to tidy up the work's multiplicity, I emphasize it. I devote six class meetings to *Troilus and Criseyde* in Transforming Desire, a seminar exploring representations of secular and sacred love from Vergil to John Donne. By the time we read the poem, my students have talked about epic and romance and the protocols of *fin'amors*; they have begun to consider the relations among the workings of desire, the enactment of agency, and the articulation of self. When we plunge into *Troilus and Criseyde,* I invoke Mikhail Bakhtin's notion of heteroglossia—the idea that a narrative may be shaped from the reproduction of multiple, contestatory discourses (70)—to suggest one way of dealing with the clamorous voices of this work. Noting how much of the poem represents the direct speech of its characters, I propose that genre lenses implicit in various voices generate competing interpretive frames and allow Chaucer to tell more than one story at once.

A useful starting point for this approach to the poem is book 1's "Canticus Troili" (1.400–20). I distribute copies of Robert Durling's translation of Petrarch's *Rime sparse* 132, describe the main characteristics of Petrarch's lyric sequence, and then invite my students to ponder the implications of Chaucer's translation/quotation of this particular poem at this particular moment. We discuss the way the interpolated lyric emphasizes the divided self of the speaker and turns away from direct contemplation of the lady to address the paradoxical experience and expression of desire itself. Troilus is locked in a kind of lyric stasis, paralyzed by oxymoron: "For hote of cold, for cold of hote, I dye" (1.419–20). His song affords a useful touchstone for thinking about his agency (or lack of agency) in the work; as our exploration of *Troilus and Criseyde* continues, students notice his continuing recourse to certain kinds of lyric apostrophe—in particular after Criseyde's departure from Troy (see, e.g., 5.218–45, 540–53, 638–44). I also encourage the class to think about the charged intersection between the Petrarchan vocabulary of the divided (or paralyzed) self and the idealizing language of *fin'amors*. Doing so offers students a useful lens through which to consider Troilus's later resistance to Pandarus's suggestion that he abduct Criseyde: "I moste hire honour levere han than me / In every cas, as lovere ought of right / Thus am I with desir and reson twight" (4.570–72).

Troilus's tendency to sound like a lyric speaker unhappily trapped in a narrative universe is emphasized by the contrast offered in book 1 between his inward-turning imagination and the desire for narrative process and progress voiced by Pandarus. Students are quick to notice the narrator's positioning of Pandarus as a rival maker in the poem; I also encourage them to consider Pandarus, wooing his niece for Troilus, as the shaper of a romance text in which he offers Criseyde a role. We will have discussed the nature and importance of "aventure" in Chrétien de Troyes's romances: Pandarus's meditations on "goodly aventure" (2.281–87) and his desire that Criseyde seize the "aventure" that has come to her (2.288–91) will thus seem rather significant— especially as his visit interrupts the reading of a mere text of romance (2.100). Carefully constructing Troilus as a model of chivalry (2.190–207), Pandarus offers Criseyde two different parts to play in his own fiction: the woman who offers *routhe* to a worthy suitor or the *belle dame sans merci* who has the power to kill the romancer as well as the lover.

When I last taught the poem, Pandarus's romancing provoked a wide-ranging discussion of Chaucer's inflection of Criseyde's agency. Students compared Pandarus's coercive construction of her options in book 2 with the larger narrative context in which she is bound to betray Troilus (both by the opening lines of book 1's proem and by Chaucer's sources). Some of them argued that Criseyde only has the appearance of free choice and that, although the poem repeatedly depicts her as weighing alternatives, she is always hemmed about by men's fictions. Pandarus's tales of Poliphete's persecutions (which beget her first meeting with Troilus) and of Troilus's jealousy of her supposed kindness to Horaste (which bring about the lovers' union in Criseyde's bed) consistently "pre-scribe" her actions. When we reached book 5, one student helpfully observed that the urbane Diomede combines speech characteristics of both Troilus and Pandarus. Self-consciously couching his suit in the language of idealizing *fin'amors*, but also insisting that to keep faith with any lover in doomed Troy is futile, he too presents Criseyde with drastically limited options.

One consequence of my particular approach to the poem is to raise the question of whether Criseyde has any access to a discourse of her own. Does Chaucer offer her a space for speech and agency outside the constraints not only of his sources but also of the various scripts in which she is inscribed by his male characters? I like to focus on her response to her first sight of Troilus in book 2: "Who yaf me drynke?" (2.651). Noting that Chaucer here supplements Boccaccio and dramatizes Criseyde's independent experience of the spontaneous birth of desire, I invite my students to gloss her words. The class may end up debating whether Criseyde in fact owns her desire, since her exclamation, although different from the cautious responses she has offered to Pandarus's solicitations thus far, positions her as the victim of an intoxicant or love potion offered by a third party. This might lead us to readdress the different scenarios offered by the conversion experiences of hero and heroine. Troilus is punished for his original crimes against Cupid by being struck down by love's arrow as he looks on Criseyde; he then announces his new identity (and interiority) by singing a Petrarchan lyric. Criseyde is more gradually drawn to the point where she "wex somwhat able to converte" (2.903) not only by beholding Troilus but also by hearing her niece sing someone *else*'s verses.

I have always encouraged my students to set Antigone's song (2.827–75) in dialogue with book 1's "Canticus Troili" and with Troilus's subsequent Petrarchan excurses. The song's female-voiced vision of mutuality and security and its testimony to the morally elevating effects of earthly love operate in marked contrast to Troilus's Petrarchan poetics of frustration, absence, and self-division, as well as to the poetic narrative's larger anatomy of betrayal. We're offered another discursive lens through which to view experience: Antigone attributes the song to a noble female author, and it is not present in *Il Filostrato*. Are we getting a gendered lyric alternative to the Troilus voice, which might inflect Criseyde's own experience of desire (or at least suggest a revisionary ending to the narrative in which she is inscribed)? I encourage the class to keep coming back to this textual moment and invite them to consider whether Troilus and Criseyde themselves ever seem to speak Antigone's language. Is her discourse recapitulated in the blissful consummation episodes of book 3? Is it completely vitiated by the Christianizing account of the imperfect nature of earthly love offered at the conclusion to book 5?

The question of Criseyde's access to a language of her own may be revisited in discussions of book 4 when Pandarus, preparing his niece for a last tryst with Troilus, turns *her* into romancer and script maker: "shapeth how destourbe youre goynge . . . Women ben wise in short avysement" (4.934, 936). I invite my class to look at Criseyde's speech describing her plans for returning to Troy (4.1254–1414), asking them to consider her diction and rhetoric and the ways in which she imagines her own agency. Students usually observe that the speech is full of echoes of "Pandar-speak"; they also note Criseyde's rambling and contradictory descriptions of her imagined stratagems. One group found it very telling that Criseyde lays claim to a Pandaric power to "enchaunten" Calkas with her "sawes" (4.1395)—and that she recapitulates Pandarus's emotional blackmail of *her* when she responds to Troilus's gentle criticism of her plans by declaring that his distrust will bring about her death (5.1604–10).

Examining this part of book 4, students tend to seize on the defense of Criseyde's "entente" and "purpos" in the stanza following her long speech

(4.1415–21) and worry about the relation between Criseyde's words and the narrator's commentary on them. I use the tension between Criseyde's expressed intent and what one might call the "authorized ending" (evoked by the narrator's very act of interrogating his sources) to provoke discussion of the competing ends implicit in or explicitly articulated by the competing discourses of the poem. Pandarus has argued that "th'ende is every tales strengthe" (2.260) but has proved unable to cope with the fact that the consummation of the affair between Troilus and Criseyde is not the end of their story. I invite the class to consider what happens to Pandarus and his plotting in books 4 and 5 (and what this might suggest about the poem's critique of romance). Criseyde tells Troilus, apropos of her "enchanting" of Calkas, that "as me lyst, I shal wel make an ende" (4.1400). If I'm lucky, a student will notice that the only end she invokes in book 5 is her own embeddedness in a canonical and source-determined text of betrayal: "thise bookes wol me shende. / O, rolled shal I ben on many a tonge!" (5.1060–61). Surveying the poem's multiple end-directed discourses, students may also notice book 4's return to the epic narrative ostensibly left behind in book 1 (implicit in Calkas's foreknowledge of the fate of Troy—which shapes his desire to bring Criseyde to the Greek camp), the "wo" to "wele" to "wo" cyclicity of Fortune suggested by book 1's first stanza, and Troilus's muddled Boethian meditations on divine foreknowledge and free will (4.958–1078). All these matters may be reinvoked as we discuss the poem's closing moves.

In teaching book 5, I often speed to its final stanza and speak to the narrator's imagination of an artist-God who is "[u]ncircumscript, and al maist circumscrive" (5.1865). Given that narrative closure seems so difficult for the earthly author, it is useful to raise the whole question of circumscription in this work. I ask my students to think about other attempts at circumscription or containment evident in the poem, and the ensuing discussion can take various tacks. Undergraduates are always alert to Pandarus's addiction to proverb and maxim, and we might ponder the repeated attempts by all the poem's characters (including its narrator) to fix and stabilize fickle earthly experience and the vicissitudes of earthly love by way of such apothegms. We also look back at the many embedded lyrics in the poetic narrative and their particular circumscription of experience—and at this point I would probably nudge us toward Troilus's hymn to "Love, that of erthe and se hath governaunce" (3.1744–71). I try to unpack the complex heteroglot moment in which Chaucer's pagan hero voices Boethius's celebration of heavenly love (on more than one occasion this has produced a lively argument about the degree of conscious irony with which it is framed). We may discuss, too, Troilus's helpless and anachronistic suggestion that he found a kind of scriptural stability within Criseyde's pledge of faith ("I wende . . . / That every word was gospel that ye seyde" [5.1264–65]) and move on from there to the new perspective on "blynde lust" his ghost achieves after his death in battle (5.1814–27). I might then ask why Chaucer doesn't offer this as the conclusion to his poem and raise the issue of Troilus's own "circumscription" within the quotation from Boccaccio's *Teseida* and within a pagan postmortem destination presided over by Mercury.

As our discussion of book 5 continues, I point to Chaucer's difficulties in ending this poem, encouraging the students to explore the various strategies and vocabularies deployed in his proliferating concluding gestures. When we focus on the explicitly Christian moralizing of lines 1835–69, there are always objections to these stanzas from readers annoyed by what they perceive as a clumsy cut-and-paste job, a kind of moral imposition; this, to be sure, invites consideration of the degree to which the rest of the poem makes the relation of earthly to heavenly love an active issue in its competing discourses. And when we return to the stanza praising the circle of the Trinity, I talk a little about the fact that (as Chaucer recites Dante's words) we have one last instance of heteroglossia. Why can this work only be completed by "re-voicing" a moment from *Il Paradiso*? And does the divine circumscription invoked at the last indeed manage to contain what has gone before?

This account of my pedagogy risks misrepresenting an always perplexed exploration of the work's many voices as something relatively tidy and linear. (Classes are typically thoroughly embroiled, for example, in the poem's mutually entangled sacred and secular, Christian and pagan vocabularies of love from the moment we read the narrator's introductory "bidding prayer" [1.22–49]; the question of their precise relation to each other doesn't wait until we read book 5!) My practice of teasing out the work's multiple discourses may indeed provoke people to dilate on the ones *they* find most compelling. Last fall, the poem took on a very particular shape because three sharp students were fascinated with the nuances of Pandarus's manipulative fiction making and with his voyeuristic intimacy with the real-life bodies whose encounter he plots. On another occasion, a (largely female) seminar was more interested in exploring Chaucer's representation of Criseyde's speech and agency. To teach *Troilus and Criseyde* is always to be provoked and intrigued by whatever new circumscription of its competing histories a room full of novice readers will attempt.

Philology, History, and Cultural Persistence: *Troilus and Criseyde* as Medieval and Contemporary

Peggy A. Knapp

The beauty and accessibility of *Troilus and Criseyde* makes it one of the most teachable poems of the English Middle Ages. In addition to introducing students to medieval culture, the poem can be used to illuminate generic structures, modes of characterization, linguistic change, and the usefulness of various interpretive styles. I use the much-pilloried designation *philology* in my title, not in opposition to *theory*, but as the term that best signals the close examination of the words of a text in order to restore as much as possible "of their original life," as Jan Ziolkowski puts it in *On Philology* (7). Such a reanimation of the semantic dimension of *Troilus and Criseyde* involves contemporary modes of historical study, rather than the *gran récit* called by Raymond Williams "epochal analysis" (*Marxism* 121). The fact that we *can* reanimate this lovely poem suggests the third of my terms, *cultural persistence*: some medieval strands of thought and feeling have had a long life in our social and discursive traditions and continue to demand our attention. In this essay, I discuss approaches to the poem in two pedagogical contexts: an upper-division undergraduate-graduate seminar in Chaucer and a senior seminar called Past and Present: Early Texts and Contemporary Interpretations.

In the Chaucer course, I begin with *The Canterbury Tales*, so students are accustomed to reading Middle English when we take up *Troilus and Criseyde*. Each student has researched the social role of one of the pilgrims and developed a sense of the pilgrim's potential responses to each of the tales. As a result, students are reading from both a "medieval" and a contemporary vantage point when we turn to *Troilus and Criseyde*. We have, by this time, a shared sense of the range of generic effects Chaucer commanded and of the nuanced way he used language. The overarching question posed in this part of the course is, therefore, how do the various genres and historical traditions involved in the poem—tragedy, epic, romance, Boethian allegory of Fortune—contribute to a reading of the whole? The critical record is invoked to show how theories of tragedy are called into play both by claimants to "historicist" readings (Robertson, *Preface*) and by proponents of an Aristotelian (and modern) sense of noble projects betrayed by an inscrutable universe (Aers, "Chaucer's Criseyde"). These general issues are raised in class and anchored by selected secondary sources.

Questions about generic shape like these become a framework for reading passages closely, often through single words. Here philology in its most literal sense kicks in. When Polonius asks, "What do you read, my lord?" Hamlet answers, "Words, words, words" ([ed. Evans] 2.2.191–92). The ideas, plots, and tones of a text—the "matter" Polonius asks about next—is necessarily read through a specific vocabulary. This is true of any complex text, but it is especially important to examine vocabulary closely when as much linguistic change has occurred as it has since Chaucer.

Especially instructive are those words that occur both early and late in the poem and that can be used to mark the stages of the narrative. "Thrift," for example, appears to be a greeting or mild oath ("Good thrift have ye!" or "by my thrift") but darkens when Pandarus congratulates Criseyde on her "right good thrift" on catching Troilus's interest (2.582). "Corage" is another focus word that repays close attention. Early in the poem it seems cognate with modern *courage* or *encourage*. Elsewhere in Chaucer, it has to do with will, particularly in connection with sexual desire. Chaucer's Merchant describes January's "greet corage . . . to ben a wedded man" as sexually motivated (*CT* 6.1254), but he needs a concoction to increase it on his wedding night (1808). The Merchant's Tale treats this pun comically, but when Criseyde's "corage" is described as "slydyng" (5.825) the various meanings from valor to lust merge ominously.

This classroom emphasis leads to a paper assignment on *Troilus and Criseyde* for which students are asked to choose a particular word or phrase. They check the word's range of meaning in the *Oxford English Dictionary* or the *Middle English Dictionary*, follow it through the poem with the help of the Chaucer concordance, and then comment on how their analysis contributes to a reading of the poem. The overarching questions posed earlier can be addressed individually in this paper and collectively in the discussions that follow from it. Attention to this interpretive style is informed by Hans-Georg Gadamer's formulation of "horizons of understanding" and his contention that a "fusion of horizons," a mitigation of the historical distance between present audiences and those of a previous era, is effected through an understanding of shared language. "Reality does not happen 'behind the back' of language" but "precisely *within* language" (35). Although we can never fashion a complete image of the past, we can attain genuine (though corrigible) knowledge of it. The specific focus on Chaucer's lexicon in this course teaches close attention to the ways language registers medieval cultural understandings. It is equally a philological enterprise and a historical one. Gadamerian fusions of horizons are used to connect the semantic and social patterns of the late fourteenth century with our own. It is not just that we learn something valuable about Chaucer's world through language but that some linguistically encoded features of his imagination have persisted over the centuries.

Such persistence is the focus of the differently organized seminar Past and Present: Early Texts and Contemporary Interpretations, in which Chaucer is one of several early authors. The purpose of this seminar is to implicate early texts in our understanding of our own cultural moment—again with reference to Gadamer's fusion of horizons. Each of the four sections of the seminar surrounds medieval texts with both contemporary criticism on them and recent imaginative literature related to them, taking both as commentary. *Troilus and Criseyde* appears in the section Cultural Persistence and Sexual Love. The point of this section is that some medieval preoccupations remain in the picture throughout the centuries, attended by different ethical assessments but answering similar "structures of feeling" (a term I take from Raymond Williams). The section begins with Gottfried von Strassburg's *Tristan* and Denis de Rougemont's *Love in the Western World*. The "Tristan myth"—that passionate love is irresistible to "noble hearts"—is treated with delicate ambivalence by Gottfried (more ambivalence than Rougemont concedes, since he was using primarily French sources). The myth nonetheless reaches deep into cultural imagination and persists. We take up *Troilus and Criseyde* to continue the discussion of Western attitudes toward sexual love, concluding the section with Scott Spenser's 1979 novel *Endless Love* as a contemporary novelistic appropriation of such attitudes. A small group of students are commissioned to begin class discussions on Rougemont's theory before we read *Troilus and Criseyde*, and another group reports later on echoes of Chaucer's poem in the diction and plotting of *Endless Love*. In some ways, *Troilus and Criseyde* appropriates the themes and strategies of earlier "courtly love" writing: love sickness, idolatry, secrecy, and the like. Yet it can also be seen as a critique of the rhetoric that, by the 1380s, had come to accompany these conventional associations.

There are several ways to frame the hermeneutic problems—for us and for Chaucer's first audiences—presented by the text. First, we pose the issue as that of Chaucer's recounting a story from antiquity to a Christian audience. (This entry point underlines the grand theme of the course in stressing a series of appropriations rather than an authoritative source.) The antique past was a fascinating and prestigious monument for medieval Europe, yet it was also the era before the age of grace. This ambivalence creates an opportunity to dignify the love affair: just as the potion in *Tristan* renders the lovers helpless to resist love, the pagan setting releases *Troilus and Criseyde* from ecclesiastical strictures applicable in fourteenth-century England. The text produces powerful aesthetic effects that connive with the lovers without directly indicting their love as sinful.

We use Morton Bloomfield's "Distance in *Troilus and Criseyde*" to focus on this aspect of the text. Bloomfield's essay introduces the knotty issue of the narrator's double relation to the plot, at once the Godlike knower of its outcome and the mortal interpreter reacting to ongoing experience. Chaucer's narrator cannot create the plot, as Bloomfield points out, but he can control the tone of the telling. The vividness of Troilus's first sight of Criseyde and the crafted suffering-to-joy representation of the love tryst in book 3 place the distanced narrator in a tense and conflicted relation to his tale.

Second, we consider the hermeneutic possibilities from the logic of a cultural idealism completely dominated by a Boethian distrust of passionate love as the gift of untrustworthy Fortune. A forceful statement of the poem as an elaborated exemplum is that of D. W. Robertson's *A Preface to Chaucer*, from which we read a hefty excerpt demonstrating that "the poem itself is one of the most moving exemplifications of Boethian ideas ever written" (473). This position simplifies the conflicts and ambivalences of the narrator's self-presentation by making him a straw man, drawn by imaginative vision into sympathy with the lovers. Even knowing the end of an overcommitment to loving, Robertson's argument implies, does not always prevent a crushing disappointment. Chaucer's medieval readers were being warned against what was clearly a sin in their own world, even though it may not have been one in the virtual world of the poem. This position rings yet another change on the uses of history for textual explication.

Yet a third contemporary perspective on the poem confronts the narrator's role from a different angle. Carolyn Dinshaw's "Reading like a Man" from *Chaucer's Sexual Poetics* takes up the problem of a Christian author telling a pagan tale. Dinshaw's emphasis is on the vigor and delight with which the telling enters the world of the female, only at the end moralizing Criseyde as the stand-in for the false felicity of the world. In our course, we regard her argument as a meditation on reading both literary text and historical imagination, especially on the issue of sexual love. Dinshaw's conclusion is that when Criseyde allows herself to be traded and seeks the protection of Diomede, she recognizes her duty to the patriarchal system that trades women for *its* political advantage. Her very " 'slydyng' can be read as proving 'trewe' to patriarchal society" (62). This reading relates the poem to large-scale social history rather than to doctrinal or intellectual history. From this perspective, it is possible to see Chaucer the author as highlighting the injustice of Criseyde's situation, since his narrator stresses the double bind in which Criseyde is placed.

On the one hand, *Troilus and Criseyde* can be taken to elaborate the love myth of an idealized, irresistible, life-enhancing force that nonetheless inevitably entails suffering. Instead of regarding Troilus as an ideal hero before he loves (as Robertson seems to do), we might see that his commitment to Criseyde makes his a more "noble heart," more considerate to women, more dutiful to his country (3.1772–75), more courteous in his speech (3. 1786), and more successful in avoiding vices (3.1805–06).

On the other hand, many details specifically refute the myth. The helpfulness of Pandarus looms large among these. At first, his aid may be regarded as loyal friendship, but his scheming begins to wear the face of voyeurism, and his implication in the traffic in women becomes increasingly evident. For Troilus, love is represented as irresistible, both in the compelling freshness of his first sight of Criseyde and in his inability to cure himself of its effects. But Criseyde's falling in love is more gradual, taking up nearly the whole of book 2 and involving a less spontaneous response to Troilus. The concerns of this course highlight the contrast between this slow, probing examination of interiority and the sudden, mutual capitulation of Tristan and Isolde in Gottfried's tale. *Tristan* creates the myth of transcendence, whereas *Troilus and Criseyde* is rich in the psychological details and social contexts. In short, these two influential medieval "founders" of the Western love tradition diverge in important ways, demonstrating both the continuity and the variety of medieval approaches to love.

These twentieth-century critical perspectives on the poem are followed by our consideration of Spencer's *Endless Love*. Spencer's novel, like the medieval tales, is tragic. In it, David Axelrod's love for Jade Butterfield defines his identity and absorbs his entire vantage point in a similar manner to the experience of Tristan and Troilus:

> From the time I learned to love Jade . . . there was nothing in my life that wasn't alive with meaning, that wasn't capable of suggesting weird and hidden significances, that didn't carry with it the undertaste of what for lack of anything better to call it I'll call The Infinite. (23)

This young man is overwhelmed by a creature instead of the Creator—just the capitulation Boethius warned against. Like *Troilus and Criseyde*, Spencer's novel is also in some ways a critique of the persistent myth of idealized, irresistible, life-enhancing love in the West. David's testimony closes the novel, as Troilus's does the poem, but *Endless Love* does not "despise / This wrecched world" or hold it "vanite" in the light of transcendence (5.1816–17). Just the opposite. David writes for Jade,

> I am standing on a long black stage, with a circle of light on me, which is my love for you, enduring. I have escaped—or have been expelled— from eternity and am back in time. But I step out once more to sing this aria, this confession, this testament without end. (418)

For David the view from eternity was connected with Jade—an exact reversal of Troilus's rejection of his love for Criseyde from the eighth sphere.

This intricate interlace is the meaning of my term *cultural persistence*. The Gadamerian notion of horizon basic to both courses is situational—a horizon defines what can be seen from a particular place in a certain light. The texts and commentaries I have taken up in these courses are specific to the way our students have been introduced to literary forms and to my own understandings of past and present social formations—these will vary from college to college and from decade to decade. The interweaving of a focus on the otherness of images from the past with a focus on their relevance and force in the present has many instantiations.

Chaucer and Gender Theory

Angela Jane Weisl and Tison Pugh

The broad phrase in our title, "gender theory," refers to a critical stance that provides a variety of pedagogical approaches to Chaucer's *Troilus and Criseyde* and the shorter poems, allowing readers to examine the ways these poems both assert and challenge gendered and sexual constructions of normativity. By revealing the myriad ways femininity and masculinity are constructed in a patriarchal society, gender theory lays a road map for opening up Chaucer's literature. These poems' most prominent characters are defined through conflicting constructions of gender, resulting in the confusion of desires in their plots; such tensions create difficult gender paradigms for students to negotiate if they are to understand the unfolding of the poems. Because students typically *think* they understand gender, since they are so deeply tied to their own gender narratives and expectations, their assumptions can provide a useful opening point for discussing the poems' many complications.

A clear path through *Troilus and Criseyde*'s assumptions demands the use of more recently defined gender theories to examine the full context of gender in Chaucer's romance. The foundational works of Judith Butler (*Gender Trouble* and *Bodies That Matter*) in gender theory and of Eve Kosofsky Sedgwick (*Between Men* and *Epistemology of the Closet*) in queer theory emphasize the illusory quality of gender and desire, delimiting the fantastic construction of gendered and sexual normativity yet also highlighting the very real ramifications that these fantastic constructions bear. The various incarnations of gendered identities, including those of Criseyde, Troilus, and Pandarus, as well as of the poem's minor characters, create a gendered and sexualized battleground on which opposing ideological constructions of femininity and masculinity come head to head. Gender and queer theories provide crucial hermeneutics for students to understand the frailty of gender in the world of the poem, where courtly love constructs paradigms of gendered behavior but where characters at times display an arbitrary understanding of their roles. These issues can be addressed with simple questions that generate topics for discussion and research: in Chaucer's fictional worlds, what are the paradigms of gender and sexual normativity? and how do various characters construct or resist the force of the normative?

For example, as a widow, how typical is Criseyde's role in her society? What freedoms and limitations does she find in this status? As feminist critics such as Carolyn Dinshaw (*Chaucer's Sexual Poetics*) and Elaine Tuttle Hansen (*Chaucer and the Fictions of Gender*) have shown, Criseyde is constructed through her relationships to men—and indeed she maintains little identity apart from the roles (daughter, lover, trade bait) imposed on her. Her behavior and her voice constrained, she becomes the text itself, written on rather than writing her own destiny. *Troilus and Criseyde* highlights a range of shifting gender relations and assumptions within the poem since Criseyde's profoundly gendered position takes place in a complex of identities that are inhabited and performed but also concealed.

To keep students from descending too deeply into stereotypes while interrogating Criseyde's position in the poem, teachers can provide them with background reading on women in the Middle Ages. Christiane Klapisch-Zuber's *Silences of the Middle Ages* (the second volume in *A History of Women in the West*) offers a historical view of the multiple roles of and assumptions about women. Students can draw on this work to consider the positions Criseyde occupies in the poem, since the essays in Klapisch-Zuber's volume offer a fairly complex reading of secular women's positions in medieval life and society, including both war and love. Criseyde's shifting back and forth between the threatened pawn of war, who quivers at Hector's feet, and the powerful lady of romance, who demands of Troilus, "Is this a mannes game?" (3.1126), makes her difficult to define.

If students see Criseyde as a cipher, they often see Troilus as a wimp. His lovesickness and his inability to pursue his amatory objectives appear to students as passive, if not emasculated. Although Troilus's excessive stasis provides certain opportunities for comedy, it also raises key issues about the definition of masculinity in medieval romance. Through such initial interpretations, students typically express their modern perspective on medieval love. But as they learn to shift their perspective to one that more fully recognizes a medieval context, they begin to realize that Troilus's hypermasculine prowess in battle is not incongruous with his passivity as lover. The conflation of Rambo warrior with retiring lover may initially be surprising, but it yields the necessary insight that a modern perspective on medieval masculinity is limited. The structure and ideological force of gendered normativity have shifted considerably over the centuries, which necessitates that our students confront the ways in which courtly love calls forth both familiar and unfamiliar performances of gendered identities. Students must link their modern day conceptions of masculinity to one in accordance with Andreas Capellanus's *Art of Courtly Love* to understand that medieval masculinities reflect varying cultural norms.

From this vantage point, instructors can expand the lesson to examine how gender acts in accordance with or resistance to other cultural entities. For example, some of the poem's tension and its complexities can be organized by considering the structures of masculinity and femininity in the two competing discourses of the poem, love and war. As the poem shifts generically between romance and epic, the characters are controlled by conflicting sets of assumptions. Intersections of public and private (such as Criseyde's view of Troilus through the window of her closet) and of national and personal (for instance, the movement in book 4 from the parliament to the bedroom) can elucidate these constructs in tension.

Building on these perspectives, students should recognize the ways in which gender bleeds beyond bodies to actions and social forms. In war, for example, male and female are defined by violence and vulnerability; Troilus is the warrior second only to Hector, whereas Criseyde is trade bait. In love, these structures are reversed. Yet in the poem, the two worlds cannot help penetrating each other and upsetting power dynamics previously in play. A key example is Criseyde's dream, which is enacted on the stage of love. Yet in this dream, Troilus is figured as the powerful eagle ripping out the heart of a singing nightingale, figured as Criseyde. The impacted nature of these definitions is again revealed at the point of consummation, when Troilus declares, "Now be ye kaught" (3.1207), and when Chaucer comments, "What myghte or may the sely larke seye, / Whan that the sperhauk hath it in his foot?" (3.1191–92). Who holds the power in this scene—the courtly lady or the masculine warrior? And how do these moments lay the groundwork for subsequent inversion and irony?

The image from the dream of the eagle's penetration can be seen as a metaphor of gender normativity. Although Troilus is often figured as a simulacrum of Troy, the powerful warrior city undone by a woman, Criseyde serves as an image of Troy in its vulnerability. Criseyde appears in a series of small, enclosed spaces (like the walled city). Each space however, turns out to be penetrable. Pandarus for example, intrudes into Criseyde's private quarters to thrust Troilus's letter into her bodice and again appears through the trap door in his own house—and he possibly violates Criseyde after her night with Troilus. Troilus's vision appears through the window of Crisyde's closet as he rides home from war, enters the little room drawn by Pandarus and literally penetrates Criseyde's body. These metaphoric Trojan horses play significant roles in the eventual downfall of Criseyde, the poem, and the city itself. However, the structures of penetration are not univalent: Troilus is made vulnerable by the penetration of Cupid's arrow and his resultant love for Criseyde, and the images of Pandarus's penetration of the lovers' privacy again complicate normative gender assumptions in *Troilus and Criseyde*. Pandarus's polymorphous and destabilizing desires undermine attempts to see any normativity in desire at all. His desires seek to perpetuate the lover's pleasures through endless deferral more than through carnal fulfillment. This discussion will draw students' attention to the slippery nature of gender and desire. It is effective to start from the text, asking students to discuss these recurring images and their interlocking and contradictory meanings.

Although we have used *Troilus and Criseyde* as our primary example in this essay, the question of gendered normativity is no less useful to apply to Chaucer's other works, including *The Book of the Duchess*, *The Parliament of Fowls*, *The Legend of Good Women*, and *The House of Fame*. Each of these texts proves frustrating to modern conceptions of gender and sexuality. Students are often troubled by the melancholic view of courtly love and the weary masculinity of *The Book of the Duchess*, amused by the bickerings of the gendered birds in *The Parliament of Fowls*, ensnared in the debate about women that occasions *The Legend of Good Women*, and intrigued by the masculine construction of authorship in *The House of Fame*. But to what extent are any of these gendered depictions normative?

A range of pedagogical activities can fruitfully bring the topic of gender to the Chaucer classroom. Short student reports, classroom discussions, and research papers can all require students to use medieval hermeneutics to justify their responses to medieval gender. As students research medieval expectations of behavior for men or women (or for femininity, masculinity, and sexuality), they must ponder moments in Chaucer's texts when depictions of gender agree or disagree with their expectations and then theorize the ways in which this incongruency generates meaning.

It is valuable to provide some background for students as a way in to understanding both medieval and their own attitudes toward gender normativity. Establishing definitions of gender roles in a class of contemporary students can be both frightening and illustrative, particularly if instructors have the luxury of introducing outside sources that provide a sufficiently nuanced sense of medieval gender assumptions. There are many valuable resources for this, both books and Web sites; selections from Eileen Power's *Medieval Women*, Priscilla Martin's *Chaucer's Women*, D. M. Hadley's *Masculinity in Medieval Europe*, and Peter Beidler's *Masculinities in Chaucer* provide terminology for the class to work from. Examining the poem then reveals the way each character does and does not represent normative gender assumptions throughout the narrative.

For teachers who wish to engage their students in this topic in writing, one basic assignment can be adapted to all the texts discussed here:

> The concept of femininity/masculinity in Chaucer's works is established not by means of individuals but through a dialogue between a variety of types. Chaucer's ideas of womanhood/manhood thus must be sought in a tense harmony of opposites. As you read through the poem, different images of femininity/masculinity assert themselves, often in contrast to earlier examples. Discuss the progression that you see developing in the poem(s). What are the different images of femininity/masculinity that Chaucer offers up to his reader, and how are they treated in the texts? What suggestions does Chaucer seem to be making about femininity/masculinity? Be sure to draw some conclusions about how Chaucer indicates a position in this dialectic.

Whether offered as an essay prompt or an exam question, students addressing these issues are forced to engage the very questions that gender theory opens up for the poems. Their answers can easily provide the fodder, mentioned at the start of this essay, for beginning this challenging yet rewarding inquiry into Chaucer's *Troilus and Criseyde* and shorter poems.

By focusing on the issue of normativity in this essay and in our pedagogical practice, we reify an instructive illusion—that the normative can be pinned

down and scrutinized. The normative is always shifting, ever various, and mul-
tiform. As we look to the normative, however, we can better understand the
ways in which its shifting parameters perpetually fail to account for the vast
array of characters and experiences of medieval fiction, if not also of medieval
and modern fact. Helping students analyze the ways gendered normativity
constructs the experiences of fictional characters can assist them in under-
standing how ideological force bears similar gendered pressures on their own
lives.

"Made and Molded of Things Past": Intertexuality and the Study of Chaucer, Henryson, and Shakespeare

Roger Apfelbaum

My first opportunity to teach a special-topics graduate seminar allowed me to create an ideal syllabus, which studies Chaucer's *Troilus and Criseyde*, Henryson's *Testament of Cresseid*, and Shakespeare's *Troilus and Cressida*. My book *Shakespeare's* Troilus and Cressida: *Textual Problems and Performance Solutions* considers the stage history of editorial problems in Shakespeare's *Troilus and Cressida*. I also discuss early versions of the legend as a way to foster a dialogue between editorial choices and performance history. Tracing the resonances of a moment in Shakespeare's play back through the legend is to me as important and as interesting as pursuing the moment forward in time through performances. The way different cultures produce different versions of a similar plot and characters encourages the study of historical and contemporary culture as a part of literary analysis. There is hardly a more rewarding and complex literary heritage to explore than the legend of Troilus and his variously named lover.

In a Chaucer course that has just a week or two for Shakespeare's play or in a Shakespeare course that touches on Chaucer as an example of sources, I recommend studying select passages that open up comparisons between the lovers and their Pandarus. I would also spend time considering war as a setting for the lovers and look at the different roles of Calkas. For courses with a broader scope or less advanced students than the graduate seminar I am describing, I still hope a selection from my choice of criticism, editions, and pedagogy is relevant.

I wanted the seminar to be as cyclical as possible, allowing for more complex readings as we returned to passages covered or passed over in an initial reading of Chaucer, Henryson, and Shakespeare. My overall plan was to read Shakespeare's play quickly over the first two weeks, study Chaucer's poem over six weeks, discuss Henryson's poem for a week, and then return to Shakespeare's play for a six-week study using different scholarly approaches, especially editorial, intertextual, performance-history, and theorized critical perspectives.

Reading Shakespeare's play in the first two weeks provided an introduction to the legend and the issues we would return to and allowed for reference to Shakespeare's play as we read Boccaccio, Chaucer, Henryson, and excerpts from their predecessors and heirs. Focusing mostly on the love story in a first reading of Shakespeare's play, I encouraged thinking (and writing and talking) about Cressida and Pandarus watching the return of Troilus from battle (1.2), issues of spectatorship and voyeurism, the references in the play to the char-

acters' legendary status (especially 3.4), and the common moments in Shake-
speare and Chaucer (see table).

Similar Passages in Chaucer and Shakespeare[1]

Chaucer	Shakespeare
1.547–1061	1.1.1–84
2.155–210	1.2.38–88
2.610–86	1.2.218–86
2.1247–60	1.2.219–31
3.1422–70	4.2.1–15
3.512–1309	3.2.38–206
3.1555–75	4.2.24–34
4.666–72, 736–99, 1128–414	4.4.1–56
4.1485–596	4.4.57–105
5.1051–631	5.2.121–87, 5.3.97–111

Studying the way Chaucer, Henryson, and Shakespeare borrow, translate,
and adapt versions of the legend shows how source study can lead to critical,
literary, and cultural readings. I wanted to make use of the incredibly rich
scholarly tradition that reflects the kinds of shifts in cultural interest that are
also seen in the literary works. Students wrote for an electronic forum and
presented their ideas about the texts through a variety of tasks that gave them
experience with different scholarly approaches. On their own and in small
groups, their weekly responses centered on close readings, but I asked them
to alternate approaches and to, for example, comment on published explica-
tions, respond to recent theorized criticism, engage with sources and source
studies, establish a text and other editorial tasks (such as writing annotations
and introductions), read and respond to relevant cultural and literary texts,
and do the work of theater historians and performers. For formal papers,
students were encouraged to use an approach of their choice, but with the
weekly postings I wanted scholarly experimentation that extended their ex-
perience, expertise, and critical vocabulary. Bringing together these ap-
proaches created a kind of class variorum, where passages from the poems
and play opened up into different students' presentations. Two especially good
examples of this kind of study are the problematic texts and inventive per-
formances of Cressida and Pandarus as they watch Troilus and the other sol-
diers return from battle (1.2 in Shakespeare, with similar passages in Chaucer
starting at 2.610 and 2.1247) and Pandarus bringing the lovers together (3.2
in Shakespeare; 3.512 in Chaucer).[2]

Recent considerations of intertextuality provide a framework for under-
standing questions of influence and textual juxtaposition. Barbara Bowen's
Gender in the Theater of War: Shakespeare's Troilus and Cressida and Mihoko
Suzuki's *Metamorphoses of Helen: Authority, Difference, and the Epic* both

turn to Thomas Greene's *The Light in Troy: Imitation and Discovery in Renaissance Poetry.* Suzuki describes Greene's work as having

> broken new ground in the study of the relationships between Renaissance texts and their antecedents. Going beyond a traditional study of "sources" or "influences," Greene insists on an understanding of an imitative literary work through its "subtext," which is not external to it but which constitutes an essential component of its verbal structure. (9–10)

While Suzuki's chapter on Shakespeare's *Troilus and Cressida* only briefly touches on the relation between Chaucer, Henryson, and Shakespeare's works, Bowen offers an insightful and theoretically informed chapter, "Representations, Performance, Narrative: Truth Tired with Iteration," which summarizes how recent criticism has moved beyond Harold Bloom's "anxiety of influence":

> Thomas Greene and Ann Rosalind Jones have demonstrated in their studies of Renaissance lyric [that] the range of imitation in the period was much greater than the Bloomian model permits, varying with historical and gender difference. Greene's *Light in Troy* . . . reverses a Burckhardtian picture of the Renaissance as a time of untroubled cultural rebirth and claims instead that humanism was characterized above all by a deep anxiety about its relation to antiquity . . . [and] a powerful sense of remoteness from the past to which he gives the name "historical solitude." (145–46)

Bowen goes on to give an account of the "feminist scholars [who] have identified in the act of translation itself the kind of eroticism between source-text and reader, authorial text and writer that seemed to be present in Shakespeare's handling of the Homeric and Chaucerian scenes of spectatorship" (146). Such complex considerations of intertextuality and context can set up a reading of the most compelling issues in literature, criticism, and culture.

Some of the influential work on the relationship between Shakespeare and Chaucer includes the essay by Muriel Bradbrook, "What Shakespeare Did to Chaucer's *Troilus and Criseyde,*" which works well with a reading of C. S. Lewis's seminal source study, "What Chaucer Really Did to *Il Filostrato.*" These two essays are certainly dated in a number of ways, but Bradbrook quickly and interestingly characterizes the relationship of the texts and authors to open up key issues about narrative choices and the similarities and differences in character and focus. Most important is her notion that Shakespeare's "Pandarus and Cressid distort Chaucer's two subtlest creations, for neither, in their Chaucerian form, is to be found in *Il Filostrato* or any of the earlier accounts; it was precisely to the most original parts of Chaucer that Shakespeare turned for his bitterest refashioning" (319).

Rather than recount a selection of the history of scholarship on Shakespeare and Chaucer, I want to briefly discuss two book-length studies that remain the most extensive comparisons: Ann Thompson's *Shakespeare's Chaucer: A Study in Literary Origins* and E. Talbot Donaldson's *The Swan at the Well: Shakespeare Reading Chaucer*. After tracing the critical history of observations on Shakespeare's potential use of Chaucer, Thompson observes that "it is common for Renaissance-centered critics to misunderstand Chaucer's poem and misread it in the light of Shakespeare's play, which is particularly hazardous when the play is seen as a 'problem' and the sources are studied in order to solve it" (115). The early critical (mis)understanding of *Troilus and Cressida* as a "problem play" and the scholarly focus on trying to discern what Shakespeare read or had open on his desk leads to a school of red herrings. Early in the course, I use Thompson's caveat not only to let my students know about the critical history but also to encourage them to find approaches that positively engage with the work through literary and cultural analysis rather than through a kind of puzzle-solving simplification.

Thompson's remarks help stress the importance of understanding critical perspectives. At the risk of pigeonholing two versatile critics, Thompson can be seen as a Shakespearean looking at the relationship between Shakespeare and Chaucer whereas Donaldson offers a Chaucerian's perspective. Other critical approaches can be instructively informed by trying to understand some of the critical and cultural factors at play in different considerations of the texts. Donaldson's chapters are insightful and provide important models for focused critical commentary. Thompson, however, provides a more methodical analysis and includes sections on the Chaucerian connections for the eight scenes or groups of scenes in Shakespeare's play that feature the lovers. She moves from poet to playwright in what students agree is a clear and perceptive analysis, offering extended quotations and discussions about similarities and differences in both theme and narrative.

Two recent outstanding scholarly editions of Shakespeare's play are of great help to teachers and students. David Bevington's Arden edition, third series, and Anthony Dawson's New Cambridge Shakespeare edition both have insightful and well-referenced sections on Shakespeare's sources. Bevington's edition is certainly more extensive on the overall influences on Shakespeare's love and war plots, but both have about the same space dedicated to Chaucer's and Henryson's influence on Shakespeare. While both editors give a brief general account of the relation between the two versions of the legend, Bevington is somewhat more exact in identifying parallel passages (see table). However, both recent editors show how Shakespeare "digested" Chaucer: Dawson writes of the "compression" (255), and Bevington of how "Shakespeare telescopes events, as he so often does in working with his sources" (385). Dawson is particularly insightful about Pandarus, Cressida, and the tone of both works. After considering the difference in narrative and Shakespeare's compression of time, Dawson stresses that "Chaucer's attitude mixes sympathy with genial detachment; his irony is softer and subtler than Shakespeare's and he provides no precedent for Shakespeare's bitter satire" (255).

Dawson and Bevington are clearly influenced and impressed by Donaldson. They summarize Donaldson's view that Shakespeare perceptively determined that Henryson's *Testament* was tacked onto Chaucer's poem, despite the fact that editions before and during Shakespeare's lifetime did not distinguish between Chaucer's work and Henryson's poem, which immediately followed. Dawson calls Donaldson's work "brilliant and indispensable—both as source study and as criticism" (254n1), and it is with such evaluations that I try to get my students thinking about what, specifically, we can find in Donaldson that deserves praise.

Studying Henryson provides an opportunity to read and comment not only on his extension of Chaucer's narrative but also on Henryson's diseased misogyny, which is either indirectly or very directly addressed in later ballads, literary works (by Lydgate, Caxton, and others), and plays (not just in Shakespeare's *Troilus* and Heywood's *Iron Age* plays, but in Shakespeare's and his contemporaries' references to Cressida as proverbial). Each author provides a different woman to judge, and each engages with a form of Ulysses's question to Troilus, "What has she done, Prince, that can soil our mothers?" (5.2.140).

NOTES

[1]This table, meant as a rough guide rather than an extensive comparison, is derived from Bevington (Shakespeare, *Troilus and Cressida* 383–84).

[2]For a feminist stage history of Shakespeare's 1.2, see especially Barbara Hodgdon; for an insightful reading of 3.2, see Elizabeth Freund.

Triform Chaucer: Deconstruction, Historicism, Psychoanalysis, and *Troilus and Criseyde*

James J. Paxson

Although the heyday of deconstruction in postmodern American literary criticism has certainly passed, its tools have entered into what are now conventionalized regimes of critical reading. Cultural studies, feminist and gender criticism, postcolonial theory, identity studies, and postmodern rhetoric depend on the exposure of the logical binary oppositions and the tropes or figures that tacitly organize systems of meaning in works of literature. Such exposure shows not the closure of meaning but the openness of texts. Chaucer criticism continues to benefit from this critical revolution, although the rigorous rhetorical readings instituted by Paul de Man never quite took off in Chaucer studies (Paxson 206–07).

In addition, deconstruction seems to stand in conflict with two other vertices in a triangular map of major critical practices—historicism and psychoanalysis. Historicism includes all varieties of critical reading intended to clarify the historical context of the literary text's production; psychoanalysis includes the articulation of human cognition as expressed in the text, especially as it is modeled through statements about the unconscious propounded by Sigmund Freud, Jacques Lacan, and their imitators. The struggle among deconstruction, historicism, and psychoanalysis emerged because of the emphases each approach put on the eccentric understanding of language as a kind of "machine," the collective agency of humans acting in and through time, and the individual agency of the unconscious. Rhetoric and history, or psychology and history, or deconstruction and psychology have suffered tensions (Waters xliv–lii; Melville 84–114); but the best thinking in contemporary criticism still must offer to mitigate these tensions and to more fully employ the theoretical tools we already have in hand. Literary theory is of use when it proves it can help us to get the critical job done.

It would be instructive in the special instance of *Troilus and Criseyde* to blaze a (still) new trail by showing the convergences of these approaches in order to promote the future of theoretically enriched Chaucer criticism. I therefore focus on a singular and thematically unusual moment in Chaucer's romance to demonstrate its philosophical and semiological potentials. These potentials stage the conflict or tension, yet also the structural interdependence, of rhetorical (or deconstructive), historical, and psychological energies that constitute Chaucerian poetics. Only one moment in the poem's long narrative, and a seemingly minor scene at that, will occupy my whole analysis in this brief but hortatory essay.

Writing exists to supplement human speech. It thus marks off the short-comings of human knowledge and experience while it seeks to clarify what lies inside the human mind or soul; it represents, for Plato, a secondarily shadowed step away from the primacy of thought and thought's *first* emana-tion or "filiation," speech, even though it must be taken as a complicit and equivalent version of the logos that Plato imagined was at the core or root of all human psychic, social, and textual being (Derrida, *Dissemination* 75–84). We thus must pay special attention to moments in *Troilus and Criseyde* in which writing is dramatized. Letters of any kind, but especially love letters, which purport to capture the lover's innermost essence for the beloved, take primacy of place in this Platonic filiation.

But what, really, should we call that written thing produced by Troilus under the close tutelage of Pandarus in book 2 of *Troilus and Criseyde*? Nominally, it is a love letter, in which the hero confesses his true feelings for Criseyde. The letter seems to be a supercharged version of the Ovidian epistle written under duress, as seen in the Roman love poet's fictional collections *Amores* and *Heroides*. Yet it is not the actual content of Troilus's letter that strikes us as peculiar. The physical composition of the document—more specifically, Pandarus's guidance of Troilus—oddly signifies the value of writing and in-tention. Pandarus advocates that his pupil Troilus dress up his Ovidian love letter for maximal effect on Criseyde:

> Towchyng thi lettre, thou art wys ynough,
> I woot thow nylt it dygneliche endite,
> As make it with thise argumentes tough;
> Ne scryvenyssh or craftily thow it write;
> Biblotte it with thi teris ek a lite;
> And if thou write a goodly word al softe,
> Though it be good, reherce it nought to ofte.   (2.1023–29)

Most of Pandarus's advice (1023–43) concerns matters of content, though he does give this minimal direction about the documentary or material condition of the actual letter. The effect of tears on the paper shows the importance of producing a letter that is authentic—one not only that is up-front and honest but also that bears some bodily proof of the writer's sincerity on its surface. The coached authenticity of the letter features formally in the neo-Ovidian discourse of courtly love literature. Pandarus advocates spilling tears to over-determine the truthful emotions behind the letter. The tears are meant to verify its message.

Since the letter's blotting with tears is highly contrived, is not the letter in part a forgery of sorts? Pandarus spends a good deal of breath telling Troilus not to jam the letter's form, that is, its rhetorical or poetic structure, with too much artifice because doing so will jeopardize Criseyde's acceptance of its *content*. Yet the authenticity is indeed compromised—certainly to us as desir-ing readers of a love text—because we have witnessed the advocating of tampering with its medial or material structure. This would be the first moment in the poem where, as deconstructive critics put it, an aporia or cognitive fissure, a hole, opens: the binary opposition of content/form dismantles itself.

Deconstruction often proceeds by showing how the basic units of logical relations in linguistic utterances, the binary oppositions of abstract categories, undo themselves even as they try to assure conceptual closure. The main opposition in this instance dismantles itself because the structurally enveloping container of the letter's form—the container of that which is supposed to be the container (not too-crafty or "scryvenyssh" phraseology) of the letter's content or message (authentic feelings of devotion and desire)—now becomes a content itself, one that is at odds with the impulse behind its usurping container's making. This minimally deconstructive state of affairs goes for any such contrived letter in the poetry of Ovid, Propertius, Boccaccio, or Chaucer.

But Chaucer goes further. We must remember that there may be a division between what Pandarus recommends about the formal features of the letter and what he might just mean by his statement that Troilus should sprinkle the letter with tears. In lines 1023–26, he addresses the abstract business of arranging language in the epistolary form. So what if his urging that Troilus "blot with tears" the letter is a metaphorical expression—and one that the young novice at love misapprehends, taking the expression literally and not figuratively? "Blot it with your tears a little" might mean, "put more feeling into the content precisely by avoiding 'crafty' phrasing"! This potential mistaking of a figurative expression for a literal one would not be an isolated blunder by one of Chaucer's characters. The binary opposition literal/figural occupies the same semiotic place as content/form (for both dichotomies resolve into a more fundamental oppositional pair—primary/secondary), and thus Chaucer's text can be said to thematize and deconstruct such basic units of language and the discourse of literature.

Once Troilus has composed his letter, pretty much following what Pandarus had advocated (2.1065–85), he blunders another way. He "be-blots" not the ink inscription on the paper directly, which would prove the tears fell during the writing process; rather, he blots his signet ring, the instrument used for the verifying of letters (another inscription of authentication), presumably after they are sealed:

> And with his salte teris gan he bathe
> The ruby in his signet, and it sette
> Upon the wex deliverliche and rathe.
> Therwith a thousand tymes er he lette
> He kiste tho the lettre that he shette.   (2.1086–90)

The bathing of the signet ring before the sealing of the wax and then the smearing of the *outside* of the sealed letter could not perforce produce a blotted Ovidian letter of true feelings. At most, a name we might presume was inscribed on the outside (*Criseyde*?) might have been smeared into illegibility.

Here is the point at which the Chaucerian text achieves a semiotic and philosophical complexity that preceding love narratives, with their own tear-stained love letters, never attain. The material sign of the letter's emotional and psychic authenticity, the symbol of what Jacques Derrida would call Platonism's desire for primary and pure presence as opposed to discursive or textual (and thus temporal) mediation, was supposed to be the *tear stains*. In the Platonic system, thought and feeling precede and are superior to speech, which is superior to writing. Each successive phenomenon emanates from its prior, more authentic form. Troilus's "salty tears," arising from within the body, are supposed to shortcut the whole mediational edifice of writing. From the genuine inside of the human body, the tears signify that which biophysically precedes speech or writing but really cannot. Such hierarchizing of human cognitive phenomena, acts of inscription, and even bodily secretion, however, always already disclose no more than the varieties of logos or meaning making. The smeared liquid of the tears would equally exist as writing; as a kind of bodily ink or inscription; or as the fluid ingredient of a sign system materially committed by custom to a surface of skin, the lover's cheeks or back of his or her hand (for parchment too is indeed skin prepared for inscription). The effluvia of the body's interior domain of erotic authenticity, which in the Platonic scheme of things is constitutive of Chaucer's great romance and domain of the unconscious, wishes to circumvent the materiality and temporality of writing but manages to fall into it. If for Freud the unconscious could be construed poetically as the turbulent domain of desire for bliss—the hidden reservoir of salt waters—that turbulent domain threatens to spill out and overtake the cognitive supremacy of writing's ratiocinative regime. Perhaps this hydraulic scenario may remind us of another of Derrida's thought games concerning poetic language's desire to represent the unrepresentable act of pure presence, of unmediated human psychic encounter—his perfect desire machine:

> Let's imagine a kind of machine, which by definition is an impossible one, that would be like a machine for ingrammatizing [*engrammer*] everything that happens and such that the smallest thoughts, the smallest movement of the body, the least traces of desire, the ray of sunlight, the encounter with someone, a phrase heard in passing, are inscribed somewhere; imagine that a general electroencephalocardiosomatopsychogram were possible: at that moment my desire would be absolutely fulfilled—and finitude accepted (and by the same token indeed). (*Points* 143–44)

It took until the twentieth century to produce modern medicine's ECG or EEG machines, but Derrida here fantasizes the Western metaphysical tradition's (i.e., Platonism's) magical "EECSPG" machine in terms that the text of

Chaucer's *Troilus and Criseyde* would recognize: the hydraulic "writing" produced by the subject who exposes his oceanic interior onto the physical textures of rhetorical and graphic inscription. Desire wants to be instantly and perfectly fulfilled, even though it could never be.

In yet another turn of irony, the tears aren't mingled with the lines of script contrived carefully by the devoted Troilus. They have ended up on the exterior of the letter's own "body"; they mingle not with the ink that has flowed from his stylus but with the wax pressed before Troilus's eager lips that smeared the tears on the unmarked parchment's outer shell. Like a face stained with the tears of its own eyes, a face harboring a verbal message inside that is as yet unspoken, unconveyed, and like the two young Trojans awaiting their first face-to-face encounter, embrace, and kiss, Troilus's letter awaits reading by Criseyde. The implicit conception of the letter as a tear-stained face may be the most remarkable "paraprosopopeia," to use J. Hillis Miller's coinage (228), in medieval literature.

Fuller semiotic importance of this deconstructive picture lies still further— at a point where its rhetorical and psychological features must intersect with historical imperatives about images of and beliefs about written documents themselves. Troilus's strangely "be-blotted" letter, a little body or face in allegorical terms, suffers its watery incursions from the outside when Troilus actually wets it. Has the damaging of the letter rendered it an artifact of graphic inscription, one intended to communicate mainly as a graphic object? Perhaps this letter-writing scene in *Troilus and Criseyde* tacitly calls up the historical experience of fourteenth-century documentary culture. Troilus's tear-blotted palimpsest—a concocted sign or figure of absolute, unmediated presence desired by him in its watery reinscription to shortcut the time of writing and reading—phenomenologically comes to resemble the water-blotted, damaged documents of antiquity obsessed over in the later Middle Ages and especially in the English fourteenth century. Blotted rolls and sealed letters of parchment serve in nascent fourteenth-century English historiography as tokens of temporal passage, of ruin or the danger of information's loss through time and neglect.

Exemplary of clerical culture's concern with damaged documents are the sophisticated ruminations of Chaucer's contemporary, Thomas Burton of Meaux, an English chronicler who despaired over the aging, neglect, and authenticity of the chronicle documents housed in his Yorkshire abbey. Thomas rescued many old manuscripts—house charters, contracts, licenses, histories, and chronicles—especially those defaced by rain that presumably penetrated the abbey's interiors from lack of building integrity and foundation leakage (Gransden 361). Water too that surged in the well-known inundations from the Humber and Hull Rivers, floods that Thomas well chronicled himself (Gransden 356, 358), must have found its way into the storage crypts—which were sometimes literally hidden holes in the broken or rotted walls and ceilings—used to store abbey rolls and codices (Gransden 362). From Thomas's chronicle, as recapitulated in Antonia Gransden's study, one gets a feel for dank interiors like those of Mervyn Peake's *Gormenghast*.

In suggesting that Thomas's observations might serve as a phenomenological and historical analogue to Troilus's tear-blotted document production, I underscore the value in showing how fourteenth-century anxieties over the authenticity, the integrity, the faithfulness of old and sealed documents that were possibly forged (Grandsen 351–52; Petrarch 621–25) or, more important at this juncture, that were blotched or defaced by water that had seeped in from their outsides, find recurring representation in historiography *and* in poetry. Pandarus, that arch mediator, prescribes the creation of a mediation-free signifying surface—one authenticated by the flows from the interior of the lover's body. This interior domain of the unconscious often contains what Derrida has termed the "crypt" of repressed or incorporated cognition: a submerged, hidden, and foreign body or site deep within the body of the desirer (Derrida, "Fors" xiv–xvii). Ironically—and felicitously—Thomas's time-ravaged texts reside in the crypts of English ecclesiastical and governmental buildings. The ruins of time transform the metaphysical dream of atemporal, pure presence, for hydraulic action wants to serve as the sign of instantaneous fluid contact and union. Such action serves as the historically describable means of separating a text's medial or material nature from its form and, in turn, from its content. If we can no longer read or read well enough to understand an inscription, time can be said to have infinitely distanced writing from its moment (and intent) of inscription. This transformation gets voiced by Shakespeare's icon of fourteenth-century English society, John of Gaunt, in *Richard II*: "England, bound in with the triumphant sea, / Whose rocky shore beats back the envious siege / Of watery Neptune, is now bound with shame, / With inky blots, and rotten parchment bonds" ([ed. Evans] 2.1.61–64). Shakespeare too deconstructs the levels of analogization conceivable among living landscape, collective people, or body politic; and representationally inscribed text that hopes to name the Edenic locus of happiness, or *jouissance*, but that succumbs to the ravages of physical and moral decay, of the ravages of time and fraud.

A deconstructive analysis of writing in *Troilus and Criseyde*, one that accommodates psychoanalytic models of mind and the textual tradition of love literature, must come to terms with corollary images of writing, time, and natural effect (rain and decay) to chart the parameters of fourteenth-century textual culture and to demonstrate the superior achievements of complex Chaucerian poetics. I therefore see the continued need in our training of scholars of medieval literature to sharpen the tools that the high theory of the 1970s, 1980s, and 1990s has left to us in a rich critical legacy.

NOTE

My thanks to John Leavey and Dean Swinford for suggestions and ideas.

A Primer for Fourteenth-Century English and Late Medieval English Manuscript Culture: Glossing Chaucer's "An ABC"

Martha Rust

This essay describes an exercise that introduces students to the medieval practice of glossing a text while providing them with an opportunity to engage and then build on a detailed study of Middle English grammar. To begin the exercise, each student receives one or more stanzas of "An ABC" printed double-spaced, in a relatively large font, on an otherwise blank sheet of paper.[1] In the first stage of the glossing process, students provide their stanzas with an interlinear gloss, labeling characteristic features of Middle English grammar and morphology; in two subsequent stages, students exchange their "manuscript pages," adding illustrations and specified kinds of commentary. In addition to facilitating an appreciation of the structure and theme of "An ABC"—one that is grounded in a secure grasp of the poem's linguistic features—this exercise facilitates a tangible though simulated encounter with medieval manuscript culture, that matrix of social and material practices that underwrote medieval literature.

Introducing "An ABC"

While this glossing exercise may be profitably conducted using a wide range of texts, certain links between Marian devotion and elementary medieval education make the particular activity of glossing "An ABC" especially appropriate. Before students embark on the glossing exercise itself, then, an account of these links is in order. I begin this explanation by showing students images of the opening pages of primers, the books used to provide late medieval children with instruction on the alphabet and on basic Christian prayers and doctrine.[2] Two characteristics of these pages are of particular import: first, the alphabet is bracketed by a cross at the beginning and an "amen" at the end; second, it is placed at the top of the page, where it takes visual precedence over the Lord's Prayer and the Hail Mary. With these two aspects of primer pages in view, students quickly discern the prayerlike quality the alphabet would have assumed for a novice medieval reader.[3]

Although such primer pages inscribe an unmistakable association between reciting the alphabet and saying one's prayers, a close alignment between elementary education and devotion to Mary in particular is revealed in the iconography of the education of the Virgin, which depicts a school-aged Mary being taught to read by her mother, Anne.[4] A look at images from this tradition makes way for the recognition that Chaucer's alphabetical prayer to the Virgin evokes the close ties between devotion to Mary and devotion to learning to read. In this way, adult medieval readers may have been drawn into Chaucer's alphabetical prayer to Mary through a memorial link, forged both by Marian iconography and by readers' elementary education, which connected meditation on the Virgin to the kind of focused concentration they once dedicated to learning their letters.

Having discussed the relations between Marian devotion and alphabetic literacy, I draw students' attention to their academic kinship with medieval students of "letters," for despite their temporal distance, our students and their medieval counterparts do share common ground. Both groups are students of a new language: medieval students would go on to read Latin after learning the alphabet; our students are just beginning to read Middle English. I then inform students that their assignment for "An ABC" features some of the strategies that medieval students of language and literature used in their study and, furthermore, that in the process of completing the assignment, they will create a "medieval" glossed page and explore some of the complexities of medieval textual transmission those pages engineered. This announcement prompts some expressions of doubt but also plenty of curiosity; the "ancient book"—full of inscriptions that seem as magical as they are indecipherable— has held a perennial allure both in literature and popular culture, and I draw on this appeal as I turn to a discussion of the medieval practice of glossing and introduce the first stage of this primer on fourteenth-century English, glossing Chaucer's "An ABC."

Three Layers of Glossing, Three Views of the Text

The definition of the word *gloss* in *The Oxford English Dictionary* provides an efficient means both to describe the practical range of medieval glossing and to give students an overview of the project they are to undertake. A gloss is defined as "a word inserted between the lines or in the margin as an explanatory equivalent of a foreign or otherwise difficult word in the text"; it is "a comment, explanation, interpretation"; and the word has "a sinister sense: A sophistical or disingenuous interpretation." Along with these definitions, I show students images of both interlinear and marginal glosses in all their enchanting variety.[5]

Students are now ready to try glossing themselves, beginning with one or more stanzas of Chaucer's "An ABC." For this initial step, I ask students to accomplish several tasks: to provide synonyms for unusual or archaic words that are not already glossed in our edition of the poem (for this task, I show students how to use the online *Middle English Dictionary*); to indicate the Middle English pronunciation of at least one line of their text (using any version of phonetic spelling they devise); and to label words and phrases that exemplify typical Middle English morphology or syntax. For instance, a good candidate for a syntactical gloss is the line "[v]enquisshed me hath my cruel adversaire" (8), which could be glossed with a *V* over "venquisshed," an *O* over "me" and an *S* over "adversaire," indicating that it is an example of the inversion of subject-verb-object word order that frequently appears in Middle English verse. Or, students might concentrate on verbs to find examples of Middle English morphology: for instance, the verbs "axeth" (12), "makest" (69), and "chasen" (15) could receive labels that indicate their person and number. This final task is the most challenging part of the first glossing assignment, but students also enjoy the opportunity to work closely with a short text.

Having had the chance to become familiar with some of the patterns of Middle English, students are well prepared to proceed to a consideration of their stanzas as poetry during the next class meeting. In the relatively small corpus of scholarly writing on Chaucer's "An ABC," it has been frequently observed that each stanza of the poem works as an independent unit; the poem reads as if it were "twenty-three different poems, each . . . a complete prayer to and praise of Mary" (Reiss 57). Since each student will have worked closely with one or two of these "different poems," this characteristic of "An ABC" may quickly become evident; asking students to discuss the imagistic or emotive center of gravity in their stanzas draws on their detailed study even as it calls forth a more holistic analysis and begins to shed light on the thematic threads—the law court, the speaker's sense of spiritual peril, the intercessory power of Mary—that string the stanzas together.

A consideration of the poem as a string of separate supplications makes way for the next layer of glossing: providing the poem with marginal commentaries and illustrations. To launch this stage of the project, I explain that after medieval students were able to construe Latin grammar and had a grasp of its basic vocabulary, they moved on to rhetorical analysis—a study that would be taken up in the margins of a text. I then explain that medieval students would also learn to decipher the textual commentary provided by images accompanying a text; here I offer examples of manuscript illustrations, including inhabited or historiated initials and border art.[6]

Students then exchange pages and are given the mission to supply their new texts with both analyses of its figures of speech and an illustration that brings out, elaborates on, or comments in some way on an aspect of the text.[7] Here I also take a moment to note that exchanging pages approximates the passing of books from reader to reader during the Middle Ages, one of the customs that led to medieval texts' accumulation of commentary, sometimes over the course of centuries. For this stage of the glossing project, students are also asked to write a short paragraph that explains their intentions with the illustrations they devise; this additional element of the assignment tips its weight away from decoration and toward an engagement with a genuinely medieval mode of reading, one in which seeing the page is as important as reading the text.[8]

For the final step in this project, students venture into the paradoxical effects of the activity of glossing, experimenting with the ways that marginal commentaries function to erode the authority of a text even as the very presence of a gloss signals a text's cultural value.[9] After exchanging pages once more, students work on three new kinds of commentary. First, I ask them to write a gloss that either identifies one of Chaucer's sources or allusions or notes a work that deals with related material (medieval or modern). Then I ask them to write a marginal paraphrase of a difficult passage either in the voice of the author or of another persona altogether. As Christopher Baswell has pointed out, this kind of commentary subtly undermines a text's authority by creating "a second, concurrent version of the *auctor* and his dramatic imagination, inscribed now parallel in the margin" ("Talking Back" 127). Finally, I ask them to write a commentary that disagrees (even disingenuously) with a previous commentary. Students are again asked to write a separate short paragraph that provides a critical account of the intended effects of their marginal commentaries.

On the day students turn in their well-filled manuscript pages, they are intrigued by the diversity of voices that now occupy their pages, and many are curious about what has become of pages they worked on at earlier points in the process. Giving students a chance to view all the pages—by spreading them out on desks or taping them to the walls for a brief gallery effect— makes way for a final discussion of the poem and of students' experiences with this simulated version of manuscript culture.

By the time students have completed this glossing project, they will have had a chance to explore Chaucer's "An ABC" in great detail and will have had a primer on several other topics pertinent to a study of Chaucer and Middle English. By means of their interlinear glosses, students are introduced not only to the characteristics of Middle English but also—through their use of the *Middle English Dictionary*—to an important tool for further linguistic analysis. By way of their work with images and figures of speech in the second glossing campaign, they are alert to the issue of style—as the Franklin puts it, the "[c]olours of rethoryk" (5.726)—frequently raised in Chaucer's work, and they have a sympathetic patience with the ambiguity of the word *portreye* in Middle English—forever oscillating between drawing and writing. All their glossing work prepares them well for later encounters in Middle English texts with the issue of how glossing possibly interferes with textual interpretation and transmission. And last, they have a sure sense of the medieval manuscript page as a complex and multidimensional site where the sense of a text is perpetually in play.

NOTES

[1]I print stanzas on letter-size paper and then photocopy them centered onto 11-by-17-inch paper.

²For a description of primer alphabets, see Orme, *English Schools* 60–62 and *Medieval Children* 246–51; for images of primer alphabets, see Wieck (pl. 3); Wolpe (pls. 18–22); and New York, Columbia University, Rare Books and Manuscripts Library, MS Plimpton 258, folio 1. Plimpton 258 is reproduced in *Digital Scriptorium* (http://sunsite.berkeley.edu/scriptorium). See Paul Acker for a complete transcription of the primer text in Plimpton 258.

³For further discussion of the religious connotations of the alphabet in primers, see Phillips, "Chaucer and Deguileville" 8; Denley 226; and Pace, "Adorned" 89.

⁴For overviews and reproductions of images of this tradition, see Scase; Sheingorn. See also Bell (pl. 5).

⁵For numerous examples of interlinear glosses, see Backhouse. Many examples of marginal commentaries may be found in *Digital Scriptorium* by searching in the image caption field (under "text search terms") using the terms *gloss* or *commentary*.

⁶For examples of decorated letters, see Alexander; for examples of border illustrations, see Hamel; Wieck; Camille; Carruthers (pls. 20–28); and Randall.

⁷For thorough explanations of rhetorical figures of speech, students may be referred to Corbett and Connors (377–411) or to Burton.

⁸See Driver for a recent discussion of this mode of reading. I stress that artistic skill is not required for students' illustrations; even pasted-on cutouts are perfectly welcome. My inspiration for the commentary component of this assignment comes from R. Pope's discussion of "rewriting" assignments.

⁹For further discussion of these processes, see Baswell, "Talking Back"; and Irvine.

Two Forms, Two Poetic Stages, Developing Voices: *The Romaunt of the Rose* and *The Parliament of Fowls*

Alan T. Gaylord

This essay introduces the subject of Chaucerian prosody as it may be applied by beginning students to the whole task of hearing and understanding Chaucer's poetry. I take as my examples just two works—the beginning of his translation of *Le roman de la rose* (*Romaunt*, fragment A), and *The Parliament of Fowls*. A full discussion of the shorter works and *Troilus and Criseyde* from the point of view of prosodic criticism may be consulted in my two-part study *I. Out Loud with Chaucer's Shorter Poems: Adventures in Prosodic Criticism*, and *II. Out Loud with* Troilus and Criseyde *and* The Legend of Good Women: *Adventures in Prosodic Criticism*. This study includes illustrative readings on CD of most of the texts discussed here, and many more.

My discussion, then, explores how a reader may imagine the sound of the poetry and illustrates the shape of the verse in a developmental context: it concentrates here on new forms Chaucer worked with, first as a translator and then, as one might say, a "great" translator, moving at his own speed and speaking in his own voice. (For a practical guide to teaching students to pronounce Middle English, see my appendix, at the end of this volume).

Romaunt of the Rose

Fragment A is a translation of the beginning of *Le roman de la rose* from the part that was written by Guillaume de Lorris; the background for the authorship and the original context of the thirteenth-century poem can be reviewed in the notes to the *Romaunt* in the Benson *Riverside*. We don't learn the first author's name until Jean de Meun identifies himself as the continuator, shortly after his own part begins, and tells us just where Guillaume had stopped. Fascinating as the relation may be between these two parts, it is not our business here. The three fragments that have been included as Chaucer or Chaucerian still do not include the whole poem. Given that only fragment A of the *Romaunt* is taken as probably authentic by most scholars, it is clear that spending time on the prosody of the other two fragments would not be profitable. But there remain some places in A that help define Chaucer's verse as the poet begins to develop it through early acts of translation. Riming in octosyllabics, both a monument to the French-based linguistic culture in which Chaucer was nurtured and the practice in which he learned how to make the kind of English verses he found most congenial, becomes the portal through which all subsequent inquiry must pass.

My method is to move through a series of passages chosen for their prosodic interest, aiming to build up a sense of Chaucer's practice as he translated from the French into his own tongue and idiom.

Lines 1–40

The beginning is about dreams and their truth or falsity. Here the language is Latinate in form: "apparaunt" (5), "authour" (7), "avysioun" (9), "signi-fiaunce" (16), not to mention the citation of Macrobius (7). Yet even at the start, the carrying language, so to speak, is simple and colloquial, and this should not be missed. The prosody enables a certain kind of talking, absorbing some technical words without fully entering the register of science; thus in lines 11–20 the basic vocabulary is English, with only a few recent loanwords like "nycete" (12) from French. The structure is argument, a mode that will become dominant as soon as the personifications in the allegory begin to "speke their resouns." Prosodically, it is important to note that lines like these are not cramped into distichs but unfold in spoken periods or brief paragraphs, flowing over line ends toward a kind of colloquial syllogism (esp. lines 15–20).

The poet continues the traditional rhetoric of courtly oral entertainment—on the one hand speaking as if his audience is sitting before him and will hear and on the other alluding to his work as something he has written down ("this book, which is here" [37]), something that will resemble a work of Ovid's, an *auctor* studied in the universities. For Guillaume's generic word, "romanz," which does not necessarily imply a bound volume of writing, Chaucer substi-tutes "this book" (37). In short, Chaucer further shapes the French to project an image of a poet who wishes to please an audience to whom he reads a poem about love out of a book that lies before him. This is the same image that will be adopted and so richly developed in *Troilus and Criseyde*. I sum it up as a "bookish orality," a literary performance of crafted speech.

Lines 531–84

The Dreamer is now described as he comes upon the first of those personi-fications he will meet inside the garden, Idleness. Ending with "Ther nys a fairer nekke, iwys, / To fele how smothe and softe it is" (555–56), the poetry has invaded the space of social propriety to get up close—not only smelling the sweet breath of this languorous maiden but in effect reaching out to touch the fair flesh. The prosody helps construct this erotic tactility, adding the alliteration to enhance the voluptuous consonance of the inter- and labioden-tals. The effect is cousin to the lip-smacking description of Alysoun by the Miller in his tale.

Lines 669–84

The Dreamer passes over the threshold and looks and listens with wonder. Here is a place where class recitation can experiment with ambiguous tones.

These birds are first described as angelic, and then as sirenic. Does the Dreamer recognize this? Is there a tension between the naive, uncritical enthusiasm of the youth, and the older voice of experience? It will not be easy to convey in an out-loud reading a tone of naïveté, on the one hand, and moral irony, on the other! If conveying such tones appears not simply difficult but impossible (but let everyone try), the point about the rational imagination having to sort out these oral possibilities in the same manner as a reader "holding the book" is further demonstrated.

Lines 729–811

Many students are intrigued to learn that before a carol was a Christmas carol it was a "karole" (744), a courtly dance and erotic entertainment. Note how the lines move now with a sort of breathlessness, with the teasing enjambment, "whan they were / Togidre almost" (785–86). It is rare to have a verb complement split between lines, but the sly "almost" hurries us along, hungry for more details as we reach the run-ons of "they threwe yfere / Her mouthis so, that thorough her play / It semed as they kiste alway" (786–88). The chiaroscuro here functions to prevent our knowing whether "play" is a trick of pretend or a startling erotic move.

Lines 1449–1706

This passage brings the Dreamer to the Well of Narcissus and thence to the "knoppe" (1702), the rosebud he will seek to gather—at which point fragment A comes to an end. The narrative in this passage is stylistically brilliant, and it is full of changes in tone that will puzzle and/or delight the reader.

As the Dreamer continues into the garden, he is stalked by the God of Love, arrows at the ready. The voluptuousness of this garden of delights is continuously illustrated, from the pleasant "shadiness" of the groves to the amatory comfort of the grass and the company of rabbits, known for their sexual urgency. And then he comes to stand before a "welle" with the inscription, "Here starf the fayre Narcisus" (1468).

We now have a passage of Franco-Ovidian poetry, structured to move through the story of Narcissus as easy as running water. Readers reading outloud should practice reciting fluently the extended sentences of 1474–80 and 1489–98, noting especially the marked parataxis and syntactical expansion of the latter passage. This is the kind of storytelling that octosyllabic couplets are particularly designed for.

The narrator tells us that we are going to learn something from him (1626–34); indeed, somewhat mysteriously, the promise to "expound the mystery" is woven through the texture of fragment A, and Jean de Meun will continue the promise of explication. Yet in neither part of *The Romaunt of the Rose* is there any marked authorial exegesis. We can't settle the matter in the limits of fragment A, but we can see clearly enough that the authorial tease of deferred clarification is part of a thickening of the bookishness of the narrative at this point.

One will need to reflect on the last major shift in tone. Surprisingly, the narrator says: "That mirrour hath me now entriked. / But hadde I first knowen in my wit / The vertu and [the] strengthe of it, / I nolde not have mused there" (1642–45). Is this true self-knowledge (though, as usual, too late) speaking here, or just chagrin of Elde? Who is self-knowing, the young "playing" in the shadows or the adults standing in the light of day? The question points toward the approaching encounter with Reason and the Lover's responses to her, not to mention the responses of other friends of court who will approach and argue their positions.

The Lover has seen in the well an image reflected by the marvelous crystals of "a roser chargid full of rosis" (1651). The sight transforms the meanderer into a pluckster, one with a passion, a "rage," to go forward, to inhale "the savour of the rose swote" and to prepare to seize the shining red rosebud that most appeals to him. He is about to begin, or to have begun for him, his education in the art of love.

The Parliament of Fowls

The new poetic form must be examined for a proper beginning. What sort of poetic engine is this new combination of rimes and lines? And what sort of opportunities did it offer Chaucer? Chaucer would have found expanding his poetry into stanzas appealing, both for what stanzas offered structurally and for what their previous literary associations would have been. They offered the vernacular poet something that was "classic" in substance, something with more gravitas than what he had essayed to that point. This new field of play would allow him to enter with fairly stately pace and yet exit with more energetic and various rhythms, with at once greater vernacular dissonance and more-cunning thematic coherence than before. He grew further into his art.

The stanza is a container, "a little room" (one of its original Italian meanings), in which a complete idea is packed. This sense of stanza is especially evident in the opening of the poem, which plays out one continuous sentence in seven lines, a single utterance that sways with supple syntax toward closure.

The rime scheme is one that must have ticked and buzzed in Chaucer's head all through the days of his "middle period," because he went on to write many stanzas with *ababbcc*. Students assume this scheme shouldn't be too hard to write. Having two extra syllables in each line helps make it less difficult than it could be, but, to disabuse students of the idea this is an easy rhyme scheme, it's a good idea at some point early on to have the class try their hand at building their own stanzas. Rime is always some kind of ordering device. Looking at *ababbcc*, one might expect that the first four lines develop a thought, rounded off with the first couplet, and that the second couplet serves as a related generalization, not unlike the function of the couplet in so many of the Shakespearean sonnets. The stanza, in other words, is built and armed for argument; it is an engine for *sentence*. This is not a form for light work.

What Chaucer does in *The Parliament of Fowls*, however, is to play with the stanza and its internal organizations. The material he treats is suited in several ways for stanza organization. The encounter with Affrike deals with a book, its summary, and its loftiest thoughts; the entrance into the garden deals with erotic *ekphrasis*, set pieces of description adapted from Boccaccio (who Chaucer is now reading avidly); the parliament itself deals with groups or sets of birds who make formal (or very informal!) speeches.

It needs to be said that "playing" is exactly what Chaucer is doing, in several senses. It is noteworthy that, of his first five stanzas, each has a different syntactic ordering. Such variety does not testify to a hand that knows exactly what it wants for best effect: as an example of forcing or stretching to the utmost, see the stanza beginning with line 71. Milton might have liked how the form is distended so far that it is very little different from prose. The *sentence* of the stanza is not treated ironically and may well be the open statement closest to Chaucer's heart, but it could not be said that the form of the stanza enhances the prose sense with much poetry. On the other hand, compare the lines later in the poem beginning with line 561. By now Chaucer's playing has brought him a sense of ease. Logic and rhetoric are blended and proceed with humorous effect.

This point invites transition to a second sense of "playing" with the form, for it should always be kept in mind that Chaucer is not doing crossword puzzles or working out how to stuff a heap of statements into his lines and rime scheme. He wants to have the stanza enhance his poetry, wants it to seem necessary and inevitable. The setting—the fitting and the fit (the dancer and the dance?)—should have a certain radiance.

We have begun with prosodic criticism's· examination of the new stanza. What can be said, now, for the bearing of our examination on overall interpretation? Recall my examination of the stanza of heavenly advice (71–77) and how its form was described as distended so far that it is very little different from prose. The exhortations of Affrike are sublime and would once have been clothed in Ciceronian eloquence. The eloquence is not obliterated in Chaucer's stanzas, but it rests uneasy in his prosody, not quite set in place. Recall further that the later stanza examined above was from the debate of the birds (561–67) and moved with animated confidence as the goose spoke her "wisdom." One could say that common profit seems a distant goal at this point, which is part of the problem facing this assembly; but for our purposes, one can fittingly say that the "radiance" these best of lines can display is that of eloquence.

If there is a problem here, it lies in the strategy Chaucer is working out for delivering, obscuring, hiding, and radiantly exposing his meanings. But I am not trying to describe a tormented poet; Chaucer frequently describes himself as confused, anxious, and unfulfilled, and yet the problematics of his prosody bear in various measure the seal of his approval—signs that he enjoyed what he was doing. This is serious play, and (quoting Robert Frost) "for mortal stakes"—but it is play all the same.

Eloquence in the Christian tradition (following at once Quintilian, Cicero, and Augustine) was defined as combining the craft of rhetoric with moral integrity; it was a means to persuade through oratory (in the broadest sense) the infected will of humanity. I once defined prosody as "that which moves, and in moving moves us" (Gaylord, "Scanning" 22), and there the problem lies. If Chaucer intends to instruct through delighting and with moral eloquence, some of the masters he purports to serve or seems to accept without critical reservation will need to be set into some order other than indiscriminate approval. How to develop a prosody that enables such a program? And how to "move" the reader/hearer? A demonstration may be found in the stanza beginning at line 491. The noble birds have spoken, presumably with avian eloquence (except no one seems to be persuaded) and in the formulaic diction of love lyrics—each one proffering the reddest and laciest of valentines to the beloved. The response? "Com of!" The mask of nobility has been shattered with that rude shout. What is deflated, then, is the assumption that the highborn know best and can act best. "Ye wol us shende!"

Chaucer here does three things: the loud interruption provides a surprise and relief from the swooning solemnities of the preceding; the structure of the stanza retains a core of logic, for all the noisy outrage; and the theme of confusion and irresolution is continued, with a new turn. The air is now filled with the earnest sound of individual voices, speaking their piece within an approximation of parliamentary order, but speaking from the heart in animated and colloquial fashion.

It turns out the decasyllabic line is not here to give a more extended version of what octosyllabics had done; instead, it has room for speech, for talking, for shouting, for silly statements, for insults. So might it not be that Chaucer's prosodic program in this poem, working with a new stanza, would be to discover the unfinished job of deflation—which is to say, the job of stimulating the reader to a new condition of wakeful thoughtfulness (almost always in the mode of apparently light-hearted humor) based on the discovery of contradictions and ambiguities salted into the text and leading toward a critical awareness of the cultural implications of the discourses the poem has passed through? Playing within the new stanza, the poet discovers a new dimension of eloquence, one in which traditional eloquence is turned inside out and heightened speech and formal rhetoric are (largely) displaced by "com of!" and "kek kek! kokkow! quek quek!"

"In Forme of Speche Is Chaunge": Introducing Students to Chaucer's Middle English

Barbara Stevenson

As Chaucer commits his *Troilus and Criseyde* to posterity, he notes that words become "nyce and straunge" (2.24) over time, so he prays on his poem's behalf "that non miswryte the" (5.1795). Given the linguistic anxieties Chaucer expresses in *Troilus and Criseyde*, one wonders what his reaction would be to the various modern translations of his works. Many Chaucer professors are horrified by these "trots," as evidenced by the professors surveyed in *Approaches to Teaching Chaucer's* Canterbury Tales (Gibaldi 10). Teachers researching effective ways to encourage students to put down those trots and pick up *The Riverside Chaucer* will find more sources at their disposal than were available in 1980, when *Approaches to Teaching Chaucer's* Canterbury Tales was published. Now teachers have David Burnley's *A Guide to Chaucer's Language*, Arthur Wayne Glowka's *A Guide to Chaucer's Meter*, and the peer-reviewed journal *Studies in Medieval and Renaissance Teaching*, as well as many other pedagogical resources. However, most scholarship of teaching on medieval studies lacks a grounding in proven pedagogical theory and draws instead on literary criticism. The instructor looking to introduce students to the unfamiliar language of Middle English and medieval poetics must turn to the pedagogy of other fields, notably composition and rhetoric.

In class, I begin with *The Book of the Duchess* as the introduction to Chaucer's Middle English. This poem marks the beginning of Chaucer's success as an author, just as the students are at the beginning of their knowledge of his literature, and it provides an opportunity to present students to major Chaucerian discussion topics that will dominate the course, such as the nature of love. Furthermore, chances are great that this work is entirely new to the students. If I used The General Prologue to *The Canterbury Tales*, many English majors would have already studied it in high school or in an English literature survey. Modern English versions of *The Canterbury Tales* abound, so students might have of one of them. But few students seek out the Penguin edition of the love visions or download one of the translations of *The Book of the Duchess* now available over the Internet. Thus, with *The Book of the Duchess*, students are less likely to rely on a translation to avoid the Middle English.

But what can be done to overcome the "cognitive dissonance" that readers feel when they encounter Middle English for the first time and that sends students to modern renditions? If one were to read the scholarship available on the topic or to quiz colleagues at conferences, one would find that a common method of teaching Middle English is to require students to recite a passage, most often the opening lines of The General Prologue. As an assignment, it does nothing to encourage students to read Middle English, aside from the designated lines. Furthermore, this assignment is product-oriented.

In the 1960s, James Britton and other British teachers began exploring pedagogies to teach effective writing to students, who often were unfamiliar with Standard English and academic genres of composition. This research gave rise to what Maxine Hairston labeled a "paradigm shift" (qtd. in Perl xv) in American universities during the 1970s, when such influential books as Peter Elbow's *Writing without Teachers* were published. The resultant "process method" has become a staple in teaching composition. In this method, students begin with an experimental stage of brainstorming and inventing ideas, move on to writing and revising stages in which peer groups work with one another, and end with the finished product. Learning language is now recognized as an active process, recursive as opposed to linear, that takes place in a social setting as opposed to a solitary one; hence, pedagogy requires careful sequencing of collaborative activities involving peers as well as the instructor.[1]

Techniques from composition and rhetoric research are applicable to the Chaucer classroom, for, like the composition teacher, the teacher of Middle English is faced with the difficulty of making students versant in a dialect and in genres unfamiliar to them. So, rather than product-based assignments, I first implement process-based assignments.

Most important, students must believe that reading Chaucer in Middle English—aloud, no less—is important to understanding his literature. Teachers of Middle English can adapt valuable practices from research into theories of literacies, including hypertext and electronic literacy. For example, I explain to students that Chaucer was a poet who was alive to the sounds of language and that in manuscript culture orality was still central, unlike the focus in our print age on silent reading. I show students the famous image of Chaucer reading aloud that appears in the frontispiece of the Cambridge, Corpus Christi College MS 61 edition of *Troilus and Criseyde* and point out that perhaps Chaucer created *The Book of the Duchess* as part of a "later and highly elaborate annual commemoration" service for Blanche, John of Gaunt's deceased wife (Wilcockson, qtd. in *Riverside* 329).

Hypertext literacy theorists establish parallels between medieval manuscripts and current multimedia; both can employ a synthesis of word, image and icon, and sound. Contrasting pages from a facsimile of the Ellesmere manuscript with the students' own *Riverside Chaucer* edition reinforces the point, as does demonstrating the hypertext edition of *The Book of the Duchess* (McGillivray). The images from this edition are not as vivid as those in the Ellesmere, but the students can hear Chaucer's poem read aloud, illuminating the importance of sound to medieval poetry.

As the class examines the opening lines of *The Book of the Duchess*, we note spelling inconsistencies, such as *sleep* being spelled "slepe" (3) and "slep"

(5). The history of literacy explains this phenomenon: Chaucer and his scribes would have written more phonetically than we do with our standardized spellings; thus spelling is erratic and sounding out words helps—the spelling may be unfamiliar although the word itself is not. Therefore reading aloud can be important for comprehending Chaucer's vocabulary, strange as it may seem to the silent reader of the print era.

To teach students Middle English pronunciation, I distribute a copy of John Gardner's appendix on the pronunciation of Chaucer's Middle English from his book *The Life and Times of Chaucer*. *The Riverside Chaucer* charts pronunciation with International Phonetic Alphabet (IPA) values (xxxii). If students have not had a prior course in the history of the English language or in linguistics, then the professor must teach students IPA—a lengthy lesson that reduces the amount of time available for the discussion of literature—or else use a guide like Gardner's. Gardner circumvents linguistic terminology by illustrating sounds through Modern English words: "Pronounce vowels like vowels in modern European languages, especially French, German, or Italian (but resist the temptation to drag in the consonant sounds of those languages)" (315–16).

At the start of the semester, the pedagogy is teacher-centered and lecture-based, but I quickly move to reading Middle English without teachers. English composition theorists favor peer group work as a key component in mastering language skills, for language is a social act and thus better understood in a group situation. I start the assignment by modeling what I would like the groups to do. So for pronunciation, I read aloud portions from the poem's opening (or, if in a room with appropriate technology, play lines from *The Book of the Duchess* hypertext edition) and ask the students to repeat the words after me. Then, smaller groups of students read their assigned lines aloud to the class.

At the beginning of the semester, I do not call on students to read aloud, to avoid the foreign-language fear factor, the common fear among students that learning to read Middle English will be much like learning to speak a foreign language. The point I stress to students is that Chaucer's language is *their* language, not a foreign one; Middle English is an archaic dialect, with pronunciations that experts themselves cannot agree on, but it is English nonetheless. At first I read aloud (or play a sound file). Next, students read Middle English as a whole class and then as a subdivided group. It is not until much later in the semester that they are expected to read alone.

After giving an introduction to *The Book of the Duchess* and discussing and reading Chaucer's language, I model the upcoming assignment by doing a word-by-word rendering into Modern English of the opening lines from *The Book of the Duchess*, demonstrating the use of *The Riverside Chaucer*'s footnotes and glossaries. Since a word-by-word rendition can be terribly time consuming, we cannot in class do the whole work. Thus, for the rest of the first-person narrator's opening, I provide a paraphrased summary.

The remainder of the poem is subdivided according to the sections outlined in Robert Jordan's structural analysis of the poem ("Compositional Structure" 103–05) and assigned to groups of students who work together in class to summarize and to translate some passages word by word. The groups record the problems they encounter in reading, and I meet with each group to resolve the problems. Then each group reports its answers to the entire class. For instance, a group may be assigned lines 291–343, the section Jordan describes as "Dream begins. Description of dreamer's surroundings. 291–320—Auditory. 321–343—Visual" (104). That group reads the first sentence of lines 291–97 in Middle English and gives its word-by-word rendering:

> Thus I thought that it was May,
> And in the dawn I lay,
> (Thus I dreamed) in my bed naked
> And looked up, for I was waked
> By many small birds [i.e., fowls in a great heap]
> That had startled me out of my sleep
> Because of the sweet noise of their song.

For the remainder of the section, they give a synopsis of the birds' singing in harmony; of the chamber filled with glass windows depicting scenes from the story of Troy and walls painted with the *Roman de la rose*; and, for the ending, of a description of the beautiful, sunny day. The group members then present any particular problems they had, such as the confusion over the "her" in line 297 that means "their" in Modern English, an observation that triggers a discussion of the similarities and differences between Middle and Modern English pronouns. The activity focuses on the act of reading and understanding Middle English as opposed to producing an accurate translation. As students express in their evaluations, they favor my "gentle" and "nonthreatening" approach to Middle English.

Later, as we approach *The Canterbury Tales*, I have students translate a few lines on their own and then compare their translation with another one. Students may already own a translation or they can download one from the Internet. I then ask them to bring the translations to class for discussion. In groups they compare and contrast their findings and present their conclusions to the rest of the class. Peter Beidler discusses a similar exercise in his article "Chaucer and the Trots: What to Do about Those Modern English Translations," in which he illustrates inadequacies of many published translations—for example, Nevill Coghill has "the showers do the piercing," whereas Chaucer has "the personified April who pierces the dryness of March with his showers" (Beidler 291). As we discuss the students' results, I read lines aloud and have the groups read aloud as well; I also encourage individual students to read aloud words or lines in Middle English that they have questions or comments about. Some prefer their own translations, and most decide that they could read just as well on their own, without the modern rendition. Students observe that when first confronted with Shakespeare's language, they were intimidated, but that by college they had become comfortable with his archaic language; the same situation now applies to Chaucer.

Eventually, though, process must be put aside, and students must produce work that will be graded. Each student does his or her own reading of a passage aloud to the class as part of an oral presentation on a tale. To prepare for their oral presentations, some students listen to Chaucer Studio tapes and others practice with me in my office, whereas most are ready to read on their own with no assistance. My tests are structured in the same way: students write word-by-word Modern English versions of quotations, followed by an analysis that connects the quotation to the themes, writing styles, and so forth that we have been discussing in class.

In short, I take an incremental approach: I do reading and translation, then ask students to work in groups, then to read aloud on their own outside class for a grade, and finally to read in class for tests. My approach combines theories and pedagogies related to language, which are then applied to Chaucer's Middle English. As scholars, we are aware how literary theory informs medieval texts, and ideally as teachers we should be just as aware how pedagogical theory can inform classroom practices.

NOTE

[1]See both Harris and Perl for historical overviews of teaching composition and rhetoric, and Jost on active learning.

Visual Approaches to Chaucer

Glenn Davis

Instructors who want to offer their students images to illustrate a cultural context for Chaucer's *Canterbury Tales* can choose from a variety of easily accessible sources. Chaucer's pilgrims have captured the visual imaginations of artists from just after the poet's own time up through the present, resulting in a wealth of imagery directly associated with the *Tales*. Yet not all of Chaucer's works are so well represented. The teacher of *Troilus and Criseyde* and the shorter poems does not have as many immediately attractive options: like many late-fourteenth- and early-fifteenth-century English manuscripts, the manuscripts containing these poems, with the notable exception of Cambridge, Corpus Christi College MS 61, do not provide much in the way of illumination or miniature. Nor have works like *The House of Fame*, *The Book of the Duchess*, or *Troilus and Criseyde* found their way as smoothly into modern popular culture. This essay first explores the frontispiece of the Corpus Christi manuscript, and then lists other relevant visual resources. In doing so, it demonstrates how visual media can enhance students' experience with medieval literature by asking them to consider the relevance of visual formulations of Chaucer and his texts—and visual formulations of other aspects of late medieval culture—for their original audiences. It also enhances students' personal constructions of meaning through the interpretation of signs, texts, and images.

Cambridge, Corpus Christi College MS 61, which dates to the early fifteenth century, contains only *Troilus and Criseyde*; its magnificently painted frontispiece suggests that it was originally intended to be used as a presentation manuscript (Hardman 52). The frontispiece becomes a useful tool for introducing visuality into the Chaucer classroom, providing an opportunity for students to contemplate important questions about the relations between word and image, as well as between image and reality. Additionally, it underscores the importance of considering exigencies of manuscript production when studying the composition and reception of medieval literature.

The frontispiece—a rare feature for a manuscript produced at this time in England—is divided diagonally into two primary sections: the upper register depicts a noble procession leaving a castle, apparently to meet another equally noble group; the lower register illustrates an outdoor recital scene in which a bearded speaker standing at a lectern or pulpit addresses an assembled company of well-dressed men and women paying varying degrees of attention to the speech (*Troilus* 15–23).

The frontispiece raises a number of interesting and useful questions about the function of manuscript illumination and about what it can—and what it cannot—tell us about the relation between image and text. The initial questions that students viewing the frontispiece are likely to ask are journalistic: who? what? when? where? why? The first four of these questions reflect a desire to identify elements of the image's composition and situate them historically; the last is concerned with its cultural relevance and function. A look at the scholarship on the frontispiece demonstrates that early critics were eager—perhaps too eager—to explore the first four to the exclusion of the fifth. Margaret Galway, for example, identifies the characters in the lower register as members of Richard II's court and the recital scene as representing an actual historical event: the reading of Chaucer's new poem (161–77). Galway's assessment of the image sought to establish historical reality by identifying Chaucer as a court poet. This identification led to a series of concomitant interpretations about the character of his audience that for some time went unchallenged.

Yet to complicate these basic journalistic questions, as critics have done in response to Galway's totalizing theory and as more has been learned about the international character of English manuscript illumination in the fifteenth century, opens up the possible function of the image, allowing students to consider the broader cultural relevance of the miniature. And in turn, one hopes, it also encourages them to consider the broader cultural relevance of manuscript illustrations in general. Derek Pearsall, for example, works against Galway's method and provides a reason why achieving a concrete, historical understanding of an image's meaning and function is not only impossible but also undesirable:

> Nor is such speculation necessary, for once the situation is seen in terms of patterns of manuscript production and demand, and the pressure towards historical authentication removed, the picture can be recognized as fully explicable from within the poem. In other words, it represents as a reality the myth of delivery that Chaucer cultivates so assiduously in the poem, with his references to "al this compaignye" of lovers "in this place." (*"Troilus* Frontispiece" 70)

Moving beyond the quest for historical verification can lead students to a more interesting and potentially fruitful set of questions about manuscript production and manuscript culture, and also about ways that the image is intimately connected with the text it prefaces.

Another way to stimulate student interest in the frontispiece, especially the imagery of the lower register, is to situate it iconographically. A close look at the image reveals that there is no visible manuscript on Chaucer's lectern, a fact that calls into question Galway's interpretation of the speaker as court poet. Elizabeth Salter and Derek Pearsall comment on the iconographic significance of this image, identifying the author figure as a preacher:

If we now ask, more particularly, why the choice of composition was made [to depict the figure as a preacher], we find that the illustrator of such a manuscript, or the supervisor who gave him his instructions, or the patron who dealt with both, had a number of options, a number of iconographic models for frontispiece author portrayal. (Salter and Pearsall 115)

These options include the author as teacher, reader, dreamer, reporter, and protagonist. What are the interpretive consequences of the illustrator's choice? How would selection of a different option have changed the image's function? This exercise also provides an opportunity to situate the frontispiece imagery in its international context: Salter and Pearsall reproduce images from continental manuscripts that depict several of the options available to the illustrator of Corpus Christi 61 (109–22; see also Pearsall and Zeeman, pls. 10–18d).

Fortunately, the small amount of manuscript imagery directly related to *Troilus and Criseyde* and the shorter poems can be easily supplemented by the wealth of relevant visual material made available in print and Internet sources. And while the material found in these sources may not have much immediately to do with Chaucer's poetry, it can nonetheless help students consider what images might have been familiar to Chaucer and his contemporary audience. From there, students can contemplate connections between the visual and the textual. Such imagery provides students at all levels with a concrete picture of the social, economic, artistic, religious, and domestic spheres of the medieval world.

The Flowering of the Middle Ages, edited by Joan Evans, contains an extensive collection of visual images. This quarto-sized volume, which offers a mixture of full-color and black-and-white plates and illustrations, is divided into chapters that explore visual aspects of medieval architecture, religious life, education, industry and economy, and life in the court. While Evans and her contributors focus primarily on images from Insular and continental European sources, they succeed in offering a global perspective as well, providing images from around the medieval world. Derek Brewer's *Chaucer and His World* likewise presents a large number of images documenting a wide range of subjects. Most of the imagery is in black and white, though there are a total of fifteen full-color plates, including a fine reproduction of the *Troilus and Criseyde* frontispiece. The images include manuscript illuminations; landscapes and architectural features that Chaucer and his contemporaries might have witnessed; and products of artistry, including sculpture, woodcuts, tapestries, and textiles. The volume is organized according to generalizations based on various stages of Chaucer's life and aspects of his presumed experience; chapter titles include "A Fourteenth-Century Childhood" and "London, Flower of Cities All."

Richard Loomis has assembled a picture book titled *A Mirror of Chaucer's*

World, which, like Brewer's, provides images of medieval art, architecture, and manuscript illumination that relate specifically to Chaucer's life and works. Unlike Brewer, however, Loomis selects moments in Chaucer's poetry, including *Troilus and Criseyde*, *The Parliament of Fowls*, *The Romaunt of the Rose*, and *The Legend of Good Women*, that are then paired with relevant images. Each pairing is accompanied by a brief discussion of the nature of the link. Another resource is Maurice Hussey's *Chaucer's World: A Pictorial Companion*. While most images in this volume are associated directly with *The Canterbury Tales*, instructors may still find it a useful tool for providing general background information on Chaucer's England, similar to that found in Evans's and Brewer's books. The last print source I discuss here is the most recent: Matthew Boyd Goldie devotes a chapter in *Middle English Literature: A Historical Sourcebook* to medieval manuscript imagery. Each of the twelve black-and-white plates he includes, ranging from the Thomas Hoccleve portrait of Chaucer in *The Regiment of Princes* to a miniature from the Lovell Lectionary, is accompanied by a brief discussion of the image's provenance and the history of its manuscript.

Medieval images proliferate on the World Wide Web as well. There are literally hundreds of Internet sources that offer images associated with all aspects of medieval culture, many of them created and maintained by individuals, both academics and amateurs, with an interest in the Middle Ages. Rather than provide a lengthy list of these sites, I will discuss a small number that seem most useful.

The *Luminarium* Web site offers sixteen images directly related to Chaucer and his works and provides links to a much larger collection of general medieval imagery in categories such as "Medieval Manuscripts and Illuminations," "Medieval Art," "Medieval Architecture," and "Medieval Costume" (www.luminarium.org). *Early Manuscripts at Oxford University* provides complete and partial facsimiles of over eighty manuscripts held by Oxford colleges and the Bodleian Library (http://image.ox.ac.uk). The Bodleian Library's section of the Web site contains hundreds of high-quality pictures of European manuscripts from the eleventh century through the end of the fifteenth. The Web site for The Cloisters, the medieval art museum affiliated with New York's Metropolitan Museum of Art, offers fifty high-quality digital images of pieces in their collection, accessible from the Metropolitan's Web site (www .metmuseum.org). The images include metalwork dating from the late Iron Age through the fifteenth century, later medieval tapestry, woodwork, stonework, and stained glass. The Metropolitan Museum's main Web site also offers a wide range of medieval images.

Bringing images from these sources into the classroom can help students move beyond a solely textual understanding of Chaucer's lesser-taught works to a richer interpretive space that acknowledges those works' larger cultural contexts. Reading from a clean, professionally edited version of a poem makes it easy for students to forget the circumstances of its original composition, that it was part of a living, changing culture that has left other witnesses beside the textual. Students examining these images have little choice but to confront the complicated world of the Middle Ages, a realization that in turn can help improve the quality of their literary interpretations.

Teaching Chaucer without (or with) Translations: An Introduction to Othon de Grandson's "Les cinq balades ensuivans" and Chaucer's "The Complaint of Venus"

Jean-François Kosta-Théfaine

The French poets allowed Chaucer to learn about his own poetic art for a variety of reasons, including their erudition and use of technical and rhetorical conventions. My purpose in this essay is to give an introduction to the relationship between the Savoyard Othon de Grandson's "Les cinq balades ensuivans" and Chaucer's "The Complaint of Venus," since Chaucer's "Complaint" was heavily influenced by "Les cinq balades ensuivans." I begin by giving a brief overview of the French influences that can be found in other texts by Chaucer, followed by a survey of Grandson's life; a reading of the two poems in question; and some topics for classroom discussion, exercises, presentations, or papers. I end my essay by introducing primary and secondary critical materials. Through this reading of Grandson's "Les cinq balades ensuivans" and Chaucer's "The Complaint of Venus," I hope to model a method of bringing Chaucer's sources—whether translated or not—into a beneficial dialectical relationship with his resulting poetry so that students can explore the necessary transitions of translation.

A brief review of the French influences on some of Chaucer's poetry contextualizes the importance of Grandson's impact on his work. Chaucer uses Guillaume de Machaut's *Dit de la fontaine amoureuse*, in addition to Grandson's "Complainte de l'an nouvel" and "Complainte Saint Valentin," for *The Book of the Duchess* (Braddy, "Chaucer's *Book*" and *Chaucer and the French* 57–60). Chaucer's "An ABC" is a version of a part of Guillaume de Deguileville's *Le pèlerinage de vie humaine*. We find in *The Parliament of Fowls* some elements from works of Marie de France and Alain de Lille, in addition to other foreign writers such as Giovanni Boccaccio. It is also possible to find connections between *The Parliament of Fowls* and Grandson's "Songe de Saint Valentin" (Braddy, *Chaucer and the French* 64–66). Additionally, there are numerous similarities between Chaucer's "Complainte d'Amours" and Grandson's "Complainte amoureuse" (Braddy, *Chaucer and the French* 55–57). According to Haldeen Braddy,

> the larger body of Graunson's better poetry was written to celebrate festivities appropriate to Saint Valentine's Day. These French poems are built according to a traditional pattern and are full of such conventional machinery as dream visions and bird allegory. In somewhat lesser degree

Chaucer subscribed to the Valentine tradition, his *Parliament of Fowls* and *Complaint of Mars* being two of the most famous treatments in English of this theme which came to him from France. (*Chaucer and the French* 71; see also Braddy, "Chaucer and Graunson")

If the French writers' influences on Chaucer's works are clear, then it is also important to note, as Braddy has, that "the sum total of Graunson's influence on Chaucer is thus seen to be a good deal larger than hitherto has been supposed" (*Chaucer and the French* 69). From this perspective, it is apparent that bringing French texts into the classroom enlightens our students' understanding of Chaucer's literary milieu. Although the exercises I subsequently outline may not work for students unversed in French, students with the necessary linguistic skills could benefit from studying such relationships as those between Grandson and Chaucer and share their findings with the rest of the class.

Grandson was among the most famous personages of the second half of the fourteenth century. He was born Othon III de Grandson, lord of Sainte-Croix, Cudrefin, Grandcour, Aubonne, and Coppet in Savoy around 1345. Son of Guillaume de Grandson and Jeanne de Vienne, he came from the illustrious noble family of Vaud, whose family motto was "A petite cloche, grand son" ("a great sound from a small bell"). Grandson married Jeanne d'Allamand on 25 September 1365. We have no specific information concerning the events of his life before the year 1368, at which date some documents record that he took part in a battle between Burgundian and Savoyard knights. In 1372, during the French siege of La Rochelle, Grandson accompanied John Hastings, second earl of Pembroke. At this occasion, Grandson was captured by the Spanish and sent to Santander in Spain from 1372 to 1374, during which he composed "Les cinq balades ensuivans." After his captivity, he entered into the service of John of Gaunt, duke of Lancaster, but he returned to Savoy in 1379; he then participated in another English expedition in 1384. After his father's death in 1386, he returned to Savoy.

Grandson was accused of having been an accomplice in the death of Amedée VII, the so-called Red Count, on 2 November 1391. This accusation, as has been demonstrated by scholars, was false (Carbonnelli; Olivier). Amedée's death was the result of tetanus contracted in a riding accident and was not caused by poisoning. Grandson was implicated in an affair in which political intrigue was mixed with economic stakes. In 1394, Grandson returned to England to escape the hostilities that were growing around him. He entered into the service of Richard II and participated in the military campaign of Henry Bolingbroke, earl of Derby, in Prussia and Upper Palatina, from 24 July 1392 through 5 July 1393. Finally, in 1395 Grandson was exonerated by the French king Charles VI. But Gérard d'Estavayer, who took over the administration of some of Grandson's properties, revived the accusation against him.

D'Estavayer challenged Grandson to a judicial duel. The Council of Savoy, after a long delay, planned the duel at Bourg-en-Bresse on 7 August 1397. The approximately fifty-year-old Grandson was killed by the young d'Estavayer.

Though a knight, Othon de Grandson also took part in literary activities during his lifetime. This "romantic knight" built his work in connection with the topic of the sadness of love (Kosta-Théfaine "Du chant" and *Livre*), which was a popular literary subject during the late Middle Ages (Pagès "Thème"). There was a strong French influence at the court of Edward III. Many elements of protocol, such as language, customs, and etiquette, were French in origin. Thus Chaucer, having been exposed to so many French traditions at court, was likely influenced by them in his writings. A branch of Grandson's family lived in England (Galbreath), and, according to Braddy, "during Chaucer's lifetime, it is clear, that the family of Graunson had already become prominent at the English court" (*Chaucer and the French* 39). Thus Grandson was in familiar country during his journeys to England. His literary reputation was also important there, since Chaucer has qualified him in "The Complaint of Venus" as the "flour of hem that make in Fraunce" (82; see also Braddy, "Sir Oton"); from literary admiration to a friendship there was only one step (Braddy, "Messire Oton").

Having briefly addressed the French influences in some of Chaucer's works and presented a survey of the major events of Grandson's life, I can now begin the reading of Grandson's and Chaucer's texts. First, it is important to note that the structure of each poem differs from the other. "Les cinq balades ensuivans" contains decasyllabic stanzas that follow the schema *ababbccb*, whereas Chaucer's stanzas are standard iambic pentameter with minor internal variations and follow the schema *ababbccb*, with *aabaabbaab* for the envoy. There is also a difference of length between these two texts. Grandson's poem contains, as is stated in its title, five ballads, whereas there are only three in Chaucer's. Chaucer includes an envoy, which is absent in Grandson's text. Braddy suggests, as an explanation, that "[t]he three balades, each three stanzas in length, which comprise the main body of Chaucer's 'The Complaint of Venus' are freely translated from the first, fourth, and fifth of Graunson's 'Cinq balades ensuivans'" (*Chaucer and the French* 61–64). His hypothesis has influenced later scholars (Norton-Smith; Ruud). John Scattergood, however, has recently demonstrated that "in fact, Chaucer uses all five of Graunson's ballades" ("Chaucer's 'Complaint'" 175). That Chaucer uses Grandson so heavily also means in one way that Chaucer did not exaggerate when he stated in his envoy that he "folowe[s] word by word the curiosite / Of Graunson" (81–82). Asking students to analyze the differences between the texts allows them to attune themselves to the nuances of meaning in both the source and its translation.

A close look at both texts shows intriguing thematic differences in the narrator's gender. In Grandson's text, the speaker is a man, whereas the speaker is a woman in Chaucer's poem. Grandson's poem celebrates a woman who is, according to courtly topics, "si belle et plaisant dame" (Piaget, *Vie* 209, line 14). Grandson also describes his suffering when the woman does not answer to his love. This poem is, in fact, as Scattergood writes, "a poem about a situation which has a past history, but no future that can be conceived in terms other than those of present" ("Chaucer's 'Complaint' " 176). Thus, the speaking voice in Grandson's text could be interpreted to be the poet's. In Chaucer's poem, with the alteration of gender from male to female, it is impossible to identify the voice speaking with the poet's.

Although both poems celebrate love, they do so in different ways. Chaucer's "Complaint," as Scattergood notes, is "about emotional readjustment, about coming to terms with reduced expectations, not about coming to terms with no expectations" ("Chaucer's 'Complaint' " 178). In another way, the physical description in Grandson's poem does not appear in Chaucer's work, in which there is a moral description rather than a physical one. At least the woman speaking in Chaucer's poem celebrates a knight with whom she is in love.

I have only discussed here the main elements of these two poems, since my goal is to offer an introduction to them. But much more could be said and done with students. Thus, I would like to suggest some topics that could be used for discussion, exercises, presentations, or papers. Instructors can direct students to find the elements from Grandson's poem used by Chaucer or to distinguish between Grandson's physical descriptions and Chaucer's moral descriptions. In each of these cases, students would analyze both the vocabulary and the images used by the poets. Then, many other questions could be raised, such as: Why does Chaucer reduce five ballades to three? Does he succeed aesthetically in doing so? Why does Chaucer alter the genre? Was there a reason for him to do so? What is the significance of the envoy he added? The formal structure of both poems could also be discussed.

I would like to end this essay by addressing the primary and secondary materials available for the study of Grandson's work. The standard edition for Grandson's poetry is the critical one published by Arthur Piaget in 1941. It also provides a survey of the poet's life. The critical edition by Caroline A. Cunnhingam in 1987 can also be useful, although it is incomplete. But the easiest access for students to "Les cinq balades ensuivans" is James Wimsatt's *Chaucer and the Poems of "Ch" in University of Pennsylvania MS French 15* (70–74). Lastly, I would like to note that there is a small book published in 1943 by Charles-Albert Cingria entitled La complainte de Vénus *telle que la faite sire Othon de Grandson, célèbre savoisien, sous ce titre:* Les cinq ballades ensuivans *et telle que l'a translatée le grand Jauffroy Chaucer, enrichie des gloses marginales de Charles-Albert Cingria*, which is not particularly useful but does contain texts by both Grandson and Chaucer in addition to glosses by Cingria.

Concerning Grandson's life, useful and valuable works in French are those by Piaget published in the journal *Romania* in 1890 and Joseph Orsier's *Un ambassadeur de Savoie, poète d'amour au XIVe siècle. Oton de Grandson.* For those who do not read French, Sally Tartline Carden's "Oton de Grandson" in *Literature of the French and Occitan Middle Ages* and Braddy's *Chaucer and the French Poet Graunson* provide full biographical information for Grandson and an examination of the literary relation between Chaucer and Grandson. My collection of essays on Grandson, *Othon de Grandson, chevalier et poète*, contains articles in both French and English focusing on various topics. Two valuable articles have also been published on "Les cinq balades ensuivans" and "The Complaint of Venus": Helen Phillips's " 'The Complaint of Venus': Chaucer and de Graunson" and Scattergood's "Chaucer's 'Complaint of Venus' and the 'Curiosite' of Graunson."

The chief difficulty in replicating the type of study I have outlined here is that not all students will be sufficiently versed in French to analyze Chaucer's sources successfully. And, of course, this problem extends to students with insufficient exposure to Italian in regard to other Chaucerian source studies. But by inviting our students with the necessary linguistic skills to model these types of readings for the rest of the class, we make explicit the truly international flavor of Chaucer's literature.

Notes on a Journey:
Teaching Chaucer's Shorter Poems and
Troilus and Criseyde for the First Time

Jenifer Sutherland

12 September

The room feels too small to contain this giant with his aggressive tongue and enormous vision. Sixty students sit in silence behind long tables bolted to the floor, one young man at the back of the room enjoying a dinner out of several plastic containers spread over his desk. How will we work together? Once a week for three hours from September to April we'll be reading Chaucer's work. From September to December, we will focus on the shorter poems and the epic *Troilus and Criseyde.* Tonight I lose ten students without even trying. I blame it on the great vowel shift. That fifty students return next week I attribute to laughter. After the handouts and the lecture, the students read "Fortune" in small clusters. "Don't forget to roll your *r*'s," I encourage them. The room comes alive with the sound of something like Chaucer's language. Fifteen minutes later, volunteers perform. Applause. I summarize some basic pronunciation guidelines before letting them go. Smiles and chatter on the way out. Objective number one: orality.

19 September

Web of Providence. Today we've read Boethius's *Consolation of Philosophy.* The young man who dines at the back of the room claims the text, or reading, has given him a headache. I draw two concentric circles on the board and begin to talk about how fate links the hub of providence to the spinning rim of fortune, having first checked the expert to make sure I get the connections right (Magee). I contrast Boethius's providential eye, which sees out of the still center of eternity, with the preemptive justice system based on precognition in Steven Spielberg's film version of Philip K. Dick's short story, *Minority Report*. For the rest of the term, the "precogs," as Dick names his futuristic version of the three fates, help us talk about narrative perspective.

Everything will come back to the *Consolation*'s visionary wheel, and to ensure this I have asked each student to create a florilegia of passages that they connect with on their journey from *The Book of the Duchess* through *Troilus and Criseyde*. Also I have set up a class Web site. A different student each week takes minutes, then turns them into a summary, which gets uploaded, allowing me to keep track of connections and disconnections. Key words are markers for us to follow on our narrative journey from fortune, through fate, to providence. When Susan sends me the minutes for Boethius, I'm relieved. Authority and experience are already in play. I add a question that has just occurred to me: if the divine author can see events as they are happening and narrate them as they unfold, does this mean that the divine plan is a (Menippean) dialogue? I will return to this question when we take up *Troilus and Criseyde*.

26 September

Complexity. In addition to the Web minutes, students present minireports at the beginning of each class. Today's main text is *The Book of the Duchess*, and there are reports on John of Gaunt, the Black Death, and Ovid's story of Ceyx and Alcyone (in book 11 of *Metamorphoses*). Following my lecture, students discuss how the dialogue between the Black Knight and the narrator compares with that between Boethius and Philosophy. Note: next time leave more time after each group reports back for full class discussion of our differences. Complexity requires savoring each point of view before moving on to the next, then drawing a circle big enough for the differences to begin to speak to each other.

3 October

A cautionary tale. To introduce *The Parliament of Fowls*, Tim presents a report on Alain de Lille's *Plaint of Nature*. I remember being surprised by this text, which complains of a monstrous Venus that "turns 'he's' into 'she's,' and with her witchcraft unmans man" (67). Tim seemed keen on it, so I directed him to the edition with James Sheridan's translation and notes. Instead, he Googled: the result is a disaster. I'm suddenly faced with the challenge of finding a simple way to introduce Neoplatonism, the school of Chartres, and the medieval concept of nature and, at the same time, deal with medieval homophobia. We spend ten minutes comparing Alain's Nature with Boethius's

Philosophy, starting with their robes and moving to their bodies. Tim's mini-report goes up on the Web site after hours of negotiations mediated by M. D. Chenu. Note: next time you teach this, forget Alain and approach nature through Boethius's image of the caged bird (*Boece*, bk. 3, metrum 2, lines 21–31), picked up by Jean de Meun (*Romance* 13936–66) and used by Chaucer throughout *The Canterbury Tales*.

10 October

Swift wings and pileups. Today we fly in the clutches of *The House of Fame*'s windbag eagle. My focus is on experience and authority. Students brainstorm where to go after the narrative breaks off, leaving the stampede of traders, couriers, and globe-trotters climbing over one another to get the latest and hottest whiff of news. "At laste y saugh a man, / Which that y [nevene] nat ne kan, / But he semed for to be / A man of gret auctorite" (*HF* 2155–58). The presentations are hilarious; this time I've left time to process them. We work together to follow the endings back through the text, looking for narrative authority. A precog stands at the hub of providence by reading moment by moment, detail by detail.

17 October

Words, words, words. Every week I give a short quiz, alternating between a test on content and one that requires students to translate a passage. The translation quiz provides a growing list of Middle English vocabulary. *Fyn loving* is today's primary addition. We're reading *The Legend of Good Women* before *Troilus and Criseyde*, the palinode before the transgression. I have little taste for Chaucer's tales of larger-than-life-women, irony or no irony, so I focus on the prologue (F and G) to prepare the ground for Chaucer's narrative relationship with Criseyde. The first report is on Eleanor of Aquitaine; the second, Andreas Capellanus's *Art of Courtly Love*; the third, John Gower's version of Alceste's descent to redeem her husband, Admetus, in the *Confessio Amantis* (7.1917–43 and 8.2640–46). The students make the connection with Christ's descent into hell. We talk about passion and agency. I lecture on *couverture*, a medieval concept of female legal invisibility that Elizabeth Fowler argues results in women's becoming figures of self-agency ("Civil Death"). The young man who dines at the back of the room complains his headache has turned into a migraine. I suggest it's all the MSG he ingests. The minutes come back to me in indigestible lumps. Too many words. I write a retraction: *The Legend of Good Women* is about a daisy.

24 October

How could I introduce *Troilus and Criseyde* without Barry Windeatt's *Troilus and Criseyde* in the Oxford Guides to Chaucer series as guide? From his handbook to Chaucer's epic poem, I pick out a few keys to the essential

complexities I want students to savor over the next five weeks: the rich im-
agery of heaven and hell; the characterizations of Pandarus, Troilus, Criseyde;
the tension between proverbial wisdom and lived experience; shifts in narra-
tive perspective.

31 October

Book 1. Is the divine plan a dialogue? I introduce Charles Taylor's phrase,
"webs of interlocution." We are going to follow Lollius, Troilus, Pandarus,
Criseyde, and the narrator through the fall of Troy, treating each one as a
writer. We read Chaucer's translation of Geoffrey of Vinsauf (1.1065–71;
3.530). Who is building which frame? I draw the wheel of fortune with its
providential hub on the board, asking students to be aware of frames of in-
terlocution as we head off on our journey through time. Where does the
narrator stand? At the rim? At the hub? Does he move back and forth, linking
the reader in the chains of fate? This week, the plastic-container diner is on
minutes. He begins, "according to Dr. Sutherland, we're going somewhere."
Or not. A precog can only portend the stages of the journey if someone makes
it.

7 November

Orality again. Windeatt supplies a list of proverbs used throughout *Troilus and
Criseyde* (*Troilus* [1992] 346–51), and I draw on Walter Ong's statement that
commonplaces result from a tendency to shape human interaction to formulaic
treatment (84–85). I ask the students to read the proverbs in book 2 out loud,
discuss their meaning, and suggest some limitations of their formulaic treat-
ment of Troilus and Criseyde's situation. Happy approximations of Chaucer's
spoken language lift us out of the November fog.

14 November

To lecture on book 3 is a pleasure of which I am unwilling to deprive myself.
We are celebrating love, but, I warn, there are signs of trouble in paradise. I
focus on the fracture between the Boethian structures of a public, common
bond of love and the secrecy of the conventions of *fin'amors*, Pandarus's mach-
inations, and the lovers' aubade. We reread book 3 to pick out the narrator's
cautious interjections. I ask them to think through some of the ways Fortune
occupies the fracture between a Boethian cosmic love and the erotic religion
of *fin'amors*. The class ends with a discussion about the proem to Venus (3.1–
49) and the relation of Venus to Fortune. Every shift in perspective is a chal-
lenge to the Boethian framework. There's an air of excitement in the room;
we're thinking hard about things that matter—love and loss.

21 November

Fierce pain and sorrow at the *chaunge* of book 4 will be somewhat tempered,
I promise the students tonight, by our fury at our contemporary media's mis-

representation of the Middle Ages. I read them a quotation from a recent article in the *New Yorker*: "Now, democracy, individual rights, and women's sexual autonomy are concepts almost nowhere to be found, even in the West, before the eighteenth century" (Menand 98). I ask them to respond to this statement by analyzing the process of Criseyde's "exchange," paying attention to the parliament and its aftermath (4.162–210). I remind the students that universities and the British parliament both come to us from the Middle Ages. Their responses are animated. They are becoming passionate readers of Chaucer's complexity.

26 November

Tonight we hold a casting conference for the characters of Pandarus, Criseyde, Troilus, and Diomede. I object to Angelina Jolie as Criseyde, although I submit there may be a role for her in *The Canterbury Tales*. From laughter at our own cultural stereotypes, we move to sadness at Troilus's laughter. I introduce Augustine, "Scripture teaches nothing but charity and condemns nothing but cupidity" (*De doctrina Christiana* 3.10.15), as well as D. W. Robertson Jr., according to whom all medieval literature is written out of Augustine's distinction ("Doctrine of Charity"). I hand out several passages from the Song of Songs (1.2; 4.10–12; 5.2–5), together with a gloss from Bernard of Clairvaux's second sermon. In addition, I provide a photocopy of a page from a medieval Bible with *glossa ordinaria*, accompanied by a phrase from Jacques Derrida: "Language is neither prohibition nor transgression, it couples the two endlessly" (*Of Grammatology* 266). I want to end on dialogue.

3 December

Conclusion. I have asked students to come prepared to share from their florilegia of readings to help us go backward over the journey from the insomnia of the narrator of *The Book of the Duchess* to the laughter of Troilus. As the students explain their original, tentative connections with the text, we review key themes, particularly how they are informed by the Boethian distinction between fortune and providence. I insist that the providential eye is the eye of the reader who rereads, keeping the entire text in mind and never reducing it to the last word. Over the holidays, as I'm grading term papers on *Troilus and Criseyde*, I decide that my insistence on *The Consolation of Philosophy* was worth the resistance of the back-of-the-room diner. Although a few have submitted to the temptation to collapse Chaucer's great epic into Troilus's last laugh, the rich quotations I am regaled with from all over the epic work suggest the term has been a success. In January, we will shift to *The Canterbury Tales*, where the tension of sustained complexity is an essential element of the pilgrimage.

The next time I teach these pre-*Canterbury Tales* works, Boethius stays. In fact, I might put together a series of short readings from *Boece* on nature, love, fortune, and providence, to which students could expect me to refer throughout the term. In addition, since I refer so often to *Minority Report*, it would make sense to assign a viewing of the video so that all of us will be on the same page, so to speak. A printout combining quotations from *Boece* and scenes from *Minority Report* would lift my comparisons from haphazard to providential.

Next time, I would incorporate more oral Chaucer into the class. My insistence that we play together with the language and not worry too much about accuracy of pronunciation was a good beginning, but I wish I had held back a bit on the big vowel shift that introductory class in September and taken the students into the Middle Ages in stages. Maybe some of the students who left that night never to return would have stayed long enough not to think that Chaucer's genius is "noght but eyr ybroken" (*HF* 765).

I would not have students keep minutes again. Although the exercise did teach summary, I'm not sure the lesson was worth its pedagogical cost, and some students thought they could pick up the lecture on the Web site. Next time, I will have students write reports on words, creative exercises that take them into the conceptual differences of Chaucer's world, and share their research. If, at the end of the term, the students can talk about the context for the difference between *kynde* and *kind*, *daunger* and *danger*, *happe* and *sad* and *happy* and *sad*, then they have walked a little distance down the road that Chaucer paved elegantly long ago.

Overcoming Resistance to "That Old Stuff": Teaching *Troilus and Criseyde* through Journaling and Debate

Marcia Smith Marzec

A dilemma facing teachers of literature, especially teachers of "old" literature (which for some students may be as ancient as the nineteenth century), is on the one hand whether to assign for reading what we consider important and meaningful, risking in the process having students tune out and learn nothing at all, or on the other whether to give in to students' desire to read only what interests them, again risking their learning nothing at all. The challenge, of course, is to find a way of making the "old stuff" immediately interesting. This is particularly important in classes of nonmajors, who often are resistant to any literary pursuits and who would rather read about the love life of a celebrity couple than Troilus and Criseyde. It is because of my success with this particular group of reluctant nonmajors that I offer an approach that has worked for me.

In our required interdisciplinary sophomore humanities course, journaling is a major learning aid. Students are required to write a response to their initial readings of the course material and a follow-up entry after class discussion. The initial journaling encourages students to read closely, as active readers; presses them to refine their thoughts as they articulate them in writing; allows them to determine what they do *not* understand and to formulate questions ahead of class; and better prepares them for class discussion. The after-class journaling gives students the opportunity to think through and summarize the points from class and also to raise any questions they may still have. The course Web site lists for each work a number of questions designed to raise significant issues and provoke thought. These questions are phrased in a personalized way that involves the students; thus, even though it is implicitly redundant to ask, "What do you think is . . . ?," the pedagogical use of the second person is effective.

The journal questions I use for *Troilus and Criseyde* almost inevitably split the class—often, along gender lines—and generate debate. For book 1, I introduce consideration of the characters of Troilus and Pandarus, asking three sets of questions: first, how do you feel about Troilus? Does his lovesickness make you more or less sympathetic to him? Second, does your own experience make you empathize with Troilus? Why or why not? Does the narrator ever rely on your empathy and similar experiences? Third, how good a friend do you think Pandarus is to Troilus? What personality qualities do you identify in Pandarus from book 1? Do you like him? Why or why not?

The questions for book 2 prompt the students to reevaluate characters they have perhaps previously taken at face value: Has your opinion of Pandarus changed or been validated? What clues in book 1 might prepare you for his behavior in book 2? How would you describe Criseyde? Do you think Criseyde is victimized by Pandarus or just playing along? How do you interpret Criseyde's dream?

Book 3 questions focus on character dynamics and motivation: Do you think Criseyde is a hapless victim, or is she complicit in her own seduction? What do you make of Troilus's swoon? What is your impression of Pandarus throughout the love scene and in the scene the "morning after"?

Book 4 questions are geared to turn the students' attention toward their own reading of the text and reactions to it: Why doesn't Troilus object to the trade of Criseyde for Antenor? Should he object? Do you think Troilus and Criseyde should have run away together? Would you have? How grieved do you think Troilus is at the separation? How grieved is Criseyde? How grieved were you at it?

Book 5 questions introduce the notion of hindsight: How did you feel during Troilus's anguished wait for Criseyde's return? Did you anticipate Criseyde's betrayal of Troilus? Why or why not? Why is Criseyde "fooled" by Diomede? Why does the narrator spend so much time on Troilus's suffering at the wall but give only one line to his death? What was your reaction to the translation of Troilus to the eighth sphere at the end? Does it fit?

From the first day of discussion, the students are divided concerning Troilus. Some argue that he's silly and weak, others that he's a committed idealist. At this stage, I inform the class about the romance genre and the conventions of courtly love. Discussion recommences with the question, Is Troilus just a typical romance hero, or is there a realism here that goes beyond convention and negatively characterizes Troilus? If opinion is fairly evenly divided, I reconfigure the class into pro and con groups. I find that gathering together students of like opinion generates a team spirit among them, increases their investment in the discussion, and makes even the less vocal more secure about offering opinions. Meanwhile, I act as devil's advocate, helping bring up contrary evidence from the text against each side's arguments. During the exercise, students are free to change sides if they have been so persuaded; although most would not wish to capitulate the point, some do, in fact, begin the subsequent class session by making a switch of sides.

If the students are not divided on Troilus the first day, they are almost always divided on the character of Pandarus. The debate usually concerns Pandarus's motives and the quality of his friendship with Troilus. What indeed is Pandarus's motivation? Does a desire to help his friend absolve Pandarus of manipulating that friend? What possible significance is Pandarus's own failure in love? How are we to take his use of the term "game" in referring to what Troilus considers "ernest"?

When the class reconvenes after the students' reading and journaling of book 2, some will have changed sides on the Pandarus issue. Discussion may consider, for example, how Pandarus plays on Criseyde's fear, the tactics Pandarus adopts when Criseyde catches him in a lie, or Criseyde's own need for approval. Students consider the fundamental issue of whether Pandarus really believes in love's malady and its putative threat to Troilus's life, as well as what Pandarus reveals of himself in his instructions to Troilus on the writing of a love letter.

Students' discussion of Criseyde is even more animated, with students showing strong feelings for or against her. Students argue whether Criseyde actually believes Pandarus's threat that he will take his own life and whether she is sincere in lines 463–76 or rationalizing her probable involvement. They consider the implication of Criseyde's comment that Troilus is no "avantour" (2.722–28). They analyze lines 659–65 for an indication of what persuades Criseyde of Troilus's worthiness (lines that she will later contradict directly in 4.1667–73). They consider Criseyde's motivation when she returns to the subject of Troilus, asking Pandarus if he can "wel speke of love" (2.498–504). Finally, students consider what Criseyde finds appealing in Antigone's song, and what her dream reveals about Criseyde.

Student discussion of book 3 is always contentious. Some students vehemently argue that Criseyde is taken advantage of by a manipulative, lecherous voyeur and a lustful, self-serving Romeo; others insist that Criseyde is in control of the situation and, in fact, has psychically emasculated young Troilus. Students concentrate on interpreting some very problematic passages. They debate whether Criseyde knows that the evening at Pandarus's house is a setup, and, if so, why she is upset at the story of Troilus's jealousy of Horaste. They need to come to terms with lines 939–45 concerning Criseyde's motives, as well as her notions of her "honour" and Troilus's "plesaunce." Those who defend Criseyde will have to deal with her reaction to Troilus's swoon as "unmanly" (3.1125–27). Further, they must find a suitable interpretation of Criseyde's statement that she had "[b]en yold" long before (3.1210–11). Finally, students must deal with the nature of the interchange between Pandarus and Criseyde the following morning.

If the lesson goes as designed, by the end of the third day's discussion, the students may not have changed their positions on the characters, but they have moved into a new awareness of the complexity of the narrative as they encounter so much diverse and seemingly contradictory evidence, a complexity that confronts the limitations of either-or thought. Adding to their difficulties, I might assign two or three opposing scholarly articles on the character of Criseyde and ask students to journal their responses.[1]

Book 4 discussion continues our evaluation of the characters' motives, but by now the students tend to find themselves on a continuum rather than mired in a pro-con debate. The complexity of evidence in book 3 opens students to the further complexities of book 4. Those who had faulted Criseyde previously are willing to admit her powerlessness. Those who defended Criseyde are willing to question her swoon, her notion of suicide by starvation, and her overwrought pledges of fidelity. Those who defended Troilus need to ask themselves hard questions about his failure to defend Criseyde in the parliament and about his helpless capitulation to Criseyde's plan, even against his better judgment. As students find themselves of increasingly divided minds, I begin to physically reconfigure the class into a continuum, with many students arguing against both extremes of the debate.

The second half of our discussion shifts our consideration to ourselves as readers. With the debates over the characters temporarily suspended, we begin to analyze our own motivations. We discuss what the students felt in encountering the turning point and what they think of the characters' reactions. Why, I ask the students, were we all so happy in book 3 at the lovers' own felicity when we knew that things were not going to work out for the young couple and that Troilus, in becoming increasingly involved, has only opened himself to more pain? Similarly, if we know that Criseyde will betray Troilus, why are we ourselves grieved that he seems to be losing her? The students begin to sense how they as readers have been taking their cues from the narrator, even though they still at this point generally do not suspect that they are falling into the author's trap.

The discussion of book 5 continues with our reaction to the story we have read. We concentrate on Troilus's agonized wait for Criseyde, and students list ways that Chaucer elicits our sympathy. They consider how Troilus's suffering disposes us to feel toward Criseyde, who is being wooed by Diomede. However, they also consider carefully why Criseyde does not return to Troy and the legitimacy of her fears. Perhaps most troubling for the Criseyde defenders is her last letter to Troilus and her gift of the brooch to Diomede. Is there any evidence, I ask them, that Criseyde feels that Diomede is preferable to Troilus? If not, why does she take Diomede as lover, and what does it say about her?

Having determined how Chaucer uses details that we identify with to make Troilus's wait seem not only painful but endless, I ask why the narrator spends so much time on Troilus's anguish at the wall but dispatches the hero in a one-line death, in paraphrase rather than narration. Why do we not feel any pain in Troilus's death, regardless of the narrator's "weilawey" (5.1805)? Some students are quick to answer that the very nature of paraphrase short-circuits sympathy; others will insist that it is because of the immediate apotheosis of Troilus to the eighth sphere that we have no time to feel sorry for him and that we indeed feel good about his new perspective. This gets us into a discussion of how we are to take the translation of the soul of Troilus to the eighth sphere. Does it fit? Many students will be ready with the answer: only if you reread the text.

It is now that students begin to recall the Boethian messages that have been included all along but that have been deftly obscured by Chaucer through a narrator who, like Troilus, puts his hopes for happiness in "this false worldes brotelnesse" (5.1832). My students have the benefit of having previously read *The Consolation of Philosophy* and will thus recognize the Boethian references.[2] The marvel of Chaucer's artistry, students realize, is that we readers are kept oblivious to the messages that we already knew so well, or at least that we had been unconsciously taking in throughout the poem.

Finally, I pose the question, If the work is indeed about the "double sorwe" of Troilus (1.1), when is the story complete? Students come to see that the work is complete at the supposedly misplaced envoy, the ending of the narrator's "litel . . . tragedye" (5.1786). They also see that the narrator's desire to write a comedy (5.1786–88) has taken place sooner rather than later: Troilus's vision is that of Christian comedy implicit in the notion of divine providence and in keeping with Chaucer's address to the "yonge, fresshe folkes" (5.1835) to eschew "worldly vanyte" (5.1837). Just as our earthly "tragedies" are all part of God's great comedy, so is the narrator's story of *amor* within the larger story of *caritas*.

NOTES

[1]Some provocative possibilities include Aers, "Criseyde"; Slocum; Martin 156–188; Mieszkowski; Pearsall, "Chaucer's Criseyde"; David; and Wetherbee, *Chaucer and the Poets* 179–204, alongside his recent reassessment, "Criseyde Alone."

[2]Useful Boethian passages include 1.218–24; 1.730–35; 3.813–33; 3.1618–631; 3.1745–771; and 4.960–1078.

"Diverse Folk Diversely They Seyde": Teaching Chaucer to Nonmajors

Adam Brooke Davis

How shall we teach Chaucer to nonmajors? Instinctively, I think, most of us would respond: exactly as we teach it to majors. We can reject out of hand any approach that would have us accommodate the teaching of our subject to an understanding that it's really not very important compared with what the student is doing in his or her major. Our colleagues in the quantitative disciplines, for instance, feel precisely the same about the literature students who find themselves taking classes in Science Hall, and I absolutely affirm them in it. But when we insist that our subject has an integrity that compels respect, we should not confuse that conviction with a right to determine where the students will take this disciplinary knowledge and what they will do with it.

This essay is meant as an appreciation of the pleasures and possibilities available to the teacher so fortunate as to have a class of students with no intention of specializing in Chaucer, or even in English. Nonmajors can have rich, rewarding, even life-transforming experiences with Chaucer on their own terms and can be held to very high standards of rigor. Moreover, insofar as these students do not share our professional commitment and are not proper or promising objects of evangelization, they present us with a challenge we should welcome: to make the case, as John Fisher's title has it, that Chaucer is *important*.

Nonmajors, whether encountering the poetry in a survey course or gate-crashing the 300-level party, are more likely to regard the poems as individual texts and are likely to be comfortable with an idea of "literary greatness" that majors have been trained to regard critically, if not with outright disdain. They cannot have failed to note that only two single-author courses remain on the books and are in regular rotation (I think my institution is pretty standard in this), which accounts for the comparatively large number of nonmajors we see in the Shakespeare and Chaucer courses. Nonmajors understand the idea of the "great author" and, if they aren't driven away in the first week or so of the course, they want to know what these writers' greatness consists of. They even want to claim a cultural patrimony.

A lack of expertise, and the absence of the impulse to control meaning that expertise often seems to license, has its charms. I value the very naïveté of the nonmajor's approach to Chaucer. It is in these matters of purpose and meta-analysis, rather than the uncontested ground of ancillary factuality, that the purposes of majors and nonmajors diverge. The nonmajors are, I find, comparatively uninterested in questions of how the discourse of chivalry in *Troilus and Criseyde* squares with the attitudes in The Knight's Tale, in order to establish dates for composition. They have surprised me, however, by their interest in C. S. Lewis's "What Chaucer Really Did to *Il Filostrato*" (or what he did to *Teseida*, for that matter, or to Boethius; they're very drawn to that old stoic). They respond quickly to the limited sallies in biographical criticism that are possible at this historical remove and will engage at the tropological level with very little prompting—indeed, they can hardly be shaken loose from it once they get their teeth set.

What they are doing, in short, is meeting Chaucer on his own terms, as a kind of conversation partner. They are touchingly respectful of his cultural prestige, but not slavishly so; I am writing, after all, from the Show-Me State, and our students are often first-generation college students who bring with them a skepticism toward abstraction that only a foolhardy prof would mistake for lowbrow smugness.

One way of looking at the situation is to see these students, in fact, as taking Chaucer much more seriously than some narrowly professional approaches might. They are certainly not attempting to contain him within a theoretical framework that will render him untroubling and harmless. I have seen sophisticated approaches that seemed to me to have precisely that reduction of what is complex (and therefore interesting) as their aim. Nonmajors most certainly do that too, but it's a different sort of pedagogical problem with a more optimistic prognosis.

So what does classroom praxis actually look like? The familiar combination of lecture and discussion. In a full Chaucer course, I sometimes screen Pier Paolo Pasolini's film version of *The Canterbury Tales* (with due warnings about graphic content and alternative assignments for those whose academic detachment does not extend that far). I would also screen a film in a minor poems course if I knew of appropriate materials—not because students need a break but so that we can talk about the range of interpretation to which literary works are subject. Pasolini's version of *The Canterbury Tales* scandalizes less for its prurience than for its unrelenting and un-Chaucerian meanness. This contrast exemplifies the sort of thing some might see as "Chaucer Lite," but it is precisely the point at which the legitimate interests of majors and nonmajors can come together.

I typically lecture for the first week on the general background to the Middle Ages, targeting those misconceptions that experience tells me will be well established by authoritative high school teachers and even more authoritative popular culture. We explore the idea of the Middle Ages, and Norman Cantor's name comes up, along with a great many others, both in our live talks and on a select bibliography posted on the course Web site. Chaucer always expands to fill the available space, and, for this reason perhaps, our course-catalog specifies for Medieval Lit a survey of medieval writings except Chaucer. But I have never yet had a student haul me up on charges for letting Geoffrey in the back door. *Troilus and Criseyde* and the shorter poems may be undeservedly squeezed out of my Chaucer course, since *The Canterbury Tales* too expands to fill the available space.

I index the success of a given approach by the quality of student comments and questions. A well-schooled major might note that Pandarus's conduct toward his niece does not conform to the socially established norms governing such relations in the present day and those norms that might be assumed for Chaucer's period, duly recognizing that the setting of the poem is not and was never really supposed to be genuinely classical (or Bronze Age, for that matter). But I value just as highly what one young woman said, on reading how the arch-procurer thrust a letter down Criseyde's cleavage: "You know that something here is *just not right.*" Either response arrives where it should: at an understanding of the indeterminacy of Pandarus's motives, combined with deep distrust for his highly skilled maneuverings at the very edge of acceptable behavior and for his ability to maintain his victim in a state of vulnerability. And either way, we have a chance to talk about a subject that should be equally of interest to majors and nonmajors, the shift in sympathies over time among interpreters of the poem, from the abandoned Troilus to the manipulated Criseyde. In another semester, the focus may just as likely alight on Pandarus's verbal skill, and I allow that in-class conversation to touch both on other imaginative works and on collective and individual experience, in order that we might recognize our shared ambivalence toward eloquence itself. I spend a few minutes adding Richard Hofstadter's *Anti-intellectualism in American History* to that long list of things they want eventually to read. We find ourselves at some remove from Chaucer, and that's just fine. We talk and think about where our cultural attitudes come from and how Chaucer, six centuries dead, can be our interlocutor, which is the point (especially but not exclusively with reference to nonmajors). We use Chaucer to understand ourselves.

There is bibliography aplenty on those questions of gender relations and cultural attitudes in Chaucer and the Middle Ages more generally, which the majors may use to construct a history of the criticism. The nonmajors may simply observe that criticism tracks other cultural changes—no shabby insight. But they will put this observation together with the poet's peculiarly modern taste for nondecidability (which I certainly foreground in my lectures), correlating that observation further with the complexity of the relations among the rhetorical modes that frame *Troilus and Criseyde*, which are in turn analogous in certain ways to the almost mathematical qualities of the narratological frames we must consider for "Chaucer pilgrim" and "Chaucer poet," in E. Talbot Donaldson's still-useful distinction.

And some students will say, as did a nursing major I cherished, "Man, that guy was smart!" She had come to the surprising realization that merely living in the twenty-first century does not make us wiser, cleverer, more intelligent, and more insightful than those long-gone men and women who loved and worked and feared as we do.

Not all English majors arrive at such an *aha!* I fear that many of them are following professional pathways that discourage them from entertaining such a possibility; our very training can immerse us in a hermeneutic sophistication so highly wrought and internally consistent that it can inculcate in us the delusion that Chaucer was writing specifically for such as us. It can lead to interpretations of baroque complexity very far removed from nonacademic experience, readings that provoke yawns from the noninitiate. The yawn perhaps offends us, but it should disturb us more deeply if it extends to the material—if the nonmajors indeed share the delusion that Chaucer is not for the likes of them.

Those are of course abuses and caricatures of critical practices none of us would approve, and normal classroom practice involves a lot more cooperation and consensus among the sundry audiences. Majors and nonmajors alike laugh at a fart (or *humph* indignantly at same)—and in about the same proportions, as Kurt Vonnegut's *Galapagos* predicts we shall do a million years hence, when our arms will have evolved into flippers but when we remain human nonetheless.

And maybe it is good for the English majors to be exposed to nonmajors' approaches even at an advanced stage of their study. At a faculty retreat about a year ago, we were discussing the problematic third column of a rubric we use for all our degree programs, as we undertake to instill in our students certain knowledge, skills, and attitudes. I was surprised and impressed when a colleague, whose specialty runs about as far from Mark Twain as it can, quoted the passage from chapter 9 of *Life on the Mississippi*, in which Clemens counts the cost of his training as a steamboat pilot. He has *mastered* the river, with the direct result that it can never again move him to wonder and awe. My colleague was making the point that we, the professionals, came originally to literary study from a love of reading, experiences we sometimes described in terms reserved for religious experiences and affairs of the heart, and we entered the community of interpreters often at the beckoning of some admired mentor whose affirmation and affection we craved. But we also often experience some disillusionment precisely as we obtain the objectivity and methodological sophistication necessary to operate the machinery of analysis ("God I'm sophisticated," said Daisy). I wonder if there's any of us who has not read such sentiments on a student evaluation: "I used to love stories, but in here all we do is tear them apart." When I read such a line, I regret the anonymity of such evaluations, because I want to get together with that young person and show him or her that there's a mature relation with the text, a relation that has much of the old magic and warmth of regard, that lies on the other side of the growing pains.

In looking back, I see that there's a problem of nonreplicability to much of this report from the field. However, I'd have it understood that the purpose has not been to lay out particular lecture strategies, essay prompts, or bibliographic avenues but rather to describe an attitudinal orientation of presumptive respect for the motivations that bring nonmajors to Chaucer. This is of course an ideal and will encounter frustration and disappointment: back-row buzzards snoring out beer fumes beneath visor caps, people unlikely to be reading Homer decked out in the Greek alphabet. But then, that's no rare thing with majors, is it? Everyone with access gets the education she or he deserves, and, at any rate, it was never promised to us that we would see the fruits of our labors, what realization some idle remark we make today may spark twenty years from now.

Let this essay end where the course does. Assessment in the course recognizes no differences among majors and nonmajors. All must become adept at reading Middle English aloud, and the tests contain spot passages for contextualization, paraphrase, and commentary. Depending on the size of the class (I have had as many as forty-five in a class intended for about thirty), there may be a number of short papers, but there is always a substantial term paper or project. There will be what my own Chaucer teacher, Tom Garbáty, called "the house question," a default option generally laying out a well-defined conflict of critical opinion (for example, the shift, mentioned above, from Criseyde as strumpet). There is always the option for individual proposals (with a discreet note that my Googling skills are sufficiently advanced to detect a canned paper and with requirements for notes, drafts, and revisions that would make it a bad bargain anyway). The prompt sheet always has a few general ideas, some intended for majors (bibliographic inquiries, responses to individual critics, technical problems of language or prosody), and some I lay out with nonmajors in mind.

I have been struck, time and time again, by the eagerness with which the majors take up those suggestions I had initially intended for nonmajors: for example, scripting or even staging a dramatization of some portion of the poem or composing a version in a contemporary setting. Certainly a good many want to do the critical analysis, properly situated in the existing discourse. "But for the moore part they loughe and pleyde" (RvP 3858).

Are they slumming? slacking? Some of them, sometimes, maybe. But I'd like to think that, when we rightly suggest that Chaucer should be taught to nonmajors exactly as we teach it to majors, we have the flexibility of mind, the generosity of spirit, the openness that is the very essence of Chaucer himself to consider and reconsider which side of the equation we mean to be the norm, which of these is *ernest*, and which is *game*.

Chaucer's Early Poetry in Graduate Seminars: Opportunities for Training Future Chaucer Teachers and Molding "Yonge, Fresshe Folkes" into Publishing Scholars

Lorraine Kochanske Stock

Exemplifying a general pattern of marginalizing early-period course work, the curricula of most American and British departments of English literature feature one Chaucer seminar that is focused on *The Canterbury Tales* but that perhaps features a rushed, late-semester summary coverage of *Troilus and Criseyde* to represent his "minor" works. Ironically, the "yonge, fresshe folkes" (5.1835) Chaucer addresses at the end of *Troilus and Criseyde* have virtually no opportunity to study his other long poem. Because the dream visions and lyrics are even more rarely assigned in the all-purpose Chaucer seminar, Chaucer's absent other poetry is othered in graduate syllabi. Failing to expose future postsecondary teachers to Chaucer's early works in graduate school contributes to a further trickle-down elimination of this material in undergraduate Chaucer syllabi and in the high school English curricula of teachers who did not study these texts as English majors. To rectify this deficiency at all levels and to encourage early graduate student participation in activities required in the profession of English, I recommend redesigning both the content of graduate curricula and the kinds of research and writing projects assigned in Chaucer seminars. I urge English departments to offer (preferably) two cataloged Chaucer seminars separately covering *The Canterbury Tales* and the early texts. Those offering one Chaucer seminar should alternate syllabi between *The Canterbury Tales* and the early works.

This curricular change offers important professional benefits to graduate students. With the early works better showcased in the graduate curriculum, seminar members can learn Chaucer's complete poetic oeuvre and diversify their postgraduate teaching repertoire. Increased coverage of the other texts also will stimulate graduate students to choose these critically orphaned minor works as subjects of seminar writing projects, theses, and dissertations. This salutary alternative to processing (and replicating) the daunting body of received *Canterbury Tales* criticism creates more chances for "young fresh folks" to write original, potentially publishable, critical papers (Stock 12–15). Developing a more diverse teaching repertoire and producing original scholarship about the critically less-treated early works enhance the prospective success of graduate students in both the immediate postdoctoral job search and the quest for tenure after securing an academic appointment.

In the stanza of *Troilus and Criseyde* in which his narrator addresses the "young fresh folks" comprising both Chaucer's medieval audience and the targeted beneficiaries of my chapter, the narrator defines the world as a marketplace when he advises, "thynketh al nys but a faire" (5.1840), a mercantile metaphor now applied to the search for postdoctoral academic employment. I recommend assigning in the other Chaucer seminar nontraditional writing projects that promote professional development and enhance the viability of graduate students in a shrinking job "market."

Established methods of demonstrating professionalism and making the curriculum vitae of job applicants more attractive to hiring committees include presenting scholarly papers at academic conferences and, more importantly, publishing these papers before entering the job market. This is one practical aspect of graduate education that is overlooked in most content seminars in which the traditional long research paper is assigned as the course's final work product (Graff 12–13). The alternative below has been demonstrably successful for my own students.[1]

In my Chaucer seminars devoted to the other works, I have replaced the traditional term paper with a series of assignments culminating in a tightly focused, eight-to-ten page conference paper. In the six hours allocated to the last seminar meeting and the scheduled final exam, the students orally present their papers at a mock conference staged to replicate an authentic conference atmosphere, with structured theme sessions, introductions, strictly timed presentations, and critical discussion. The seminar experience thus concludes on a heady, professional note. Before presenting the conference papers, the students complete preliminary assignments that both prepare them for producing this shorter, more narrowly focused paper and that simulate the process of submitting scholarly work for acceptance at a real conference—the best venue for promoting academic professionalism through the exchange of scholarly ideas, forming professional contacts, and even securing job interviews.

In place of the term paper and final exam, I require a ten-page bibliographic essay evaluating primary texts and criticism for later use in the eventual narrowly focused paper; a one-page abstract for a conference paper; a cover letter addressed to a conference call for papers; and an oral conference paper, not to exceed twenty minutes' reading time (eight-to-ten pages).

The bibliographic essay, due at midterm, requires students to read criticism widely, and ultimately select ten items—sources, books, chapters, and articles—that cohere around a subtopic in a Chaucerian text's major or minor themes. Not an annotated catalog but a cohesive, integrated essay appraising how these items mutually conduct a critical conversation, this assignment is evaluated for how effectively it reviews and synthesizes an interrelated body of scholarship on a Chaucerian theme and identifies various scholarly lacunae that the eventual mock conference paper will fill. The exercise funnels initially broad research into a manageable corpus informing the abstract.

The one-page abstract is the most difficult challenge. To prepare for an assignment not usually required in other seminars, I review the abstract's purpose in the structure of an actual conference situation: to convey the paper's title, topic, and essential argument, concisely presented in an attractive package that makes the organizers want to place the paper in their conference. I teach strategies for composing successful abstracts: they must convey clearly the thesis of the paper and its significance—how it modifies the standard positions taken on this text or fills a scholarly vacuum or lacuna—and must demonstrate the presenter's scholarly authority. A clearly descriptive, provocative, and eye-catching title is the "hook" that grabs the attention of the reader or conferee and distinguishes one's abstract or paper from other submissions. The title and body must express the paper's scholarly position and assure achieving its promised goals in twenty minutes.

Two weeks before the scheduled mock conference, students distribute copies of their abstract to all class members for a three-hour "workshop" in which we note strengths, weaknesses, or vagueness and suggest tactics for reorganization or clarification of the abstract, refining the argument, reordering paragraphs, rephrasing sentences, and constructing a clearly articulated thesis sentence. We isolate the most interesting and exciting ideas (a single idea of the original argument might be recommended as the final focus), discarding cumbersome expositions and questioning the plausibility of presenting the proposed idea in the allotted time. "Discard the first paragraph of verbal warm-up!" becomes a mantra. We examine titles for clarity and audience appeal.

Once initial tentativeness is dispelled, students become quite frank (and good) at evaluating their classmates' abstracts. This peer review parallels the pedagogical process used by most instructors and teaching assistants in freshman composition. To their chagrin, the students admit that they are not practicing the skills they preach to their own students. The exercise of "workshopping" the abstracts also conveys a specific Chaucerian lesson. While perusing the abstracts, sometimes "mysdeming" each other's "entente," they experience firsthand Chaucer's early narrators' perennial authorial anxiety. More important, they recognize that, unless it is carefully crafted and articulated, the abstract could be "mysdemed" by their intended audience of the conference organizers, who judge the proposed paper by the one-page abstract. Failure to pitch their idea successfully at that critical juncture may result in rejection of the paper. The stakes are no longer merely a grade on a transcript but acceptance as a professional. I distribute some of my own past abstracts to show how the same topic was adjusted for pitching to sessions with different emphases and to offer a template for one-page formatting. Primed with suggestions made by their peers, the students substantially revise the abstracts. The next, considerably improved version is submitted for a grade and provides the basis of the oral conference paper. I distribute invented session topics from an imaginary conference to which students apply and for which they compose a cover letter to accompany their submitted abstract.

The limitation of the twenty-minute conference paper encourages essays of tighter focus than normally result from the traditional term-paper assignment.

I encourage seeking passages containing puzzling textual cruxes ripe for a new approach or explanation. I cover strategies for best exploiting their twenty minutes and for maximizing confidence in an intimidating presentation format. We discuss the effective use of printed handouts, especially to adduce Middle English quotations, which both defrays nervousness and saves precious speaking time. They learn to present a wealth of information efficiently in handouts. The students then prepare their conference papers.

To make the artificial conference experience as authentic as possible, I assign their abstracts into creatively constructed sessions arranged in typical conference-program format, which I print and distribute to the class audience. As session presider, I pretend to meet them for the first time, asking beforehand for real or fantasized biographical information. While some submit their actual identities, most adopt successful and productive academic personae, such as positions at esteemed universities and authorship of prizewinning books. Straight-faced, I use these hilarious blurbs to introduce them, an icebreaker that relieves mounting tension and contributes to their growing awareness of being scholars in apprenticeship. I provide a lectern and water, schedule time for discussion, and include a coffee break between sessions. The audience is encouraged to ask questions, offer suggestions for enhancement or refinement of the argument, bring up peripheral issues and texts that the papers evoke—in short, to behave as much as possible like a typical conference audience. As is true at all conferences (and in all classes), there is a mixture of quality in the resulting papers, ranging from acceptable to excellent. In addition to the oral paper, students submit a printed version, complete with endnotes and bibliography, composing half the project grade. The rest is based on their conference performance, including deportment, adherence to the time limit, and successful fielding of questions.

What is gained by adopting this outside-the-box set of written assignments? In course evaluations, students report being initially intimidated by the abstract and the oral paper. Ultimately, however, they acknowledge their value and are enthusiastic about the results of the mock conference, which serves as an intellectually exciting culmination of the seminar. Moreover, the best papers and abstracts are now ready for immediate submission and presentation at actual conferences or are nearer to being ready for submission to journals. Having participated in a realistically conducted mock conference, students are prepared to fulfill the behavioral protocols expected at a real conference, whether as session presiders or as paper presenters. Participation in a mock conference encourages students to apply to real conferences, thus enhancing their self-confidence, professionalism, skill at thinking on their feet (or at job interviews), and marketability.

Moreover, the required abstract and the restricted paper length hone writing skills, a serendipitous benefit for both the student and the instructor. Most students report that, whether a paper is geared to a conference format or not, they would write an abstract before attempting to produce all future seminar papers. All report that the three hours devoted to workshopping their abstracts taught them more about how to shape papers than anything else they had experienced in graduate school. This exercise proves to be the most valuable tool for teaching how to achieve more focus in writing at any level. Reading aloud to practice oral presentation and timing inevitably encouraged the revision of flabby or overly complex sentence structures into crisp, succinct prose. Some report that they would regularly read all future papers aloud to test for wandering or crabbed sentence structure. Moreover, one respondent felt for the first time in her graduate career that the world of professional scholarship was no longer a privileged club to which only Ivy League students need apply. Since most of us don't teach at the ivory-towered Ivy Leagues, this heightened self-esteem or empowerment is the most salutary benefit of the mock conference.

Such outside-the-box assignments will enhance the professionalism of nascent medievalists studying Chaucer's early poetry and make them more competitive in the job market and the tenure quest. In the mock conference, the student experiences hands-on learning of the practical necessities of conference presentation: professional etiquette and deportment, strategies for successful oral presentation of a complex thesis in a brief temporal space, methods of composing effective handouts, and tactics for handling difficult audience responses. This exercise initiates graduate students into their professional future as scholars. From the instructor's perspective, it results in reading critical papers that are more focused and original and instantiates a mentoring process that places graduate students on track for completing theses and dissertations on Chaucer's dream visions, lyrics, and *Troilus and Criseyde*.

NOTE

[1]Stephanie Dietrich's essay—" 'Slydyng' Masculinity in the Four Portraits of Troilus"—began as a conference paper in my seminar and was accepted for presentation at Kalamazoo, where it was heard by Peter Beidler, who solicited it for his book, *Masculinities in Chaucer: Approaches to Maleness in* The Canterbury Tales *and* Troilus and Criseyde.

APPENDIX

Suggestions for Reading Chaucer Out Loud in the Teaching of Chaucer's Poetry

Alan T. Gaylord

Aim

The aim of reading out loud in the classroom by both the instructor and members of the class should be to connect "out louding" with the imagination of spoken verse as a basis for public performance, class recitation, or silent reading. In each case the aim should be delight—through a recovery of the "shape of sound," lifting print off the page and constructing its aural dimensions, converting the text from something looked at to something heard, at once corporeal and intellectual. We "sound" the lines so they may resound in our minds.

Procedures

The teacher begins with Chaucerian phonology, then moves to scansion (drawing on syntax, semantics, and an inductive attention to possibilities of intonation), and proceeds to what I call "recital" (Gaylord, "Reading"). With beginning students one normally must start with explanations based on charts and books, supplemented with assigned listening from selected recordings; then, as soon as possible, one adds student recitation as part of recitation/ discussion in the classroom (needless to say, the students will enjoy the instructor's personal additions to the "out louding," as long as the additions don't fill up too much of the time!). Naturally, one would emphasize recitation at beginning of term and discussion once the term is well under way. In a lively discussion, students should feel comfortable reading Chaucerian examples out loud, less to perform than to illustrate a point.

Phonology

The major points to cover would include the system of stressed vowels, noting the Middle English (ME) feature of phonemic length (transformed in Present-Day English mainly into distinctions between acute and lax, diphongization, or differentiated articulations), the scribal systems of indicating (or not) pronunciation and vowel length (see Pearsall, "Chaucer's Meter"), the expedient of stressed or unstressed medial and final *e* that assists metrical regularization, and the "Germanic" fricatives that make it so much fun to pronounce words like *bright* and *though* (not to mention *laughen*).

It should be understood that the system is quite accurate historically only with reference to a *phonemic* mapping—and a simplified one at that—of the meaningful sounds of Chaucer's speech. For there can be no claim that a *phonetics* of Chaucer's idiolect (what he "really" and personally sounded like) can be reconstructed. (The controversies over this matter are reviewed in Gaylord, "Scanning" and "Reading.")

Resources for Pronunciation

For material supplementary to classroom instruction, I will mention only two kinds of printed resources, since a Chaucer course would not normally try to plug in minicourses in historical linguistics.

> Helge Kökeritz, *A Guide to Chaucer's Pronunciation*. This has the advantage of being inexpensive in its pamphlet form and has been kept in print even though it is now rather elderly. It will have the most value if students can learn the basic International Phonetic Alphabet (IPA) symbols for the ME vowel and diphthong phonemes. Modern words are supplied for American or British speakers in identifying the sound for each symbol. Very few learn pronunciation from a book; the charts are most useful in organizing the sounds to be produced and in providing a basic IPA for discussing examples in Chaucerian lines. Kökeritz provides fairly useful transcriptions for various passages, including *The House of Fame* and *Troilus and Criseyde*. He illustrates the standard practices of sounding (or not sounding) final and medial *e* sounds to help with syllabification and of lightly sounding a silent *e* (schwa) that is a final syllable at line end. Unfortunately, some of his IPA symbols are from a system different from the standard History of the English Language (HEL) texts, and the teacher will need to revise accordingly. (I do not recommend trying to track down the recordings that are mentioned in his preface.)
>
> HEL texts, such as C. M. Millward, *A Biography of the English Language*,

or John Algeo and Thomas Pyles, *The Origins and Development of the English Language*. A Chaucer course will rarely have the time to explore historical linguistics, but these standard texts can provide background and elucidation when questions arise about sounds, sound changes, and grammar. At the moment, an all-purpose, slightly simplified user's guide to the language and its sounds does not exist, but perhaps it is just as well that instructors cobble together a version of their own.

Printed materials, however, may prove less congenial to beginning students than resources on the Web. Only two Web sites need to be listed here since they provide further links to other sites for browsing.

> *"The Criyng and the Soun": The Chaucer Metapage Audio Files* (http://academics.vmi.edu/english/audio/audioindex.html). This has a generous selection of short passages by various teachers, many of whom have their own Chaucer Web sites (Alan Baragona's is particularly noteworthy). Students can be directed to various passages (the text being read is displayed) and asked to study the Middle English vowels, noting sounds and differences. And of course they can repeat a short passage as often as they want.
>
> *The Chaucer Studio Recordings* (http://english.byu.edu/chaucer). This site, maintained by Paul Thomas, provides a full list of the studio's moderately priced recordings of readings in Middle English of the dream romances and of *Troilus and Criseyde*, not to mention *The Canterbury Tales*. Chaucer Studio Press will also have my two-part monograph, *I. Out Loud with Chaucer's Shorter Poems: Adventures in Prosodic Criticism*, and *II. Out Loud with* Troilus and Criseyde *and* The Legend of Good Women: *Adventures in Prosodic Criticism*. Most of the passages discussed in my essay in this volume will be included in the CDs of representative examples.

Scansion

In a scansion exercise, one would focus on individual lines or brief segments of lines, identifying a workable syllabification and ascertaining the major stresses. The metrical norm can be described as "alternating-stress ten-syllable lines" or "loose iambics" (Frost) or "the goddam iamb" (Pound); in my edited collection, *Essays on the Art of Chaucer's Verse*, the consensus of the scholars is that an early version of iambic pentameter was the metric in most places, though some metricists allowed more variation than others (see Barney, "Meter"; E. Brown). Run-on lines will illustrate syntactical movement overflowing single lines. Notice should be given to the many places where variants for strictly alternating stresses are discovered, and these should be tied to the patterns of sense and emphasis.

Recital

Recital has more "music" in it than recitation (beginning practice) but less drama than public performance. Before entertaining audiences by reading Chaucer out loud, students should entertain themselves by hearing his verse as a construction of pleasing, provocative, and subtly shaped sounds in conversation, narration, and Chaucerian discourse. Recital is what classroom work should aim toward: ease, fluency, variety, clarity, and poetic sensitivity (Gaylord, "Reading"). The particular voice of a passage will be realized in a blending of syntax and rhetoric. The reader will seek to link phrases naturally to one another with a variety of stresses, pauses (junctures), and tones—the beginning of expressive intonation. Thus, in recital, reading out loud in a monotone can never be acceptable!

One sounds out the sense as it moves through, dances through, the itinerary of a chosen poetic form. There will be rhythm and nuance and varied chimes and rimes. And it is at this point, when choices begin to be made beyond negotiating the approximations of phonology, that discussion can begin about the rationale for a particular movement or the basis of a reader's choice for a particular stress or intonation. This is the time for sampling a variety of recordings, seeing what one likes best and least, and inquiring the reasons for such judgments.

NOTES ON CONTRIBUTORS

Roger Apfelbaum is senior lecturer in English and performance studies at De-Montfort University. He is author of *Shakespeare's* Troilus and Cressida: *Textual Problems and Performance Solutions* and of articles on performance history and theory.

Lynn Arner has published articles on *Confessio Amantis*, *Sir Gawain and the Green Knight*, and feminism in academe; she has also guest edited a special issue of *Exemplaria*. Lynn teaches at the University of Pittsburgh, where she is writing a book on Gower, Chaucer, urban literacy, and the production of consent in the wake of the English Rising of 1381.

Alison A. Baker is assistant professor at the California State Polytechnic University, Pomona. Her dissertation examines the role of scribes as the first readers of *Troilus and Criseyde*, and she is currently working on a pedagogical study aimed at improving students' ability to read early literature. Alison has been a reader in Middle English for the Chaucer Studio.

Julia Boffey is professor of medieval studies at Queen Mary, University of London. Her interests include Middle English lyrics, fifteenth- and early-sixteenth-century literature, and the history of the book in the late medieval and early modern periods. She has recently collaborated on a revision of *The Index of Middle English Verse* and is exploring the relations between manuscript and printed production of texts between 1475 and 1550.

Michael Calabrese is professor of English at California State University, Los Angeles. He is the author of *Chaucer's Ovidian Arts of Love* and has written essays on Chaucer, Langland, the *Pearl* poet, Abelard and Heloise, Boccaccio, and Marco Polo. He is an editor of the Piers Plowman *Electronic Archive*.

Susannah Mary Chewning teaches British literature, women's studies, and writing at Union County College. She has published studies on Chaucer, Shakespeare, anchoritic literature, and medieval devotional poetry, and has recently edited a collection of critical essays, *Intersections of Sexuality and the Divine in Medieval Culture: The Word Made Flesh*.

Holly A. Crocker is assistant professor of English at the University of South Carolina. She has published articles on Chaucer and Shakespeare, has edited a collection of essays entitled *Comic Provocations: Exposing the Corpus of Old French Fabliaux*, and is completing a book entitled *Chaucer's Visions of Manhood*.

Adam Brooke Davis teaches medieval studies, linguistics, and writing at Truman State University. He has published in *Chaucer Review*, *American Quarterly*, *Oral Tradition*, and elsewhere on medieval literature, critical theory, rhetoric and composition pedagogy and made forays into Mark Twain, folk medicine and magical practice, archaeology, and fiction and poetry. He is Webmaster and general editor of publications for the Missouri Folklore Society.

Glenn Davis is assistant professor of English at Saint Cloud State University, where he teaches courses in Old and Middle English language and literature. He has published articles on *Genesis B* and the Exeter Book *Riddles* and is currently working on a project that explores the Anglo Saxons' interest in physical and spiritual protection.

Alan T. Gaylord is Winkley Professor of Anglo-Saxon and English Language and Literature, emeritus, at Dartmouth College. For the Chaucer Studio, he has published "The Poetics of Alliteration" (with CD) and recorded in Middle English such works as *Pearl* and Chaucer's Knight's, Miller's, Friar's, and Monk's Tales. He has published with the Tabard Press, also with CDs, *I. Out Loud with Chaucer's Shorter Poems* and *II. Out Loud with* Troilus and Criseyde *and* The Legend of Good Women.

Warren Ginsberg is College of Arts and Sciences Distinguished Professor at the University of Oregon and head of the Department of English. He is the author of *Chaucer's Italian Tradition*, *Dante's Aesthetics of Being*, and *The Cast of Character*; he has also edited *Winner and Waster* and *The Parliament of the Three Ages* for the TEAMS Middle English Texts Series. He is currently working on a book about the links in Chaucer's *Canterbury Tales*.

Noel Harold Kaylor, Jr. is professor of English and administrative assistant for Specified University Programs at Troy University. He has edited late medieval and early modern English translations of Boethius's *De consolatione philosophiae*, written and lectured on the works of Chaucer, and is working on the tradition of the Trojan War in art and literature.

Clare R. Kinney is associate professor of English at the University of Virginia, where she teaches medieval and Renaissance literature. She is the author of *Strategies of Poetic Narrative: Chaucer, Spenser, Milton, Eliot* and of several articles on *Troilus and Criseyde*; she has also published articles on *Beowulf, Sir Gawain and the Green Knight*, Philip Sidney, Edmund Spenser, Lady Mary Wroth, and the Renaissance reception of Chaucer.

Peggy A. Knapp is professor of English at Carnegie Mellon University. She founded and for many years edited the annual book series *Assays*. She is the author of *Chaucer and the Social Contest*, *Time-Bound Words*, and articles on medieval and Renaissance authors and on contemporary writers, critics, and filmmakers. She is currently working on a book called "Chaucerian Aesthetics."

Jean-François Kosta-Théfaine is associate researcher at the Centre d'Études des Textes Médiévaux of the Université de Rennes 2. He has written articles on Christine de Pisan, Othon de Grandson, Jehan Chaperon, and medieval cookbooks and food. He has also published new editions of texts by Christine de Pisan: *Epistre a Eustace Mourel, Proverbes Moraulx*, and *Virelais*.

Scott Lightsey teaches Chaucer and Middle English at Georgia State University, Atlanta, where he is an assistant professor. He has published on Chaucer in *Studies in the Age of Chaucer* and *English Language Notes*. His research interests in medieval studies include mirabilia and technology in literature, urban history, and the image of the Scold. He is currently completing a book on medieval literary representations of man-made marvels and wonders.

Marcia Smith Marzec is professor of English at the University of Saint Francis, where she teaches medieval literature and language, as well as film studies. She also directs the university's sophomore core program. She is the founder and director of the annual Undergraduate Conference on English Language and Literature. With Cindy Vitto, she is the editor of *New Perspectives on Criseyde*. She is the author of numerous articles on medieval literature, textual studies, film, and American literature.

James J. Paxson teaches medieval literature and literary theory at the University of Florida. He is an editor of *Exemplaria* and has published *The Poetics of Personification* and articles on modern theory and medieval literature, allegory, rhetoric, and literature and science.

Tison Pugh is associate professor at the University of Central Florida. He is the author of *Queering Medieval Genres* and articles on medieval literature and sexuality. He has won teaching awards at the University of Oregon and the University of California, Irvine, as well as a University of Central Florida College of Arts and Sciences Excellence in Undergraduate Teaching Award.

William A. Quinn is professor of English and director of the Medieval and Renaissance Studies Program at the University of Arkansas, Fayetteville. His publications include *Jongleur* (with Audley Hall), *Chaucer's Rehersynges: The Performability of* The Legend of Good Women, *Chaucer's Dream Visions*, and articles in *Studies in the Age of Chaucer*, *Chaucer Review*, *Medium Ævum*, *Review of English Studies*, and *Viator*.

Martha Rust is assistant professor of English at New York University. Her recent publications include an article on a fifteenth-century abecedarius, "The ABC of Aristotle," and a study of reflections of the practice of reading marginal commentary in a Middle English *chanson d'aventure*, "Revertere."

Myra Seaman is associate professor of English at the College of Charleston, where she teaches Chaucer, Middle English, and the history of the English language. Her articles on late Middle English verse romance have appeared in *Studies in Philology* and *Fifteenth-Century Studies*. She is finishing a book, "Seeking an Audience for Late Middle English Romance in Two Fifteenth-Century Manuscripts," and is coediting a collection, "Cultural Studies of the Modern Middle Ages."

Glenn A. Steinberg, associate professor of English at the College of New Jersey, has published articles on the reception of Vergil, Dante, and Chaucer in the late Middle Ages and Renaissance. He is currently working on a critique of the traditional characterization of Chaucer as the father of English poetry by examining evidence that Lydgate influenced Renaissance poetics more than Chaucer, as well as a study of Dante's relationship to his classical and vernacular precursors.

Barbara Stevenson is professor of English at Kennesaw State University. Her research and teaching interests include Chaucer and Middle English literature, medieval women writers, and cross-cultural approaches to medieval literature. With Cynthia Ho, she is coeditor of *Crossing the Bridge: Comparative Essays on Medieval European and Heian Japanese Women Writers*.

Lorraine Kochanske Stock is associate professor of English and a women's studies affiliate at the University of Houston. She has published on medieval drama, Dante,

Chaucer, the *Gawain* poet, Langland, Froissart, Arthurian romance, and other medieval topics. She is currently completing an interdisciplinary book about medieval primitivism and the Wild Man. She has twice been awarded the University of Houston Teaching Excellence Award and once the University of Houston Humanities College Master Teacher Award.

Jenifer Sutherland teaches at Branksome Hall in Toronto. Her most recent scholarly publications are "*Repuerascere*: Christianizing Classical Rhetoric through Play in Walter of Wimborne's *De Palpone*," in *Exemplaria* and "Amplifications of the Virgin: Play and Empowerment in Walter of Wimborne's *Maria Carmina*," in *Virginity Revisited: Configurations of the Unpossessed Body*, edited by Judy Fletcher and Bonnie MacLachlan.

Karla Taylor is the director of the Medieval and Early Modern Studies Program at the University of Michigan, Ann Arbor. A member of the Department of English Language and Literature, she is also an affiliate of comparative literature and romance languages and literatures. Her work includes studies of late medieval English and Italian literature and of translation. She is the author of *Chaucer Reads* The Divine Comedy, a study of *Troilus and Criseyde*.

Carolynn Van Dyke is the Francis A. March Professor of English at Lafayette College, where she teaches composition, linguistics, medieval literature, and technology studies. She is the author of *The Fiction of Truth: Structures of Meaning in Narrative and Dramatic Allegory* and *Chaucer's Agents: Cause and Representation in Chaucerian Narrative*.

Angela Jane Weisl is associate professor of English at Seton Hall University. She is the author of *Conquering the Reign of Femeny: Gender and Genre in Chaucer's Romance* and *The Persistence of Medievalism: Narrative Adventures in Contemporary Culture*. With Cindy Carlson, she edited *Constructions of Widowhood and Virginity in the Middle Ages*.

SURVEY PARTICIPANTS

Roger Apfelbaum, *DeMontfort University*
Lynn Arner, *University of Pittsburgh*
Anne Astell, *Purdue University*
Alison A. Baker, *California State Polytechnic University, Pomona*
Louise Bishop, *University of Oregon*
Julia Boffey, *Queen Mary College, University of London*
Beverly Boyd, *University of Kansas*
Michael Calabrese, *California State University, Los Angeles*
Susannah Mary Chewning, *Union County College*
Holly A. Crocker, *University of South Carolina*
Adam Brooke Davis, *Truman State University*
Glenn Davis, *Saint Cloud State University*
Steven Epley, *Samford University*
Judith Ferster, *North Carolina State University*
Alan T. Gaylord, *Dartmouth College*
Warren Ginsberg, *University of Oregon*
Robert W. Hanning, *Columbia University*
Laura Hodges, *University of Houston*
Noel Harold Kaylor, Jr., *Troy University, Troy*
Clare R. Kinney, *University of Virginia*
Peggy A. Knapp, *Carnegie Mellon University*
M. Diane Krantz, *Weber State University*
Miriamne Ara Krummel, *University of Dayton*
Clare Lees, *King's College, London*
Scott Lightsey, *Georgia State University*
Lan Lipscomb, *Troy University, Montgomery*
Marcia Smith Marzec, *University of Saint Francis*
Erin Mullally, *LeMoyne College*
Anita Obermeier, *University of New Mexico*
James J. Paxson, *University of Florida*
William A. Quinn, *University of Arkansas, Fayetteville*
Masha Raskolnikov, *Cornell University*
Lisa Robeson, *Ohio Northern University*
Martha Rust, *New York University*
Catherine Sanok, *University of Michigan*
Myra Seaman, *College of Charleston*
Martin B. Shichtman, *Eastern Michigan University*
Diana E. Slampyak, *University of California, Riverside*
Glenn A. Steinberg, *College of New Jersey*
Barbara Stevenson, *Kennesaw State University*

Lorraine Kochanske Stock, *University of Houston*
Jenifer Sutherland, *Branksome Hall* (Canada)
John Sweeney, *Seton Hall University*
Karla Taylor, *University of Michigan*
Ingeborg Urcia, *Eastern Washington University*
Carolynn Van Dyke, *Lafayette College*
Donald T. Williams, *Toccoa Falls College*

WORKS CITED

Acker, Paul. "A Schoolchild's Primer (Plimpton MS 258)." *Medieval Literature for Children.* Ed. Daniel Kline. New York: Routledge, 2003. 143–54.

Aers, David. "Chaucer's Criseyde: Woman in Society, Woman in Love." *Chaucer, Langland and the Creative Imagination.* London: Routledge, 1980.

———. "Criseyde: Woman in Medieval Society." *Chaucer Review* 13 (1979): 177–200.

Aers, David, and Lynn Staley. *The Powers of the Holy.* University Park: Pennsylvania State UP, 1996.

Alain de Lille. *The Plaint of Nature.* Ed. James J. Sheridan. Toronto: Pontifical Inst. of Mediaeval Studies, 1980.

Alexander, J. J. G. *The Decorated Letter.* New York: Braziller, 1978.

Algeo, John, and Thomas Pyles. *The Origins and Development of the English Language.* Boston: Heinle, 2004.

Anastasas, Florence Hay, trans. *Geoffrey Chaucer:* The Legend of Good Women: *Written in Praise of Women Faithful in Love.* Hicksville: Exposition, 1976.

Andreas Capellanus. *The Art of Courtly Love.* Trans. John Jay Parry. New York: Columbia UP, 1990.

Apfelbaum, Roger. *Shakespeare's* Troilus and Cressida: *Textual Problems and Performance Solutions.* Newark: U of Delaware P, 2004.

Arrathoon, Leigh A., ed. *Chaucer and the Craft of Fiction.* Rochester: Solaris, 1986.

Artz, Frederick. *The Mind of the Middle Ages, A.D. 200–1500.* New York: Knopf, 1966.

Astell, Ann W. *Political Allegory in Late Medieval England.* Ithaca: Cornell UP, 1999.

Augustine. *Confessions.* Trans. John K. Ryan. Garden City: Doubleday, 1960.

———. *De doctrina Christiana.* New York: Prentice, 1958.

Backhouse, Janet. *The Lindisfarne Gospels.* Ithaca: Cornell UP, 1981.

Bahr, Arthur. "The Rhetorical Construction of Narrator and Narrative in Chaucer's *The Book of the Duchess.*" *Chaucer Review* 35 (2000): 43–56.

Baird, Lorrayne, ed. *A Bibliography of Chaucer, 1964–1973.* Boston: Hall, 1977.

Bakhtin, M[ikhail] M. *The Dialogic Imagination.* Ed. Michael Holquist. Trans. Caryl Emerson and Holquist. Austin: U of Texas P, 1981.

Barney, Stephen A., ed. *Chaucer's* Troilus: *Essays in Criticism.* Hamden: Archon, 1980.

———. "Chaucer's *Troilus*: Meter and Grammar." Gaylord, *Essays* 163–91.

———, ed. *Troilus and Criseyde.* By Geoffrey Chaucer. New York: Norton, 2006.

Barron, Caroline M. "The Education and Training of Girls in Fifteenth-Century London." *Courts, Counties, and the Capital in the Later Middle Ages.* Ed. Diana E. S. Dunn. New York: St. Martin's, 1996. 139–53.

Baswell, Christopher. "Talking Back to the Text: Marginal Voices in Medieval Secular Literature." *The Uses of Manuscripts in Literary Studies.* Ed. Charlotte Morse, Penelope Doob, and Marjorie Woods. Kalamazoo: Medieval Inst., 1992. 121–60.

————. *Virgil in Medieval England: Figuring the* Aeneid *from the Twelfth Century to Chaucer.* Cambridge: Cambridge UP, 1995.

Baugh, Albert C., ed. *Chaucer's Major Poetry.* Englewood Cliffs: Prentice, 1963.

Beadle, Richard. "Facsimiles of Middle English Manuscripts." *A Guide to Editing Middle English.* Ed. Vincent McCarren and Douglas Moffat. Ann Arbor: U of Michigan P, 1998. 318–31.

Beadle, Richard, and Rosamond McKitterick. *Catalogue of the Pepys Library at Magdalene College, Cambridge: Volume V: Manuscripts: Part I: Medieval.* Cambridge: Brewer, 1992.

Beidler, Peter G. "Chaucer and the Trots: What to Do about Those Modern English Translations." *Chaucer Review* 19 (1985): 290–301.

————, ed. *Masculinities in Chaucer: Approaches to Maleness in* The Canterbury Tales *and* Troilus and Criseyde. Cambridge: Brewer, 1998.

Bell, Susan Groag. "Medieval Women Book Owners: Arbiters of Lay Piety and Ambassadors of Culture." *Signs* 7 (1982): 742–68.

Benjamin, Walter. "The Task of the Translator." *Illuminations.* Trans. Harry Zohn. New York: Schocken, 1969. 69–82.

Bennett, J. A. W. *Chaucer's* Book of Fame. Oxford: Clarendon, 1968.

————. The Parliament of Foules: *An Interpretation.* 2nd ed. Oxford: Clarendon, 1965.

Benson, C. David. *Chaucer's* Troilus and Criseyde. London: Hyman, 1990.

————, ed. *Critical Essays on Chaucer's* Troilus and Criseyde *and His Major Early Poems.* Toronto: U of Toronto P, 1991.

————. *The History of Troy in Middle English Literature: Guido delle Colonne's* Historia Destructionis Troiae *in Medieval England.* Cambridge: Brewer, 1980.

Benson, C. David, and Barry Windeatt. "The Manuscript Glosses to Chaucer's *Troilus and Criseyde.*" *Chaucer Review* 25 (1990): 33–53.

Benson, Larry. *A Glossarial Concordance to the* Riverside Chaucer. New York: Garland, 1993.

————. "A Reader's Guide to Writings on Chaucer." *Geoffrey Chaucer.* Ed. Derek S. Brewer. Athens: Ohio UP, 1974.

Besserman, Lawrence. *Chaucer and the Bible: A Critical Review of Research, Indexes, and Bibliography.* New York: Garland, 1988.

————. *Chaucer's Biblical Poetics.* Norman: U of Oklahoma P, 1998.

Bird, Ruth. *The Turbulent London of Richard II.* London: Longmans, 1949.

Bishop, Ian. *Chaucer's* Troilus and Criseyde: *A Critical Study.* Bristol: U of Bristol P, 1981.

Bisson, Lillian. *Chaucer and the Late Medieval World.* New York: St. Martin's, 1998.

Blamires, Alcuin, ed. With Karen Plat and C. W. Marx. *Woman Defamed and Woman Defended.* Oxford: Clarendon, 1992.

Bloom, Harold. *The Anxiety of Influence.* Oxford: Oxford UP, 1997.

Bloomfield, Morton. "Distance and Predestination in *Troilus and Criseyde.*" *Chaucer*

Criticism: Troilus and Criseyde *and the Minor Poems*. Ed. Richard Schoeck and Jerome Taylor. South Bend: Notre Dame UP, 1967. 196–210.

Boccaccio, Giovanni. *Concerning Famous Women*. Trans. Guido Guarino. New Brunswick: Rutgers UP, 1963.

———. *The Fates of Illustrious Men*. Trans. Louis Brewer Hall. New York: Ungar, 1965.

———. *Il Filocolo*. Ed. A. E. Quaglio. Milan: Mondadori, 1964.

———. *Il Filostrato*. Ed. Vittore Branca. Milan: Mondadori, 1964.

———. *Tutte le opere di Giovanni Boccaccio*. Vols. 1–2. Ed. Vittore Branca. Milan: Mondadori, 1964.

Bodleian Library MS Fairfax 16. Introd. John Norton-Smith. London: Scolar, 1979.

Boethius. *The Consolation of Philosophy*. New York: Macmillan, 1962.

Boffey, Julia. "Annotation in Some Manuscripts of *Troilus and Criseyde*." *English Manuscript Studies 1100–1700* 5 (1995): 1–17.

———. "The Reputation and Circulation of Chaucer's Lyrics in the Fifteenth Century." *Chaucer Review* 28 (1993): 23–40.

Boitani, Piero. *Chaucer and Boccaccio*. Oxford: Soc. for the Study of Mediaeval Langs. and Lits., 1977.

———. *Chaucer and the Imaginary World of Fame*. Cambridge: Brewer, 1984.

———. *The European Tragedy of* Troilus. Oxford: Clarendon, 1989.

———. "Old Books Brought to Life in Dreams: The *Book of the Duchess*, the *House of Fame*, the *Parliament of Fowls*." Boitani and Mann 39–57.

Boitani, Piero, and Jill Mann, eds. *The Cambridge Companion to Chaucer*. Cambridge: Cambridge UP, 2003.

Bonnard, Georges, ed. *Geoffrey Chaucer:* Troilus and Criseyde. Bern: Francke, 1943.

Borges, Jorge Luis. "Funes the Memorious." *Ficciones*. Trans. Anthony Kerrigan. New York: Grove, 1962. 114–15.

Boswell, Jackson Campbell, and Sylvia Wallace Holton. *Chaucer's Fame in England: STC Chauceriana, 1475–1640*. New York: MLA, 2005.

———. "References to Chaucer's Literary Reputation." *Chaucer Review* 31 (1997): 291–316.

Bowen, Barbara. *Gender in the Theater of War: Shakespeare's* Troilus and Cressida. New York: Garland, 1993.

Bowers, Bege K., and Mark Allen, eds. *Annotated Chaucer Bibliography, 1986–1996*. Notre Dame: U of Notre Dame P, 2002.

Bradbrook, M. C. "What Shakespeare Did to Chaucer's *Troilus and Criseyde*." *Shakespeare Quarterly* 9 (1958): 311–19.

Braddy, Haldeen. "Chaucer's *Book of the Duchess* and Two of Grandson's Complaints." *Modern Language Notes* 52 (1937): 487–91.

———. *Chaucer and the French Poet Graunson*. Baton Rouge: Louisiana State UP, 1947.

———. "Chaucer and Graunson: The Valentine Tradition." *PMLA* 54 (1939): 359–68.

———. "The French Influence on Chaucer." *Companion to Chaucer Studies*. Ed. Beryl Rowland. Rev. ed. New York: Oxford UP, 1979. 143–59.

———. "Messire Oton de Graunson, Chaucer's Savoyard Friend." *Studies in Philology* 35 (1938): 515–31.

———. "Sir Oton de Graunson—'Flour of Hem That Make in Fraunce.' " *Studies in Philology* 35 (1938): 10–24.

Brewer, Derek S. *Chaucer and Chaucerians: Critical Studies in Middle English Literature*. Tuscaloosa: U of Alabama P, 1967.

———. *Chaucer and His World*. New York: Dodd, 1978.

———, ed. *Chaucer: The Critical Heritage*. 2 vols. London: Routledge, 1978.

———. "Images of Chaucer: 1386–1900." Brewer, *Chaucer and Chaucerians* 240–70.

———. *A New Introduction to Chaucer*. 2nd edition. London: Longman, 1998.

———. *The World of Chaucer*. Suffolk: Brewer, 2000.

Brink, Bernhard ten. *The Language and Metre of Chaucer*. Rev. Friedrich Kluge. Trans. M. Bentinck Smith. London: Macmillan, 1901.

Brown, Carleton, and Rossell Hope Robbins. *The Index of Middle English Verse*. New York: Columbia UP, 1943.

Brown, Emerson, Jr. "The Joy of Chaucer's Lydgate Lines." Gaylord, *Essays* 267–79.

Brown, Peter, ed. *A Companion to Chaucer*. Oxford: Blackwell, 2000.

Brusendorff, Aage. "Spurious Poems." *The Chaucer Tradition*. London: Oxford UP, 1925.

Burger, Glenn. *Chaucer's Queer Nation*. Minneapolis: U of Minnesota P, 2003.

Burnley, David. *A Guide to Chaucer's Language*. Norman: U of Oklahoma P, 1983.

Burrow, John. "Poems without Endings." *Studies in the Age of Chaucer* 12 (1991): 17–37.

Burrow, John, and Thorlac Turville-Petre, eds. *A Book of Middle English*. 2nd ed. Cambridge: Blackwell, 1992.

Burton, Gideon. *Silva Rhetoricae*. Brigham Young U. 16 June 2003 <http://humanities.byu.edu/rhetoric/silva.htm>.

Butler, Judith. *Bodies That Matter: On the Discursive Limits of "Sex."* New York: Routledge, 1993.

———. *Gender Trouble: Feminism and the Subversion of Identity*. New York: Routledge, 1990.

Butterfield, Ardis. "Pastoral and the Politics of Plague in Machaut and Chaucer." *Studies in the Age of Chaucer* 16 (1994): 3–27.

Calabrese, Michael. *Chaucer's Ovidian Arts of Love*. Gainesville: UP of Florida, 1994.

Camille, Michael. *Image on the Edge*. Cambridge: Harvard UP, 1992.

Cannon, Christopher. "Chaucer and Rape: Uncertainty's Certainties." *Representing Rape in Medieval and Early Modern Literature*. Ed. Elizabeth Robertson and Christine M. Rose. New York: Palgrave, 2001. 255–79.

———. *The Making of Chaucer's English: A Study of Words*. Cambridge: Cambridge UP, 1998.

Cantor, Norman F. *The Civilization of the Middle Ages*. New York: Harper, 1993.

Carbonnelli, G. *Gli ultimi giorni del Conte Rossa e i processi per la sua morte*. Pavie: Pinerolo, 1912.

Carden, Sally Tartline. "Oton de Grandson." *Literature of the French and Occitan Middle Ages*. Ed. D. Sinnreich-Levi and I. S. Laurie. Detroit: Gale, 1999. 141–48.

Carruthers, Mary J. *The Book of Memory: A Study of Memory in Medieval Culture*. Cambridge: Cambridge UP, 1990.

Chaucer Bibliography Online. <http://uchaucer.utsa.edu>.

Chaucer, Geoffrey. *The Riverside Chaucer*. Gen. ed. Larry D. Benson. 3rd ed. Boston: Houghton, 1987.

Chaucer: Life and Times CD-ROM. Reading, Eng.: Primary Source Media, 1995.

Chaucer MetaPage. Ed. Joseph Witting. 19 Jan. 2005. U of North Carolina. <http://www.unc.edu/depts/chaucer/>.

Chaucer Pedagogy Page. Ed. Daniel T. Kline. 1998–2005. 18 July 2006 <http://hosting.uaa.alaska.edu/afdtk/pedagogy.htm>.

The Chaucer Studio Recordings. Ed. Paul Thomas. 19 Jan. 2005. <http://english.byu.edu/Chaucer/about.htm>.

Chenu, M. D. *Nature, Man and Society in the Twelfth Century*. Toronto: U of Toronto P, 1997.

Chesterton, G. K. *Chaucer*. 1956. New York: Greenwood, 1969.

Chism, Christine. *Alliterative Revivals*. Philadelphia: U of Pennsylvania P, 2002.

Christine de Pisan. *The Book of the City of Ladies*. Trans. Rosalind Brown-Grant. New York: Penguin, 1999.

Chute, Marchette. *Geoffrey Chaucer of England*. New York: Dutton, 1946.

Cingria, Charles-Albert. La complainte de Vénus *telle que la faite sire Othon de Grand-son, célèbre savoisien, sous ce titre*: Les cinq ballades ensuivans *et telle que l'a translatée le grand Jauffroy Chaucer, enrichie des gloses marginales de Charles-Albert Cingria*. Saint-Saphorien-de-Lavaux: En l'Officine de la Marine et de l'Au-delà, 1943.

Clark, Elizabeth, et al. "Commentary." *Medieval Feminist Newsletter* 6 (1988): 2–10.

Coghill, Nevill. *The Poet Chaucer*. 2nd ed. New York: Oxford UP, 1968.

———, trans. Troilus and Criseyde *by Geoffrey Chaucer*. New York: Penguin, 1971.

Cohen, Jeffrey Jerome. "On Saracen Enjoyment: Some Fantasies of Race in Late Medieval France and England." *Journal of Medieval and Early Modern Studies* 31 (2001): 113–46.

Coleman, Joyce. *Public Reading and the Reading Public in Late Medieval England and France*. Cambridge: Cambridge UP, 1996.

Collette, Carolyn P. The Legend of Good Women: *Context and Reception*. Woodbridge, Eng.: Brewer, 2006.

Connolly, Margaret. *John Shirley: Book Production and the Noble Household in Fifteenth-Century England*. Aldershot: Ashgate, 1998.

Cook, Daniel, ed. Troilus and Criseyde *by Geoffrey Chaucer*. Garden City: Anchor, 1966.

Cook, William R., and Ronald B. Herzman. *The Medieval World View: An Introduction*. New York: Oxford UP, 1983.

Corbett, P. J., and Robert J. Connors. *Classical Rhetoric for the Modern Student*. 4th ed. Oxford: Oxford UP, 1999.

Coulton, G. G. *Chaucer and His England*. 1908. London: Methuen, 1968.

Cowen, Janet, and George Kane, eds. *The Legend of Good Women*. East Lansing: Colleagues, 1995.

Crawford, William, ed. *Bibliography of Chaucer, 1954–1963*. Seattle: U of Washington P, 1967.

Crow, Martin, and Clair Olson, eds. *Chaucer Life-Records*. Austin: U of Texas P, 1966.

Cunningham, C. A., ed. "A Critical Edition of the Poetry of Oton de Grandson." Diss. U of North Carolina at Chapel Hill, 1987.

Damrosch, David, Christopher Baswell, et al., eds. *The Longman Anthology of British Literature: Second Compact Edition*. New York: Longman, 2004.

Dante Alighieri. *The Divine Comedy*. 3 vols. Trans. Mark Musa. New York: Penguin, 1985.

———. *The* Divine Comedy *of Dante Alighieri*. Ed. Robert M. Durling and Ronald L. Martinez. New York: Oxford UP, 1996.

———. *La divina commedia secondo l, antica vulgata*. Ed. Giorgio Petrocchi. 4 vols. Società Dantesca Italiana. 1966–67. Princeton: Princeton UP, 1970–76.

———. *Vita nuova*. Ed. Domenico de Robertis. Milan: Ricciardi, 1980.

David, Alfred. "Chaucerian Comedy and Criseyde." *Essays on* Troilus and Criseyde. Ed. Mary Salu. Cambridge: Brewer, 1979. 90–104.

Davis, Norman. *Chaucer Glossary*. Oxford: Clarendon, 1979.

Dean, James M. *The World Grown Old in Later Medieval Literature*. Cambridge: Medieval Acad. of Amer., 1997.

Delany, Sheila. *Chaucer's* House of Fame: *The Poetics of Skeptical Fideism*. Chicago: U of Chicago P, 1972.

———. *Impolitic Bodies: Poetry, Saints, and Society in Fifteenth-Century England*. New York: Oxford UP, 1998.

———, trans. A Legend of Holy Women: *A Translation of Osbern Bokenham's Legends of Holy Women*. South Bend: U of Notre Dame P, 1992.

———. *Medieval Literary Politics: Shapes of Ideology*. Manchester: Manchester UP, 1990.

———. *The Naked Text: Chaucer's* Legend of Good Women. Berkeley: U of California P, 1994.

de Man, Paul. "Conclusions: Walter Benjamin's 'The Task of the Translator.'" *The Resistance to Theory*. Minneapolis: U of Minnesota P, 1986. 87–91.

Denley, Marie. "Elementary Teaching Techniques and Middle English Religious Didactic Writing." *Langland, the Mystics, and the Medieval English Religious Tradition*. Ed. Helen Phillips. Cambridge: Brewer, 1990. 223–41.

Derrida, Jacques. *Dissemination*. Trans. Barbara Johnson. Chicago: U of Chicago P, 1981.

———. "Fors: The Anglish Words of Nicolas Abraham and Maria Torok." *The Wolf Man's Magic Word: A Cryptonymy*. By Nicolas Abraham and Maria Torok. Trans. and introd. Nicholas Rand. Fwd. Derrida. Minneapolis: U of Minnesota P, 1986. xi–il.

———. *Of Grammatology*. Trans. Gayatri Chakravorty Spivak. Baltimore: Johns Hopkins UP, 1976.

———. *Points of Suspension: Interviews, 1974–1994*. Ed. Elisabeth Weber. Trans. Peggy Kamuf et al. Stanford: Stanford UP, 1995.

Dietrich, Stephanie. " 'Slydyng' Masculinity in the Four Portraits of Troilus." Beidler, *Masculinities* 205–20.

Digital Scriptorium. 20 Feb. 2004. Regents of the U of California. <http://sunsite .berkeley.edu/Scriptorium/>.

Dinshaw, Carolyn. *Chaucer's Sexual Poetics*. Madison: U of Wisconsin P, 1989.

Donaldson, E. Talbot. "Chaucer the Pilgrim." *Speaking of Chaucer*. London: Athlone, 1970. 1–12.

———, ed. *Chaucer's Poetry: An Anthology for the Modern Reader*. 1958. New York: Ronald, 1975.

———. *The Swan at the Well: Shakespeare Reading Chaucer*. New Haven: Yale UP, 1985.

Donohue, James J., trans. *Chaucer's* Troilus and Cressida: *Five Books in Present-Day English*. Dubuque: Loras Coll., 1975.

Driver, Martha W. "Reading Images of Reading." *Ricardian* 13 (2003): 186–202.

Dronke, Peter. *The Medieval Lyric*. 3rd ed. Cambridge: Brewer, 1996.

DuBoulay, F. R. H. *The Age of Ambition: English Society in the Late Middle Ages*. New York: Viking, 1970.

Durling, Robert M., ed. and trans. *Petrarch's Lyric Poems*. Cambridge: Harvard UP, 1976.

Dutschke, C. W. *Guide to Medieval and Renaissance Manuscripts in the Huntington Library*. 2 vols. San Marino: Huntington Lib., 1989.

DuVal, John, trans. *Fabliaux Fair and Foul*. Binghamton: Medieval and Renaissance Texts and Studies, 1992.

Early English Aloud and Alive: The Language of Beowulf, Chaucer, *and* Shakespeare. Prod. Simon Fraser U and Caritas Productions. Videocassette. Films for the Humanities and Sciences, 1999.

Early Manuscripts at Oxford University. Oxford University. <http://image.ox.ac.uk>.

Edwards, A. S. G. "Chaucer from Manuscript to Print: The Social Text and the Critical Text." *Mosaic* 28 (1995): 1–12.

———. "The Unity and Authenticity of *Anelida and Arcite*: The Evidence of the Manuscripts." *Studies in Bibliography* 41 (1988): 177–88.

Edwards, Robert R. *Chaucer and Boccaccio: Antiquity and Modernity*. New York: Palgrave, 2002.

———. *The Dream of Chaucer: Representation and Reflection in the Early Narratives*. Durham: Duke UP, 1989.

———. "Pandarus's 'Unthrift' and the Problem of Desire in *Troilus and Criseyde*." Shoaf and Cox 74–87.

Elbow, Peter. *Writing without Teachers*. Oxford: Oxford UP, 1976.

Eliason, Norman E. *The Language of Chaucer's Poetry: An Appraisal of the Verse, Style, and Structure*. Copenhagen: Rosenkilde, 1972.

Ellis, Steve. *Chaucer at Large*. Minneapolis: U of Minnesota P, 2000.

Essential Chaucer Bibliography. Ed. Mark Allen and John Fisher. 19 Feb. 2006 <http://colfa.utsa.edu/chaucer/>.

Evans, Joan, ed. *The Flowering of the Middle Ages*. New York: McGraw, 1966.

Fansler, Dean. *Chaucer and the* Roman de la rose. Gloucester: Smith, 1965.

Federico, Sylvia. *New Troy: Fantasies of Empire in the Late Middle Ages*. Minneapolis: U of Minnesota P, 2003.

The Findern Manuscript: Cambridge University Library MS Ff. 1. 6. 1977. Introd. Richard Beadle and A. E. B. Owen. Rpt. with amendments. London: Scolar, 1978.

Fisher, John H., ed. *The Complete Poetry and Prose of Geoffrey Chaucer*. 2nd ed. Fort Worth: Holt, 1989.

———. *The Importance of Chaucer*. Carbondale: Southern Illinois UP, 1992.

Fletcher, Bradford. Introduction. *Manuscript Trinity* xv–xxxi.

Forni, Kathleen. *The Chaucerian Apocrypha*. Gainesville: U of Florida P, 2001.

———. "Reinventing Chaucer: Helgeland's *A Knight's Tale*." *Chaucer Review* 37 (2003): 253–64.

Foucault, Michel. *The Archaeology of Knowledge and the Discourse on Language*. Trans. A. M. Sheridan Smith. New York: Pantheon, 1972.

Fowler, Elizabeth. "Civil Death and the Maiden: Agency and the Conditions of Contract in *Piers Plowman*." *Speculum* 70 (1995): 760–92.

Fradenburg, Louise O. " 'Our Owen Wo to Drynke': Loss, Gender, and Chivalry in *Troilus and Criseyde*." Shoaf and Cox 88–106.

———. " 'Voice Memorial': Loss and Reparation in Chaucer's Poetry." *Exemplaria* 2 (1990): 169–202.

Frank, Robert Worth. *Chaucer and* The Legend of Good Women. Cambridge: Harvard UP, 1972.

Frantzen, Allen. Troilus and Criseyde: *The Poem and the Frame*. New York: Twayne, 1993.

Freund, Elizabeth. "Ariachne's Broken Woof: The Rhetoric of Citation in *Troilus and Cressida*." *Shakespeare and the Question of Theory*. Ed. Patricia Parker and Geoffrey Hartman. New York: Methuen, 1985. 19–36.

Froissart, Jean. *Chronicles*. Trans. Geoffrey Brereton. 1968. London: Penguin, 1978.

———. *Dits et débats*. Ed. Anthime Fourrier. Geneva: Droz, 1979.

Frost, Robert. "Two Tramps in Mud Time." *The Poetry of Robert Forst*. Ed. Edward Connery Latham. New York: Holt, 1969. 275–77.

Furnivall, Frederick J., ed. *A Parallel-Text Edition of Chaucer's Minor Poems*. Chaucer Soc. Pubs., 1st ser. 21, 57–58. London: Trübner, 1871–79.

Fyler, John. *Chaucer and Ovid*. New Haven: Yale UP, 1979.

Gadamer, Hans-Georg. "On the Scope and Function of Hermeneutical Reflection." *Philosophical Hermeneutics*. Ed. David Linge. Berkeley: U of California P, 1976. 18–43.

Galbreath, D. L. "Les grandson d'Angleterre." *Archives héraldiques Suisses* (1927): 56–69.

Galway, Margaret. "The *Troilus* Frontispiece." *Modern Language Review* 44 (1949): 161–77.

Gardner, John C. *The Life and Times of Chaucer*. New York: Knopf, 1977.

Gaylord, Alan T. "Chaucer's Dainty 'Dogerel': The 'Elvyssh' Prosody of Sir Thopas." *Studies in the Age of Chaucer* 1 (1979): 83–104.

———, ed. *Essays on the Art of Chaucer's Verse*. New York: Routledge, 2001.

———. "Imagining Voices: Chaucer on Cassette." *Studies in the Age of Chaucer* 12 (1990): 215–38.

———. I. *Out Loud with Chaucer's Shorter Poems: Adventures in Prosodic Criticism*. The Chaucer Studio. Provost: Chaucer Studio, 2007.

———. II. *Out Loud with* Troilus and Criseyde *and the* Legend of Good Women: *Adventures in Prosodic Criticism*. The Chaucer Studio. Provost: Chaucer Studio, 2007.

———. "Reading Chaucer: What's Allowed in 'Aloud.' " *Chaucer Yearbook* 1 (1992): 87–109.

———. "Scanning the Prosodists: An Essay in Metacriticism." *Chaucer Review* 11 (1976): 22–82.

Génicot, Léopold. *Contours of the Middle Ages*. Trans. Laurence and Rona Wood. New York: Barnes, 1967.

Geoffrey Chaucer and Middle English Literature. Videocassette. Films for the Humanities, 1988.

The Geoffrey Chaucer Page. Ed. Larry D. Benson. 16 Sept. 2004. President and Fellows of Harvard Coll. 25 Oct. 2005 <http://www.courses.fas.harvard.edu/chaucer>.

Geoffreychaucer.org. Ed. David Wilson-Okamura. 12 Feb. 2005. <http://www.geoffreychaucer.org>.

Gibaldi, Joseph, ed. *Approaches to Teaching Chaucer's* Canterbury Tales. New York: MLA, 1980.

Ginsberg, Warren. *Chaucer's Italian Tradition*. Ann Arbor: U of Michigan P, 2002.

"Gloss." Def. 1. *The Oxford English Dictionary*. 2nd ed. 1989.

Glowka, Arthur Wayne. *A Guide to Chaucer's Meter*. Lanham: UP of America, 1991.

Goldie, Matthew Boyd. "Images." *Middle English Literature: A Historical Sourcebook*. Malden: Blackwell, 2003. 133–55.

Gordon, Ida. *The Double Sorrow of Troilus: A Study of Ambiguities in* Troilus and Criseyde. Oxford: Clarendon, 1970.

Gordon, R. K., ed. *The Story of Troilus*. Toronto: U of Toronto P, 1978.

Gottfried von Strassburg. *Tristan*. Trans. A. T. Hatto. New York: Penguin, 1967.

Gower, John. Confessio Amantis: *The English Works of John Gower*. Ed. G. C. Macaulay. Early English Text Society extra ser. 81. 2 vols. London: Oxford UP, 1900.

———. *Confessio Amantis*. Ed. Russell A. Peck. Toronto: U of Toronto P, 1980.

———. *Confessio Amantis*. 3 vols. Ed. Russell A. Peck. Kalamazoo: Medieval Inst. Pubs., 2003.

———. *The Tale of Tereus and Procne*. Pearsall, *Chaucer to Spenser: An Anthology* 276–86.

Graff, Bennett. Letter to the Editor. *MLA Newsletter* 26.3 (1994): 12–13.

Gransden, Antonia. *Historical Writing in England*. Vol. 2. Ithaca: Cornell UP, 1982.

Gray, Douglas, ed. *Oxford Companion to Chaucer*. Oxford: Oxford UP, 2003.

Green, Richard Firth. *Poets and Princepleasers: Literature and the English Court in the Late Middle Ages*. Toronto: U of Toronto P, 1980.

Greene, Thomas. *The Light in Troy: Imitation and Discovery in Renaissance Poetry*. New Haven: Yale UP, 1982.

Guillaume de Deguileville. *Le pèlerinage de vie humaine*. Ed. J. J. Stürzinger. London: Nichols, 1893.

Gurevich, A. J. *Categories of Medieval Culture*. Trans. G. L. Campbell. London: Routledge, 1985.

Hadley, D. M. *Masculinity in Medieval Europe*. London: Longman, 1999.

Hahn, Thomas. "The Difference the Middle Ages Makes: Color and Race before the Modern World." *Journal of Medieval and Early Modern Studies* 31 (2001): 1–37.

Hamel, Christopher de. *A History of Illuminated Manuscripts*. London: Phaidon, 1994.

Hammond, Eleanor P. *Chaucer: A Bibliographical Manual*. 1908. New York: Peter Smith, 1933.

Hanna, Ralph. "Authorial Versions, Rolling Revision, Scribal Error? Or, The Truth about 'Truth.' " *Studies in the Age of Chaucer* 10 (1988): 23–40.

———. *A Descriptive Catalogue of the Western Medieval Manuscripts of St John's College, Oxford*. Oxford: Oxford UP, 2002.

———. "The Scribe of Huntington HM 114." *Studies in Bibliography* 42 (1987): 120–33.

Hanrahan, Michael. "Seduction and Betrayal: Treason in the *Prologue* to *The Legend of Good Women*." *Chaucer Review* 30 (1996): 229–40.

Hansen, Elaine Tuttle. *Chaucer and the Fictions of Gender*. Berkeley: U of California P, 1992.

Hardman, Phillipa. "Interpreting the Incomplete Scheme of Illustration in Cambridge, Corpus Christi College MS 61." *English Manuscript Studies, 1100–1700* 6 (1997): 52–69.

Harpur, James. *Inside the Medieval World*. London: Cassell, 1995.

Harris, Joseph. *A Teaching Subject: Composition Since 1966*. Upper Saddle River: Prentice, 1997.

Harrison, Robert. *Gallic Salt: Eighteen Fabliaux Translated from the Old French*. Berkeley: U of California P, 1974.

Havely, Nicholas R., ed. and trans. *Chaucer's Boccaccio: Sources of* Troilus *and the* Knight's *and* Franklin's *Tales*. Cambridge: Brewer, 1980.

Helgeland, Brian, dir. *A Knight's Tale*. Perf. Heath Ledger, Paul Bettany, Mark Addy, Rufus Sewell, and Shannyn Sossamon. Columbia, 2001.

Hicks, Michael. *Who's Who in Late Medieval England, 1272–1485*. Mechanicsburg: Stackpole, 1991.

Higden, Ranulf. *Polychronicon*. Trans. John Trevisa. Pearsall, *Chaucer to Spenser: An Anthology* 230–31.

Hoccleve, Thomas. *The Regiment of Princes*. Ed. Charles R. Blyth. TEAMS Middle English Texts Series. Kalamazoo: Medieval Inst. Pubs., 1999.

———. *The Regiment of Princes*. Pearsall, *Chaucer to Spenser* 322–33.

Hodgdon, Barbara. " 'He Do Cressida in Different Voices.' " *English Literary Renaissance* 20 (1990): 254–86.

Hofstadter, Richard. *Anti-intellectualism in American Life*. New York: Knopf, 1963.

The Holy Bible, Translated from the Latin Vulgate: Diligently Compared with the Hebrew, Greek, and Other Editions in Divers Languages. Rockford: Tan, 1989.

Horvath, Richard P. "Chaucer's Epistolary Poetic: The Envoys to Bukton and Scogan." *Chaucer Review* 37 (2002): 173–89.

Howard, Donald R. *Chaucer: His Life, His Works, His World*. New York: Dutton, 1987.

———. "Chaucer the Man." *PMLA* 80 (1965): 337–43.

Howard, Donald R., and James Dean, eds. *Geoffrey Chaucer:* Troilus and Criseyde *and Selected Short Poems*. New York: Signet, 1976.

Hussey, Maurice. *Chaucer's World: A Pictorial Companion*. Cambridge: Cambridge UP, 1967.

Hutcheon, Linda. "The Pastime of Past Time": Fiction, History, Historiographic Metafiction." *Genre* 20 (1987): 285–305.

———. *A Poetics of Postmodernism: History, Theory, Fiction*. New York: Routledge, 1988.

Irvine, Martin. " 'Bothe text and gloss': Manuscript Form, the Textuality of Commentary, and Chaucer's Dream Poems." *The Uses of Manuscripts in Literary Studies*. Ed. Charlotte Cook Morse et al. Kalamazoo: Western Michigan U, Medieval Inst. Pubs., 1992. 81–119.

Jeffrey, David Lyle, ed. *Chaucer and Scriptural Tradition*. Ottawa: U of Ottawa P, 1984.

Johanek, Cindy. *Composing Research*. Logan: Utah State UP, 2000.

"John Ball's Sermon Theme." *Medieval English Political Writings*. Ed. James Dean. Kalamazoo: Medieval Inst. Pubs., 1996. 1 Nov. 2005 <http://www.lib.rochester.edu/camelot/teams/sermon.htm>.

Jordan, Robert. "The Compositional Structure of *The Book of the Duchess*." *Chaucer Review* 9 (1974): 99–117.

———. "Lost in the Funhouse of Fame." *Chaucer Review* 18 (1983): 100–15.

Jost, Jean E. "Teaching *The Canterbury Tales*: The Process and the Product." *Studies in Medieval and Renaissance Teaching* 8.1 (2000): 63–71.

Kaylor, Noel Harold, Jr. "Boethian Resonance in Chaucer's 'Canticus Troili.' " *Chaucer Review* 27 (1993): 219–27.

———. "Chaucer's Use of the Word *Tragedy*: A Semantic Analysis." *Language and Civilization*. Ed. Claudia Blank et al. New York: Lang, 1992. 431–44.

———. " 'The Nun's Priest's Tale' as Chaucer's Anti-tragedy." *The Living Middle Ages: Studies in Mediaeval English Literature and Its Tradition*. Ed. Uwe Böker, Manfred Markus, and Rainer Schöwerling. Regensburg, Ger.: Mittelbayerische Druckerei, 1989. 87–102.

Kelly, Henry Ansgar. *Chaucer and the Cult of Saint Valentine*. Leiden: Brill, 1986.

———. *Chaucerian Tragedy*. Cambridge: Boydell, 1997.

———. *Ideas and Forms of Tragedy: From Aristotle to the Middle Ages*. New York: Cambridge UP, 1993.

———. *Tragedy and Comedy from Dante to Pseudo-Dante*. Los Angeles: U of California P, 1989.

Kiser, Lisa. *Telling Classical Tales: Chaucer and* The Legend of Good Women. Ithaca: Cornell UP, 1983.

Kittredge, George L. *Chaucer and His Poetry*. Cambridge: Harvard UP, 1915.

Klapisch-Zuber, Christiane, ed. *Silences of the Middle Ages*. Cambridge: Belknap–Harvard UP, 1992. Vol. 2 of *A History of Women in the West*. Georges Duby and Michelle Perrot, gen. eds. 5 vols.

Kleinschmidt, Harald. *Understanding the Middle Ages*. Suffolk: Boydell, 2000.

Knapp, Peggy. *Chaucer and the Social Contest*. New York: Routledge, 1990.

Kökeritz, Helge. *A Guide to Chaucer's Pronunciation*. 1961. Toronto: U of Toronto P, 1978.

Koonce, B. G. *Chaucer and the Tradition of Fame: Symbolism in* The House of Fame. Princeton: Princeton UP, 1966.

Kosta-Théfaine, J.-F. "Du chant d'amour au chant du désespoir ou l'écriture d'une poétique de la tristesse dans la lyrique d'Othon de Grandson." *Romanistische Zeitschrift für Literaturgeschichte* 23.3–4 (1999): 297–310.

———. "*Le livre Messire Ode* d'Othon de Grandson ou l'écriture fragmentaire d'un discours amoureux." *Germanisch-Romanische Monatsschrift* 53.3 (2003): 355–61.

———, ed. *Othon de Grandson, chevalier et poète*. Orléans: Éditions Paradigme (Collection *Medievalia*), 2006.

Kowaleski, Maryanne, and Judith M. Bennett. "Crafts, Gilds, and Women in the Middle Ages: Fifty Years After Marian K. Dale." *Sisters and Workers in the Middle Ages*. Ed. Judith M. Bennett et al. Chicago: U of Chicago P, 1989. 11–25.

Krapp, George Philip, trans. *Troilus and Cressida*. 1957. By Geoffrey Chaucer. Introd. Peter G. Beidler. New York: Modern Lib., 2002.

Krier, Theresa, ed. *Refiguring Chaucer in the Renaissance*. Gainesville: U of Florida P, 1998.

The Labyrinth: Resources for Medieval Studies. Ed. Martin Irvine and Deborah Everhart. Georgetown U. 19 Jan. 2006 <www.georgetown.edu/labyrinth/labyrinth-home.html>.

Lange, Lorrayne Baird, and Hildegard Schnuttgen, eds. *A Bibliography of Chaucer, 1974–1985*. Hamden: Archon, 1988.

LeGoff, Jacques. *Medieval Civilization, 400–1500*. Oxford: Blackwell, 1988.

Lenaghan, R. T. "Chaucer's Circle of Gentlemen and Clerks." *Chaucer Review* 18 (1983): 155–60.

Lerer, Seth. *Chaucer and His Readers: Imagining the Author in Late Medieval England*. Princeton: Princeton UP, 1993.

———. *Courtly Letters in the Age of Henry VIII: Literary Culture and the Arts of Deceit*. Cambridge: Cambridge UP, 1997.

Lewis, C. S. *The Allegory of Love*. Oxford: Oxford UP, 1936.

———. *The Discarded Image: An Introduction to Medieval and Renaissance Literature*. Cambridge: Cambridge UP, 1964.

———. "What Chaucer Really Did to *Il Filostrato*." *Essays and Studies* 17 (1932): 56–75.

Leyerle, John, and Anne Quick, eds. *Chaucer: A Bibliographic Introduction*. Toronto: U of Toronto P, 1986.

Librarius. 27 Sept. 2006 <http://www.librarius.com>.

Loomba, Ania. *Colonialism/Postcolonialism*. London: Routledge, 1998.

Loomis, Richard. *A Mirror of Chaucer's World*. Princeton: Princeton UP, 1965.

Love, Nicholas. *The Mirror of the Blessed Life of Jesus Christ*. Pearsall, *Chaucer to Spenser: An Anthology* 313–18.

Lynch, Andrew. *Reading of* The Legend of Good Women: *Selections*. By Geoffrey Chaucer. The Chaucer Studio. Occasional Readings 22. Rec. at U Radio SUV, Adelaide U, 1997.

Lynch, Kathryn, ed. *Dream Visions and Other Poems*. By Geoffrey Chaucer. New York: Norton, 2007.

Lumiansky, R. M., trans. *Geoffrey Chaucer's* Troilus and Criseyde: *Rendered into Modern English Prose*. Columbia: U of South Carolina P, 1952.

Luminarium. Ed. Anniina Jokinen. <http://www.luminarium.org>.

MacCracken, Henry. "King James' Claim to Rhyme Royal." *Modern Language Notes* 24 (1909): 31–32.

Machaut, Guillaume de. The Fountain of Love (La fonteinne amoureuse) *and Two Other Love Vision Poems*. Ed. and trans. R. Barton Palmer. Garland Lib. of Medieval Lit. 54, ser. A. New York: Garland, 1993.

Magee, John C. "The Boethian Wheels of Fortune and Fate." *Mediaeval Studies* 49 (1987): 524–33.

Manly, John M., and Edith Rickert, eds. *The Text of the* Canterbury Tales. 8 vols. Chicago: U of Chicago P, 1940.

Manuscript Bodley 638: A facsimile: Bodleian Library, Oxford University. Introd. Pamela Robinson. Facsim. Ser. of the Works of Geoffrey Chaucer. Norman: Pilgrim, 1982.

Manuscript Pepys 2006: A Facsimile: Magdalene College, Cambridge. Introd. A. S. G. Edwards. Facsim. Ser. of the Works of Geoffrey Chaucer 6. Norman: Pilgrim, 1985.

Manuscript Tanner 346: A Facsimile: Bodleian Library, Oxford University. Introd. Pamela Robinson. Facsim. Ser. of the Works of Geoffrey Chaucer 1. Norman: Pilgrim, 1982.

Manuscript Trinity R. 3. 19: A Facsimile: Trinity College, Cambridge University. Introd. Bradford Fletcher. Facsim. Ser. of the Works of Geoffrey Chaucer 5. Norman: Pilgrim, 1987.

Martin, Priscilla. *Chaucer's Women: Nuns, Wives, and Amazons.* Iowa City: U of Iowa P, 1990.

Mate, Mavis E. *Women in Medieval English Society.* Cambridge: Cambridge UP, 1999.

Matthews, David. "Speaking to Chaucer: The Poet and the Nineteenth-Century Academy." *Studies in Medievalism* 9 (1997): 5–25.

McAlpine, Monica. *The Genre of* Troilus and Criseyde. Ithaca: Cornell UP, 1978.

McCall, John P. *Chaucer among the Gods.* University Park: Pennsylvania State UP, 1979.

———. "Five-Book Structure in Chaucer's *Troilus.*" *Modern Language Quarterly* 23 (1962): 297–308.

McFarlane, Kenneth Bruce. *Lancastrian Kings and Lollard Knights.* Oxford: Clarendon, 1972.

McGillivray, Murray, ed. *Geoffrey Chaucer's* Book of the Duchess: A Hypertext Edition. 2nd ed. CD-ROM. Calgary: U of Calgary P, 1999.

McKisack, May. *The Fourteenth Century, 1307–1399.* Oxford History of England 5. Oxford: Clarendon, 1959.

McMillan, Ann, trans. *The Legend of Good Women.* By Geoffrey Chaucer. Houston: Rice UP, 1987.

Meale, Carol M. "The Tale and the Book: Readings of Chaucer's *Legend of Good Women* in the Fifteenth Century." *Chaucer in Perspective.* Ed. Geoffrey Lester. Sheffield: Sheffield Academic, 1999. 118–38.

Melville, Stephen. *Philosophy beside Itself: On Deconstruction and Modernism.* Minneapolis: U of Minnesota P, 1986.

Menand, Louis. "What Comes Naturally: Does Evolution Explain Who We Are?" *New Yorker* 25 Nov. 2002: 96–101.

Middleton, Anne. "Chaucer's 'New Men' and the Good of Literature in the *Canterbury Tales.*" *Literature and Society: Selected Papers from the English Institute, 1978.* Ed. Edward W. Said. Baltimore: Johns Hopkins UP, 1980. 15–56.

Mieszkowski, Gretchen. "Chaucer's Much Loved Criseyde." *Chaucer Review* 26 (1991): 109–32.

Miller, J. Hillis. *Versions of Pygmalion.* Cambridge: Cambridge UP, 1990.

Miller, Robert P., ed. *Chaucer: Sources and Backgrounds.* New York: Oxford UP, 1977.

Mills, Maldwyn, ed. *Troylus and Criseyde.* By Geoffrey Chaucer. London: Everyman, 2000.

Millward, C. M. *A Biography of the English Language.* Fort Worth: Harcourt, 1996.

Minnis, Alastair J. *Chaucer and Pagan Antiquity.* Cambridge: Brewer, 1982.

———. With V. J. Scattergood and J. J. Smith. *The Shorter Poems.* Oxford Guides to Chaucer. Oxford: Clarendon, 1995.

Miskimin, Alice S. *The Renaissance Chaucer*. New Haven: Yale UP, 1975.

Morrison, Theodore, trans. *The Portable Chaucer*. Rev. ed. New York: Penguin, 1977.

Mossé, Fernand. *A Handbook of Middle English*. Trans. James Walker. Baltimore: Johns Hopkins UP, 1952.

Mosser, D. W. "The Scribe of the Chaucer Manuscripts Rylands English 113 and Bodleian Digby 181." *Papers of the Bibliographical Society of America* 82 (1988): 604–11.

Muscatine, Charles. *Chaucer and the French Tradition*. Berkeley: U of California P, 1957.

Myers, Alec. *London in the Age of Chaucer*. Norman: U of Oklahoma P, 1972.

Neuse, Richard. *Chaucer's Dante: Allegory and Epic Theater in* The Canterbury Tales. Berkeley: U of California P, 1991.

Nolan, Barbara. *Chaucer and the Tradition of the Romans Antique*. Cambridge: Cambridge UP, 1992.

The Norton Anthology of English Literature. Ed. M. H. Abrams, Stephen Greenblatt, et al. 7th ed. Vol. 1. New York: Norton, 2000.

Norton-Smith, John. *Geoffrey Chaucer*. New York: Routledge, 1974.

O'Donnell, James. *Avatars of the Word: From Papyrus to Cyberspace*. Cambridge: Harvard UP, 1998.

Oizumi, Akio, ed. *A Complete Concordance to the Works of Geoffrey Chaucer*. Programmed by Kunihiro Miki. 10 vols. Zurich: Olms, 1990.

Olivier, M. E. "Amedée VII de Savoie, le comte rouge, est-il mort empoisonné?" *Revue Historique Vaudoise* (1932): 257–78.

Olson, Glending. "Deschamps' 'Art de dictier' and Chaucer's Literary Environment." *Speculum* 48 (1973): 714–23.

———. "Making and Poetry in the Age of Chaucer." *Comparative Literature* 31 (1979): 272–90.

Ong, Walter J. *The Presence of the Word*. New Haven: Yale UP, 1967.

Orme, Nicholas. *English Schools in the Middle Ages*. London: Methuen, 1973.

———. *Medieval Children*. New Haven: Yale UP, 2001.

Orsier, Joseph. *Un ambassadeur de Savoie, poète d'amour au XIVe siècle. Oton de Grandson*. Paris: Champion, 1909.

Ovid. *Heroides*. Trans. Harold Isbell. New York: Penguin, 1990.

———. *Metamorphoses*. Trans. Alan Mandelbaum. New York: Harcourt, 1993.

The Oxford Anthology of English Literature. Ed. Frank Kermode, John Hollander, et al. Vol 1. New York: Oxford UP, 1973.

Pace, George B. "The Adorned Initials of Chaucer's 'ABC.'" *Manuscripta* 23 (1979): 88–98.

———. "The True Text of 'The Former Age.'" *Medieval Studies* 23 (1961): 363–67.

Pace, George B., and Alfred David, eds. *The Minor Poems*. A Variorum Edition of the Works of Geoffrey Chaucer 5. Norman: U of Oklahoma P, 1982.

Pagès, A. "Le thème de la tristesse amoureuse en France et en Espagne du XIVème au XVème siècles." *Romania* 57 (1932): 29–43.

Palmer, R. Barton, ed. *Chaucer's French Contemporaries: The Poetry/Poetics of Self and Tradition*. New York: AMS, 1999.

Parkes, M. B. *English Cursive Bookhands, 1250–1500*. 1969. London: Scolar, 1979.

Patch, H. R. *The Goddess Fortuna in Medieval Literature*. Cambridge: Harvard UP, 1927.

Patterson, Lee W. "Ambiguity and Interpretation: A Fifteenth-Century Reading of *Troilus and Criseyde*." *Speculum* 54 (1979): 297–330.

———. *Negotiating the Past: The Historical Understanding of Medieval Literature*. Madison: U of Wisconsin P, 1987.

Paxson, James J. "The Semiotics of Character, Trope, and Troilus: The Figural Construction of the Self and the Discourse of Desire in Chaucer's *Troilus and Criseyde*." *Desiring Discourse: The Literature of Love, Ovid through Chaucer*. Ed. Paxson and Cynthia Gravlee. Selinsgrove: Susquehanna UP, 1998. 206–26.

Payne, F. Anne. *Chaucer and Menippean Satire*. Madison: U of Wisconsin P, 1981.

Pearsall, Derek, ed. *Chaucer to Spenser: An Anthology of Writings in English, 1375–1575*. Oxford: Blackwell, 1999.

———, ed. *Chaucer to Spenser: Critical Reader*. Malden: Blackwell, 1999.

———. "Chaucer's Criseyde." *Studies in the Age of Chaucer Proceedings* 2 (1986): 17–29.

———. "Chaucer's Meter: The Evidence of the Manuscripts." Gaylord, *Essays* 131–44.

———. "The English Chaucerians." Brewer, *Chaucer and Chaucerians* 201–39.

———. "The Future of Chaucer Studies." *Poetica* 50 (1998): 17–27.

———. Introduction. Pearsall, *Chaucer to Spenser: An Anthology* xv–xviii.

———. *The Life of Geoffrey Chaucer: A Critical Biography*. Oxford: Blackwell, 1992.

———. "The *Troilus* Frontispiece and Chaucer's Audience." *Yearbook of English Studies* 7 (1977): 68–74.

Pearsall, Derek, and Nicolette Zeeman, eds. *English and International: Studies in the Literature, Art and Patronage of Medieval England*. Cambridge: Cambridge UP, 1988.

Percival, Florence. *Chaucer's Legendary Good Women*. Cambridge: Cambridge UP, 1998.

Perl, Sondra. "Writing Process: A Shining Moment." *Landmark Essays on Writing Process*. Ed. Perl. Davis: Hermagoras, 1994. xi–xx.

Petrarch, Francis. *Letters of Old Age: Rerum Senilium Libri I–XVIII*. Trans. Aldo S. Bernardo, Saul Levin, and Reta A. Bernardo. Vol. 2. Baltimore: Johns Hopkins UP, 1992.

Phillips, Helen. "Chaucer and Deguileville: The *ABC* in Context." *Medium Ævum* 62 (1993): 1–19.

———. " 'The Complaint of Venus': Chaucer and de Graunson." *The Medieval Translator, IV*. Ed. Roger Ellis and Ruth Evans. Binghamton: Medieval and Renaissance Texts, 1994. 86–103.

———. "Fortune and the Lady: Machaut, Chaucer and the Intertextual 'Dit.' " *Nottingham French Studies* 38 (1999): 120–36.

Phillips, Helen, and Nicholas R. Havely, eds. *Chaucer's Dream Poetry*. New York: Longman, 1997.

Piaget, Arthur. "Oton de Granson et ses poésies." *Romania* 19 (1890): 237–59, 403–48.

———, ed. *Oton de Granson: Sa vie et ses poésies*. Lausanne: Payot, 1941.

The Pierpont Morgan Library Manuscript M. 817. Facsim. Ser. of the Works of Geoffrey Chaucer 4. Introd. Jeanne Krochalis. Norman: Pilgrim, 1986.

Poetical Works: A Facsimile of Cambridge University Library MS Gg. 4. 27. Introd. M. B. Parkes and Richard Beadle. 3 vols. Cambridge: Brewer, 1979–80.

Pollard, A. W. and G. R. Redgrave, eds. *A Short-Title Catalogue of Books Printed in England, Scotland and Ireland and of English Books Printed Abroad, 1475–1640*. Rev. W. A. Jackson, F. S. Ferguson, and K. F. Pantzer. 3 vols. London: Bibliog. Soc., 1976–91.

Pope, Alexander. *The Poems of Alexander Pope*. Ed. John Butt. New Haven: Yale UP, 1963.

Pope, Rob. "Re-writing Texts, Re-constructing the Subject: Work as Play on the Critical-Creative Interface." *Teaching Literature: A Companion*. Ed. Tanya Agathocleous and Ann Dean. New York: Palgrave, 2003. 105–24.

Power, Eileen. *Medieval Women*. 1975. Ed. M. M. Postan. Cambridge: Cambridge UP, 1995.

Preminger, Alex. "Averroes: Introduction; the Middle English Commentary on the *Poetics* of Aristotle." Preminger, Hardison, Kerrane 341–82.

Preminger, Alex; O. B. Hardison, Jr.; and Kevin Kerrane. *Classical and Medieval Literary Criticism: Translations and Interpretations*. New York: Ungar, 1974.

Pugh, Tison. "Queer Pandarus? Silence and Sexual Ambiguity in Chaucer's *Troilus and Criseyde*." *Philological Quarterly* 80 (2001): 17–35.

Quinn, William A. *Chaucer's Dream Visions and Short Poems: Basic Readings in Chaucer and His Times*. New York: Garland, 1990.

———. *Chaucer's Rehersynges: The Performability of* The Legend of Good Women. Washington: Catholic U of America P, 1994.

Randall, Lilian. *Images in the Margins of Gothic Manuscripts*. Berkeley: U of California P, 1966.

Reiss, Edmund. "Dusting Off the Cobwebs: A Look at Chaucer's Lyrics." *Chaucer Review* 1 (1966): 55–65.

Richmond, Velma. *A Prologue to Chaucer*. Prod. U of California, Berkeley. Videocassette. Films for the Humanities and Sciences, 1989.

Robbins, Rossell Hope, and J. L. Cutler. *Supplement to the Index of Middle English Verse*. Lexington: U of Kentucky P, 1965.

Robertson, D. W., Jr. "Chaucerian Tragedy." *Chaucer Criticism*. Ed. Richard J. Schoeck and Jerome Taylor. Vol. 2. Notre Dame: Notre Dame UP, 1961. 86–121.

———. "The Doctrine of Charity in Medieval Literary Gardens: A Topical Approach through Symbolism and Allegory." *Essays in Medieval Culture*. Princeton: Princeton UP, 1980. 21–50.

———. *A Preface to Chaucer*. Princeton: Princeton UP, 1962.

Robinson, F. N., ed. *The Works of Geoffrey Chaucer.* 2nd ed. Boston: Houghton, 1957.

Le Roman de la rose. By Guillaume de Lorris and Jean de Meun. Ed. Armand Strubel. Paris: Générale Française, 1992.

The Romance of the Rose. By Guillaume de Lorris and Jean de Meun. Trans. Charles Dahlberg. Princeton: Princeton UP, 1971.

Root, Robert Kilburn, ed. *The Book of* Troilus and Criseyde *by Geoffrey Chaucer.* Princeton: Princeton UP, 1926.

———. Introduction. Root, *Book* xi–lxxxix.

———. *The Manuscripts of Chaucer's* Troilus, *with Collotype Facsimiles of the Various Handwritings.* London: Paul, 1914.

———. *The Textual Tradition of Chaucer's* Troilus. London: Paul, 1916.

Rougemont, Denis de. *Love in the Western World.* New York: Harcourt, 1940.

Rowe, Donald. *O Love, O Charite! Contraries Harmonized in Chaucer's* Troilus. Carbondale: Southern Illinois UP, 1976.

———. *Through Nature to Eternity: Chaucer's* Legend of Good Women. Lincoln: U of Nebraska P, 1988.

Rowland, Beryl. *Companion to Chaucer Studies.* Rev. ed. New York: Oxford UP, 1979.

Rudd, Gillian. *The Complete Critical Guide to Geoffrey Chaucer.* London: Routledge, 2001.

Ruud, Jay. *"Many a Song and Many a Lecherous Lay": Tradition and Individuality in Chaucer's Lyric Poetry.* New York: Garland, 1992.

Salter, Elizabeth, and Derek Pearsall. "Pictorial Illustration of Late Medieval Poetic Texts: The Role of the Frontispiece or Prefatory Picture." *Medieval Iconography and Narrative.* Ed. Flemming G. Andersen et al. Odense: Odense UP, 1980: 100–23.

Salu, Mary, ed. *Essays on* Troilus and Criseyde. Cambridge: Brewer, 1979.

Saunders, Corinne, ed. *Chaucer.* Blackwell Guides to Criticism. Oxford: Blackwell, 2001.

Scase, Wendy. "St. Anne and the Education of the Virgin: Literary and Artistic Traditions and Their Implications." *England in the Fourteenth Century.* Ed. Nicholas Rogers. Stamford: Watkins, 1993. 81–96.

Scattergood, John. "Chaucer's 'Complaint of Venus' and the 'Curiosite' of Graunson." *Essays in Criticism* 44.3 (1994): 171–89.

———. "The Short Poems." Minnis, *Shorter Poems* 455–512.

Schless, Howard H. *Chaucer and Dante: A Reevaluation.* Norman: Pilgrim, 1984.

Schoeck, Richard, and Jerome Taylor, eds. *Chaucer Criticism:* Troilus and Criseyde *and the Minor Poems.* South Bend: U of Notre Dame P, 1990.

Sedgwick, Eve Kosofsky. *Between Men: English Literature and Male Homosocial Desire.* New York: Columbia UP, 1985.

———. *Epistemology of the Closet.* Berkeley: U of California P, 1990.

Seymour, M. C. *A Catalogue of Chaucer Manuscripts.* 2 vols. Aldershot: Scolar, 1995.

Shakespeare, William. *Riverside Shakespeare.* Ed. G. Blakemore Evans. Boston: Houghton 1974.

———. *Troilus and Cressida*. Ed. David Bevington. Arden Shakespeare. 3rd ser. New York: Nelson, 1998.

———. *Troilus and Cressida*. Ed. Anthony Dawson. New Cambridge Shakespeare. Cambridge: Cambridge UP, 2003.

———. *Troilus and Cressida*. Ed. Kenneth Palmer. Arden Shakespeare. 2nd ser. 1982. London: Methuen, 1997.

Shannon, Edgar. *Chaucer and the Roman Poets*. New York: Russell, 1964.

Sheingorn, Pamela. " 'The Wise Mother': The Image of St. Anne Teaching the Virgin Mary." *Gesta* 32 (1993): 69–80.

Shoaf, R. A., ed. *Troilus and Criseyde*. By Geoffrey Chaucer. East Lansing: Michigan State UP, 1989.

Shoaf, R. A., and Catherine Cox, eds. *Chaucer's* Troilus and Criseyde*: "Subgit to alle Poesye": Essays in Criticism*. Binghamton: Center for Medieval and Early Modern Studies, 1992.

Skeat, Walter W. *The Complete Works of Geoffrey Chaucer*. 1899. 2nd ed. 7 Vols. Oxford: Clarendon, 1972.

Slocum, Sally. "Criseyde among the Greeks." *Neuephilologische Mitteilungen* 87 (1986): 365–74.

Spencer, Scott. *Endless Love*. Hopewell: Ecco, 1979.

Spurgeon, Caroline F. E. *Five Hundred Years of Chaucer Criticism and Allusion, 1357–1900*. 3 vols. 1925. New York: Russell, 1960.

Stanley-Wrench, Margaret, ed. and trans. *Troilus and Criseyde*. By Geoffrey Chaucer. London: Centaur, 1965.

Steadman, John M. *Disembodied Laughter:* Troilus *and the Apotheosis Tradition*. Berkeley: U of California P, 1972.

Steinberg, Glenn. "The True Well of English Undefyled?: Chaucer, Spenser, and Lydgate." Unpublished essay, 2003.

Stillinger, Thomas C. *Critical Essays on Geoffrey Chaucer*. New York: Twayne, 1998.

St. John, Michael. *Chaucer's Dream Visions: Courtliness and Individual Identity*. Burlington: Ashgate, 2000.

St. John's College, Cambridge, Manuscript L. 1: A Facsimile. Introd. Richard Beadle and Jeremy Griffiths. Facsim. Ser. of the Works of Geoffrey Chaucer 3. Norman: Pilgrim, 1983.

Stock, Lorraine Kochanske. "Writing the Publishable Seminar Paper." *College English Association Forum* 12 (1981): 12–15.

Stone, Brian, trans. *Love Visions:* The Book of the Duchess, The House of Fame, The Parliament of Birds, The Legend of Good Women. By Geoffrey Chaucer. Harmondsworth: Penguin, 1983.

Strohm, Paul. *Social Chaucer*. Cambridge: Harvard UP, 1989.

Suleri, Sara. *Meatless Days*. Chicago: U of Chicago P, 1989.

Suzuki, Mihoko. *Metamorphoses of Helen: Authority, Difference, and the Epic*. Ithaca: Cornell UP, 1989.

Tatlock, John, and Arthur Kennedy, eds. *A Concordance to the Complete Works of Geoffrey Chaucer and to the Romaunt of the Rose*. Gloucester: Smith, 1963.

Taylor, Charles. *Sources of the Self: The Making of the Modern Identity*. Cambridge: Harvard UP, 1989.

Taylor, Karla. *Chaucer Reads* The Divine Comedy. Stanford: Stanford UP, 1989.

———. "*Inferno* 5 and *Troilus and Criseyde* Revisited." Shoaf and Cox 239–56.

Thompson, Ann. *Shakespeare's Chaucer: A Study in Literary Origins*. New York: Barnes, 1978.

Thomson, Leslie. *Fortune: All Is but Fortune*. Seattle: U of Washington P, 2000.

Trapp, J. B., Douglas Gray, and Julia Boffey, eds. *Medieval English Literature*. New York: Oxford UP, 2002.

Traversi, Derek. *Chaucer: The Early Poetry: A Study in Poetic Development*. Newark: U of Delaware P, 1987.

Trigg, Stephanie. *Congenial Souls: Reading Chaucer from Medieval to Postmodern*. Minneapolis: U of Minnesota P, 2002.

Troilus and Criseyde: A Facsimile of Corpus Christi College Cambridge MS 61. Introd. M. B. Parkes and Elizabeth Salter. Cambridge: Brewer, 1978.

Vergil. *Aeneid*. Trans. Robert Fitzgerald. New York: Random House, 1990.

Vitto, Cindy, and Marcia Smith Marzec, eds. *New Perspectives on Criseyde*. Asheville: Pegasus, 2004.

Wagenknecht, Edward. *The Personality of Chaucer*. Norman: U of Oklahoma P, 1968.

Wallace, David. *Chaucer and the Early Writings of Boccaccio*. Cambridge: Brewer, 1985.

———. *Chaucerian Polity: Absolutist Lineages and Associational Forms in England and Italy*. Stanford: Stanford UP, 1997.

Wallace, Michele. *Invisibility Blues: From Pop to Theory*. London: Verso, 1990.

Warrington, John. *Geoffrey Chaucer:* Troilus and Criseyde. London: Dent, 1953.

Wasserman, Julian N., and Robert J. Blanch, eds. *Chaucer in the Eighties*. Syracuse: Syracuse UP, 1986.

Waters, Lindsay. "Paul de Man: Life and Works." *Critical Writings, 1953–1978*. By Paul de Man. Ed. Waters. Minneapolis: U of Minnesota P, 1989. ix–lxxiv.

Waugh, Patricia. *Metafiction*. New York: Routledge, 1984.

Weisl, Angela Jane. *Conquering the Reign of Femeny: Gender and Genre in Chaucer's Romance*. Cambridge: Brewer, 1995.

Westrem, Scott D. *The Hereford Map*. Turnhout, Belg.: Brepols, 2001.

Wetherbee, Winthrop P. *Chaucer and the Poets: An Essay on* Troilus and Criseyde. Ithaca: Cornell UP, 1984.

———. "Criseyde Alone." Vitto and Marzec 299–332.

Wieck, Roger S. *Painted Prayers: The Book of Hours in Medieval and Renaissance Art*. New York: Braziller, 1997.

Williams, Raymond. *Marxism and Literature*. Oxford: Oxford UP, 1977.

———. "Traditions, Institutions, and Formations." Williams, *Marxism* 115–20.

Wimsatt, James I. "Chaucer and French Poetry." *Geoffrey Chaucer*. Ed. Derek Brewer. Athens: Ohio UP, 1975. 109–36.

———. *Chaucer and the French Love Poets*. Chapel Hill: U of North Carolina P, 1968.

————. *Chaucer and His French Contemporaries: Natural Music in the Fourteenth Century.* Toronto: U of Toronto P, 1991.

————. *Chaucer and the Poems of "Ch" in University of Pennsylvania MS French 15.* Cambridge: Brewer, 1982.

————. "Guillaume de Machaut and Chaucer's Love Lyrics." *Medium Ævum* 47 (1978): 76–78.

Windeatt, Barry A. *Chaucer's Dream Poetry: Sources and Analogues.* Cambridge: Brewer, 1982.

————. "The Scribes as Chaucer's Early Critics." *Studies in the Age of Chaucer* 1 (1979): 119–41.

————. "The Text of the *Troilus.*" *Essays on* Troilus and Criseyde. Ed. Mary Salu. Cambridge: Boydell, 1979. 1–22.

————, ed. Troilus and Criseyde: *A New Edition of* The Book of Troilus. Harlow: Longman, 1984.

————. *Troilus and Criseyde.* Oxford Guides to Chaucer. Oxford: Clarendon, 1992.

————, trans. Troilus and Criseyde: *A New Translation.* By Geoffrey Chaucer. Oxford: Oxford UP, 1998.

Winny, James. *Chaucer's Dream-Poems.* London: Chatto, 1973.

Wolpe, Berthold. "Florilegium Alphabeticum: Alphabets in Medieval Manuscripts." *Calligraphy and Paleography.* Ed. A. S. Osley. London: Faber, 1965. 69–74.

Wood, Chauncey. *The Elements of Chaucer's* Troilus. Durham: Duke UP, 1984.

Woolf, Rosemary. *The English Religious Lyric in the Middle Ages.* Oxford: Clarendon, 1968.

The Works of Geoffrey Chaucer and The Kingis Quair: *A Facsimile of Bodleian Library, Oxford, MS Arch. Selden. B. 24.* Introd. Julia Boffey and A. S. G. Edwards. App. by B. C. Barker-Benfield. Cambridge: Brewer, 1997.

Wu, Duncan, ed. *Poetry from Chaucer to Spenser.* Oxford: Blackwell, 2002.

Ziolkowski, Jan. *On Philology.* University Park: Pennsylvania State UP, 1990.

INDEX

Harvey, Gabriel, 88
Hastings, John, 155
Havely, Nicholas R., 5, 8, 13, 102
Hawes, Stephen, 88
Helgeland, Brian, 24, 76–80
Henry IV, 77, 85
Henryson, Robert, 3, 4, 15, 25, 122–26
Hereford Map, 63
Herzman, Ronald B., 9
Hesiod, 31
Heywood, Thomas, 126
Hicks, Michael, 70n2
Higden, Ranulph, 51, 54n3
Hoccleve, Thomas, 50, 54, 54n2, 88, 152
Hodgdon, Barbara, 126n1
Hodge, Laura, 12
Hofstadter, Richard, 172
Holinshed, Raphael, 87
Holton, Sylvia Wallace, 19, 89
Homer, 174
Horace, 13, 31
Horvath, Richard P., 76
Howard, Donald, R., 5, 8–9, 79
Hussey, Maurice, 152
Hutcheon, Linda, 97–98

Irvine, Martin, 137n9

Jacobus de Voragine, 8
Jean de Berry, 33
Jean de Meun, 8, 31, 138, 140–41, 161
Jeanne d'Allamand, 155
Jeanne de Vienne, 155
Jeffrey, David, 13
Jerome (saint), 104, 105
John of Gaunt, 34, 67, 69, 80, 132, 145, 155, 160
Jordan, Robert, 97, 147
Jost, Jean E., 148n1
Julian of Norwich, 51
Juvenal, 13, 62, 63

Kane, George, 103–04
Kaylor, Noel Harold, Jr., 23, 43, 44, 48
Keats, John, 52
Kelly, Henry Ansgar, 15, 18, 43
Kempe, Margery, 51
Kennedy, Arthur, 19
Kinney, Clare R., 24–25
Kiser, Lisa, 18, 103
Kittredge, George Lyman, 79, 80, 87, 91
Klapisch-Zuber, Christiane, 118
Kleinschmidt, Harald, 9
Kluge, Friedrich, 14
Knapp, Peggy A., 14, 25
Kökeritz, Helge, 181
Koonce, B. G., 18

Kosta-Théfaine, Jean-François, 25, 156
Kowaleski, Maryanne, 71
Krapp, George Philip, 6
Krier, Theresa, 14
Kynaston, Francis, 89

Lacan, Jacques, 127
Lange, Lorrayne Baird, 20
LeGoff, Jacques, 9
Lenaghan, R. T., 77
Langland, William, 96, 104
Lerer, Seth, 14, 58, 59, 80, 88
Lewis, C. S., 3, 9, 34, 36, 38, 124, 171
Leyerle, John, 20
Lightsey, Scott, 23–24
Loomba, Ania, 75n2
Loomis, Richard, 151–52
Love, Nicholas, 54n2, 55n5
Lumiansky, R. M., 6
Lydgate, John, 15, 54, 54n2, 57–58, 85, 87–88, 103, 126
Lynch, Andrew, 104
Lynch, Kathryn, 5

Machaut, Guillaume de, 5, 12, 14, 29, 30, 31, 33–34, 102, 154
Macrobius, 5, 8, 139
Magee, John C., 160
Manly, John M., 60n8
Mann, Jill, 3, 8
Marie de France, 154
Martin, Priscilla, 120, 169n1
Marx, Karl, 72
Marzec, Marcia Smith, 17, 26
Mate, Mavis E., 71
Matthews, David, 90
McAlpine, Monica, 15
McCall, John P., 43, 103
McFarlane, Kenneth Bruce, 77
McGillivray, Murray, 12, 145
McKisack, May, 9
McMillan, Ann, 6, 104
Meale, Carol, M., 58
Melville, Stephen, 127
Menand, Louis, 163
Middleton, Anne, 34
Mieszkowski, Gretchen, 169n1
Miller, J. Hillis, 131
Miller, Robert P., 8
Mills, Maldwyn, 3–4
Millward, C. M., 181–82
Milton, John, 142
Minnis, Alastair, 19, 33–34, 62
Miskimin, Alice S., 14, 88
Morrison, Theodore, 6–7
Mosser, D. W., 60n6
Muscatine, Charles, 13–14, 33, 36
Myers, Alec, 9

Neuse, Richard, 13
Nolan, Barbara, 14, 33
Norton-Smith, John, 96, 156

Oizumi, Akio, 19
Olivier, M. E., 155
Olson, Clair, 9
Olson, Glending, 34
Ong, Walter J., 162
Orme, Nicholas, 137
Orsier, Joseph, 157
Ovid, 5, 8, 12, 13, 16, 29–31, 52–53, 62, 97, 98, 99, 101, 103–05, 129, 139, 160

Pace, George B., 57, 78, 95, 137
Pagès, A., 156
Palmer, R. Barton, 33
Parkes, M. B., 56, 57, 60n5
Pasolini, Pier Paolo, 171
Patch, H. R., 64
Patterson, Lee W., 3, 59, 91
Paxson, James J., 25, 127
Payne, Anne, 13
Peake, Mervyn, 132
Pearl poet (*see also Gawain* poet), 96
Pearsall, Derek, 7, 8, 51–52, 54–55, 75n1, 77, 87, 91, 150–51, 169n1, 181
Peck, Russell A., 54, 63
Percival, Florence, 18, 103
Perl, Sondra, 145, 148n1
Petrarch, 13, 48, 85, 107–08, 132
Philip de la Vache, 59, 86, 93
Philippa of Hainault, 67
Phillips, Helen, 5, 33, 102, 137n3, 158
Piaget, Arthur, 157
Plato, 75, 128, 130
Pollard, A. W., 60
Pope, Alexander, 89–90, 137
Pope, Rob, 137n8
Power, Eileen, 71, 120
Preminger, Alex, 43
Propertius, 129
Pugh, Tison, 25, 35
Pyles, Thomas, 182
Pynson, Richard, 59

Quick, Anne, 20
Quinn, William A., 17–18, 23, 24, 104
Quintilian, 143

Raleigh, Walter, 52
Randall, Lilian, 137n6
Redgrave, G. R., 60n3
Reiss, Edmund, 135
Richard II, 66, 67, 69, 85–86, 105, 150, 155
Richmond, Velma, 11

Rickert, Edith, 60n8
Robbins, Rossell Hope, 60n3
Robert de Vere, 69
Robertson, D. W., Jr., 48, 91, 112, 115, 163
Robinson, F. N., 3, 53, 92
Root, Robert Kilburn, 5, 56, 58, 60
Rougemont, Denis de, 114
Rowe, Donald W., 15, 18, 103
Rowland, Beryl, 8
Rudd, Gillian, 19
Rust, Martha, 25
Ruud, Jay, 156

Salter, Elizabeth, 56, 57, 150–51
Salu, Mary, 17
Saunders, Corinne, 18, 97
Scase, Wendy, 137n4
Scattergood, John, 19, 33, 156, 157, 158
Schless, Howard H., 13
Schnuttgen, Hildegard, 20
Schoeck, Richard, 18
Scogan, Henry, 58–59, 77–78
Seaman, Myra, 24
Sedgwick, Eve Kosofsky, 117
Seneca, 31
Seymour, M. C., 19, 60n8
Shakespeare, William, 25, 54, 93, 122–26, 132, 148, 170
Shaner, M. C. E., 102
Shannon, Edgar, 13
Sheingorn, Pamela, 137n4
Sheridan, James, 160
Shirley, John, 30, 85–86
Shoaf, R. A., 3–4, 17
Skeat, Walter W., 3, 4, 102
Skelton, John, 88
Slocum, Sally, 169n1
Smith, M. Bentinck, 14
Spencer, Scott, 114, 116
Spenser, Edmund, 54, 88
Spielberg, Steven, 160
Spurgeon, Caroline F. E., 19, 85–86, 87–89, 90, 95
Stanley-Wrench, Margaret, 6
Statius, 12, 13, 16, 28, 30
Steadman, John M., 16
Steinberg, Glenn, 24, 54
Stevenson, Barbara, 25
Stillinger, Thomas C., 17
St. John, Michael, 17, 99–100
Stock, Lorraine Kochanske, 26, 175
Stone, Brian, 6
Straw, Jack, 67
Strohm, Paul, 69, 77
Suleri, Sara, 38
Sutherland, Jennifer, 26, 162
Suzuki, Mihoko, 123–24

Modern Language Association of America

Approaches to Teaching World Literature

Joseph Gibaldi, series editor

Shorter Elizabethan Poetry. Ed. Patrick Cheney and Anne Lake Prescott. 2000.
Ellison's Invisible Man. Ed. Susan Resneck Parr and Pancho Savery. 1989.
English Renaissance Drama. Ed. Karen Bamford and Alexander Leggatt. 2002.
Works of Louise Erdrich. Ed. Gregg Sarris, Connie A. Jacobs, and
    James R. Giles. 2004.
Dramas of Euripides. Ed. Robin Mitchell-Boyask. 2002.
Faulkner's The Sound and the Fury. Ed. Stephen Hahn and Arthur F. Kinney. 1996.
Flaubert's Madame Bovary. Ed. Laurence M. Porter and Eugene F. Gray. 1995.
García Márquez's One Hundred Years of Solitude. Ed. María Elena de Valdés and
    Mario J. Valdés. 1990.
Gilman's "The Yellow Wall-Paper" *and* Herland. Ed. Denise D. Knight and
    Cynthia J. Davis. 2003.
Goethe's Faust. Ed. Douglas J. McMillan. 1987.
Gothic Fiction: The British and American Traditions. Ed. Diane Long Hoeveler
    and Tamar Heller. 2003.
Hebrew Bible as Literature in Translation. Ed. Barry N. Olshen and
    Yael S. Feldman. 1989.
Homer's Iliad *and* Odyssey. Ed. Kostas Myrsiades. 1987.
Ibsen's A Doll House. Ed. Yvonne Shafer. 1985.
Henry James's Daisy Miller *and* The Turn of the Screw. Ed. Kimberly C. Reed and
    Peter G. Beidler. 2005.
Works of Samuel Johnson. Ed. David R. Anderson and Gwin J. Kolb. 1993.
Joyce's Ulysses. Ed. Kathleen McCormick and Erwin R. Steinberg. 1993.
Kafka's Short Fiction. Ed. Richard T. Gray. 1995.
Keats's Poetry. Ed. Walter H. Evert and Jack W. Rhodes. 1991.
Kingston's The Woman Warrior. Ed. Shirley Geok-lin Lim. 1991.
Lafayette's The Princess of Clèves. Ed. Faith E. Beasley and
    Katharine Ann Jensen. 1998.
Works of D. H. Lawrence. Ed. M. Elizabeth Sargent and Garry Watson. 2001.
Lessing's The Golden Notebook. Ed. Carey Kaplan and Ellen Cronan Rose. 1989.
Mann's Death in Venice *and Other Short Fiction*. Ed. Jeffrey B. Berlin. 1992.
Medieval English Drama. Ed. Richard K. Emmerson. 1990.
Melville's Moby-Dick. Ed. Martin Bickman. 1985.
Metaphysical Poets. Ed. Sidney Gottlieb. 1990.
Miller's Death of a Salesman. Ed. Matthew C. Roudané. 1995.
Milton's Paradise Lost. Ed. Galbraith M. Crump. 1986.
Molière's Tartuffe *and Other Plays*. Ed. James F. Gaines and
    Michael S. Koppisch. 1995.
Momaday's The Way to Rainy Mountain. Ed. Kenneth M. Roemer. 1988.
Montaigne's Essays. Ed. Patrick Henry. 1994.
Novels of Toni Morrison. Ed. Nellie Y. McKay and Kathryn Earle. 1997.
Murasaki Shikibu's The Tale of Genji. Ed. Edward Kamens. 1993.
Pope's Poetry. Ed. Wallace Jackson and R. Paul Yoder. 1993.

Proust's Fiction and Criticism. Ed. Elyane Dezon-Jones and
    Inge Crosman Wimmers. 2003.
Novels of Samuel Richardson. Ed. Lisa Zunshine and Jocelyn Harris. 2006.
Rousseau's Confessions *and* Reveries of the Solitary Walker. Ed. John C. O'Neal
    and Ourida Mostefai. 2003.
Shakespeare's Hamlet. Ed. Bernice W. Kliman. 2001.
Shakespeare's King Lear. Ed. Robert H. Ray. 1986.
Shakespeare's Othello. Ed. Peter Erickson and Maurice Hunt. 2005.
Shakespeare's Romeo and Juliet. Ed. Maurice Hunt. 2000.
Shakespeare's The Tempest *and Other Late Romances*. Ed. Maurice Hunt. 1992.
Shelley's Frankenstein. Ed. Stephen C. Behrendt. 1990.
Shelley's Poetry. Ed. Spencer Hall. 1990.
Sir Gawain and the Green Knight. Ed. Miriam Youngerman Miller and
    Jane Chance. 1986.
Song of Roland. Ed. William W. Kibler and Leslie Zarker Morgan. 2006.
Spenser's Faerie Queene. Ed. David Lee Miller and Alexander Dunlop. 1994.
Stendhal's The Red and the Black. Ed. Dean de la Motte and Stirling Haig. 1999.
Sterne's Tristram Shandy. Ed. Melvyn New. 1989.
Stowe's Uncle Tom's Cabin. Ed. Elizabeth Ammons and Susan Belasco. 2000.
Swift's Gulliver's Travels. Ed. Edward J. Rielly. 1988.
Thoreau's Walden *and Other Works*. Ed. Richard J. Schneider. 1996.
Tolstoy's Anna Karenina. Ed. Liza Knapp and Amy Mandelker. 2003.
Vergil's Aeneid. Ed. William S. Anderson and Lorina N. Quartarone. 2002.
Voltaire's Candide. Ed. Renée Waldinger. 1987.
Whitman's Leaves of Grass. Ed. Donald D. Kummings. 1990.
Woolf's To the Lighthouse. Ed. Beth Rigel Daugherty and Mary Beth Pringle. 2001.
Wordsworth's Poetry. Ed. Spencer Hall, with Jonathan Ramsey. 1986.
Wright's Native Son. Ed. James A. Miller. 1997.